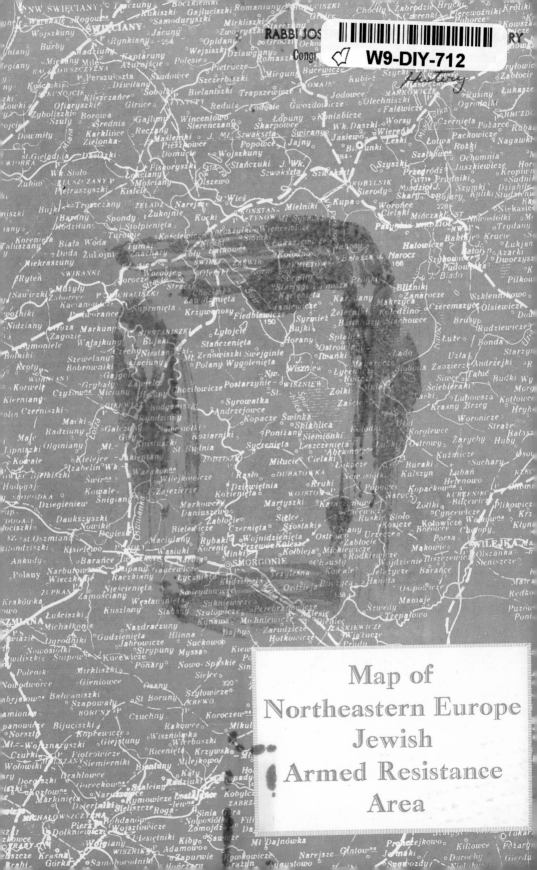

Map of
Northeastern Europe
Jewish
Armed Resistance
Area

A Secret Press in Nazi Europe

"The disruption of enemy rail communications throughout Occupied Europe, by the organized forces of the Resistance, played a very considerable part in our victory."

Gen. Eisenhower

A SECRET PRESS IN NAZI EUROPE

The Story of a Jewish
United Partisan Organization

By

Isaac Kowalski

Central Guide Publishers, Inc.
NEW YORK

Instead of a Foreword

To evaluate the importance of Isaac Kowalski's achievements, it is sufficient to quote a fragment of Kaczerginski's* book, *Partisaner Gehen . . .* (Partisans are coming . . .), as he tells it in the chapter, "White Weapons":

"The leaders of the Vilna Gestapo, with **Weiss, Kittel, Neugebauer, Falhaber** at the head, wracked their brains: where could they find the secret press which issued anti-Hitler newspapers and appeals in Polish, Lithuanian, Russian and German?

"They would have showered gold upon anyone who would at least provide a clue leading to the printing plant or to those who operated it. But even the distributors could not be found. On going into the street in the morning, you would see the doors covered with placards, calling the people not to go to the black dungeons of Germany but to hide themselves in order to avoid being drafted into the army. There was a call to the German soldiers, a call to the workers to slow down and to sabotage. It frequently happened that Weiss saw such a poster on his own door, on Kasztan Street. Nor were they pasted only on walls and doors. Gestapo officers often found copies of the appeals in the pockets of their soldiers.

"The terror failed. The sudden check-ups in the print shop and the threats to the printers did not help.

"The 'white weapon,' which these anti-Hitleristic publications were called, did its work. The Hitlerites continued to wrack their brains: how to catch the underground band?

"The influence of the Partisan appeals was tremendous. They went from hand to hand, from pocket to pocket. Where 'hot' weapons could not reach, or could do little, the 'white' weapon, the weapon of the Jewish partisan, Isaac Kowalski, succeeded."

THE PUBLISHERS

*Szmerke Kaczerginski was one of the most prolific partisan writers. He was killed in April, 1954, in an airplane crash in Argentina.

Acknowledgments

I WISH to express my deepest appreciation to Nahum Guttman, Miriam Ginsburg, Jacob Chernofsky, and Esther Zweig for undertaking the enormous task of translating this book from Yiddish and other languages. I am indebted to Mr. Guttman for valuable editorial advice and for proof-reading the final pages; to Professor David Wdowinski (a top commander and one of the survivors of the Warsaw ghetto uprising) for reading the manuscript and giving me his constructive opinions; and to attorney Paul Goldman, for reading the pageproofs and rendering legal advice.

I also wish to thank the following who have so graciously read this book in pageproofs and offered valuable suggestions:

Joseph Foxman, scholar, a survivor of the Vilna ghetto; Dr. Joseph B. Schechtman, noted historian and author of many books; Dr. Philip Paneth, noted writer; Dr. Jacob Rubin, radio commentator and writer; Jerry Stolls, journalist; Professor Dr. Leon Bernstein (Chicago), one of the partisan commanders in the Vilna ghetto; and Pesia Sheinbaum-Bernstein (Chicago), wife of a commander who fell in battle in the Vilna ghetto. I must thank Chaim Lazar (Israel), a writer and former partisan commander, for loaning me many photos; likewise, thanks to Abraham Sabrin, a former partisan commander, for some of his pictures. I also thank those whose names appear on various documents that I found in different archives and other places.

I am especially grateful to Yad Vashem for the use of some of their documents; to the library of the Herzl Institute in New York for friendly cooperation; to the World Publishing Company in New York for permitting me to reprint "The War: 1941-1945" by Ilya Ehrenburg, the account of the Vilna battle; to Memorial Foundation for Jewish Culture for the fellowship grant which facilitated the preparation of this book; to Leon Uris for reading the proofpages and encouraging this work by writing a special commentary; to Benjamin Katz, for his valuable technical advice; to my wife Masha, herself a "graduate" from Auschwitz and many other concentration camps, for encouraging me and doing some of the typing; to my daughter Ruth, a freshman of Brooklyn College, for the index; to the many colleagues and former partisans who gave me pictures and information as far back as July 1944 with my promise to them to write and publish the story of our resistance to the Nazis; and to the Book Committee which cares for the success of this book.

Preface

I STARTED collecting documents and pictures immediately after Vilna was liberated from the Nazis, in the latter half of 1944. When I left Vilna in January, 1945, the war was still raging in full fury, and millions of people were still dying. I managed to reach Romania, and finally Italy. En route, I saw many cities and villages destroyed by the military activity. I was constantly on the move, rarely spending the night in a spot where I spent the day. When the war ended, I found myself in Italy. Then I began to make more trips to various countries, to collect material for this book.

From time to time I was short of funds for my minimum necessities, but as I flew from one country to the next, I never left behind my possessions, the collection of raw materials I had so painstakingly assembled for a record of this epoch. From boundary to boundary, I lugged my valuables, regardless of cost. I used a small portion of this material in a Yiddish volume published in New York in 1953. I am using most of it in this expanded volume.

* * *

Once, when I was travelling toward Denmark, through part of Germany then occupied by American troops, I saw some United States military police on the train, looking for black marketeers. They saw a couple of big valises on the shelf and asked me to open them up. I asked them to take the valises down, and gave them the keys. The M.P.'s must have thought that they had a big haul, because of the extraordinary weight. It was too heavy for cigarettes—it must be full of solid gold . . .

When they opened the valises, they saw only a lot of scribbled papers, and scraps of paper. One of them asked me what it was all about and I gave him a sheet with my Yiddish handwriting on it. He held it upside down. I explained what this "contraband" was, but apparently he did not believe me. The police took a good look, inspecting every stitch of the valises and at last returned my keys and left the train.

* * *

I have used, as far as possible, the native spelling for names of persons and places. Since this book had four translators, some variations in spelling will occur. In general, I have used the word "ghetto" with a lower case "g" but in official documents it appears with a capital letter. I have used Estonia and Esthonia,

Tatar and Tartar interchangeably. The military ranks also present a problem. For example, in the Gestapo there was no such rank as captain (Hauptman) or sergeant (Feldvebel) which are army titles, but I used them as approximations for the benefit of the general reader.

Some Polish letters have special accent signs, which I have spelled out in a form more familiar to English readers: Dabrowski becomes Donbrowski. A slave laborer in the ghetto was called a "brigadier" (foreman), but this is not to be confused with the brigadier rank in the army.

In chapter headings, I have used the expression "First," as in "First Mine" or "First Saboteur," to indicate that this was the first time such an action was performed. Later, similar actions of this type, performed by our partisans, are mentioned without detailed description.

The index at the back of this volume does not contain the history work of A. I. Grodzenski and the list of partisans. Some of the pictures used in the book are not of first quality, but I felt they must be included for the sake of completeness; nor do the sizes of the photos as they appear on these pages, indicate the relative importance of the personalities involved—for technical reasons the sizes may vary, but the men and women who lived through these events were of equal importance, in my eyes. An exception are the pictures of Joseph Glazman, Itzik Wittenberg and the Vilna Gaon. For them I intentionally reserved full pages. Most of the photos were taken before the war except for the partisans, who were photographed during and after the war.

It has not been my intention to single out any particular group or party for special commendations. If I did write less about any group or party, it is simply a matter of chance or because I happened to be better acquainted with some than with others.

*   *   *

In general, when speaking of distances, I used the kilometer rather than the mile, as I am more used to this measurement. The distances are approximate in many cases, and are used to give the reader a rough idea of the location of an event.

I have used the term "Gestapo" quite broadly, to encompass the SS, SD and other Nazi criminals, because by now most Americans know this name of the "bad guys."

Contents and Plates

PART FOUR
FORESTS

Documents

Glossary

HEBREW WORDS

Bar Mitzva—Age of 13 when Jews assume moral responsibility, p. 99

Eretz Israel—Land of Israel, p. 132

Gabai—Beadle, p. 99

Gaon—Genius, p. 27

Golem—Legendary brute created by a mystic p. 24

Hasidism—A Jewish sect distinguished by religious ecstasy, p. 398

Kibbutz—A collective settlement, p. 154

Maharal—Creator of the "Golem" p. 24

Malina—Hideout, p. 85

Mishna—Comentary on the Bible, p. 23

Naturei Karta—"Guardians of the Wall"—extremist orthodox Jews, p. 294

Nekama—Revenge, p. 386

Rashi—A noted Medieval commentator p. 23

Shul—Synagogue, p. 99

Simcha—Festive occasion, p. 409

Talmud—Commentary on the Bible, p. 24

Torah—Bible (Old Testament), p. 24

Yad Veshem—"Place and Name"—A memorial, p. 143

Yeshiva—Religious Academy, p. 138

Yishuv—The Jewish community of Israel, p. 407

GERMAN WORDS

Der Stuermer—Anti-semitic magazine, p. 174

Fuehrer—Leader, p. 47

Gestapo—*Geheime Statspolizei* (Secret State Police), p. 45

Herrenfolk—Superiority Nation, p. 21

Judenrat—Jewish Council, p. 47

Nicht wahr?—Not so?, p. 143

S.D. *Sicherheitsdienst*—Security Service, p. 138

S.S. *Schutzstaffel*—Elite guard (Special Police.), p. 22

Strasse—Street, p. 205

Wehrmacht—German army, p. 40

OTHER LANGUAGES

Action or Selection—Name given by the Germans to any operation regarding Jews (deportation, shooting, etc.)

Sam Naczalnik—A chief by oneself, p. 260

Shikses (Yiddish)—Camouflaged Jews, posing as Aryan (A slang expression), p. 263

Wszystkich Swietych (Polish)—All the Hollies, p. 217

Organizations

ACHDUT HAAVODA (Poale Zion)—Socialist Labor section of the Zionist movement.

AGUDAH—Religious (Orthodox) non-Zionist movement.

AKIBA—Zionist youth organization.

AMERICAN JOINT DISTRIBUTION COMMITTEE—The main collecting and distributing agency, founded in 1914, by American Jews for relief and rehabilitation for overseas Jews.

BETAR—Brith Trumpeldor, youth movement of the Zionist-Revisionists.

BUND—Familiar name of the General Jewish Labor Union of Poland founded in 1897. Socialist, anti-Zionist, anti-Communist in orientation.

DROR—Zionist youth organization, affiliated with Hechalutz.

ENDEK—Acronym for National Democrats, a Polish political party with a reactionary and anti-Semitic program.

GENERAL ZIONISTS—Non-Socialist division of the Zionist movement.

GORDONIA—Zionist youth group, affiliated with Poale Zion.

IRGUN ZVAI LEUMI—Military arm of the Zionist-Revisionists.

HANOAR HATZIONI—Zionist youth group, affiliated with Hechalutz.

HASHOMER HATZAIR—Socialist Zionist youth group, with many sports clubs and training farms.

HECHALUTZ—Zionist Pioneer youth movement, founded in 1905, emphasizing need for emigration and the building of agricultural settlements in Palestine.

HITACHDUT—Zionist youth group,

POALE ZION—Labor section of the Zionist movement.

REVISIONISTS—Followers of Vladimir Jabotinsky, advocated non-cooperation with the British mandatory power in Palestine; strongly anti-Socialist.

INTRODUCTION

THE partisan movement is not a latter-day phenomenon. Partisan activities date back over a long stretch of history. They were known in the Napoleonic era, in pre-revolutionary Russia and in other countries. Here in America, partisans, known as Rangers, made their appearance during the French and Indian Wars, which lasted from 1754 to 1763. Rangers were also part of the Confederate army during the Civil War. The concept of Rangers as irregular forces was given impetus when the Partisan Ranger Act was passed by the Confederate Congress in 1862.

Whatever their scope and extent, partisan tactics have usually conformed to the same pattern.

A partisan army or band differs from a regular army in several respects: it may be small in number; it often lacks adequate arms and it seeks to avoid frontal attacks; it operates mostly under cover of dark, frequently in hills and forests; in general, it does not take prisoners and must avoid capture at all cost. Unlike a regular army, it is composed of volunteers; it never remains too long in any one spot, keeping ever on the move; its weapons are acquired in the course of fighting by disarming enemy soldiers and by sudden raids on enemy ammunition depots. While the formations are similar to those in a regular army, from the bottom up to the general staff, discipline is looser. Partisans do not have military uniforms or regulation dress and they wear whatever they happen to have.

Where a partisan group has become exceptionally strong, its members may wear the uniforms and insignia of the country in which they are operating. Food is requisitioned from the civilian population. Payment is made only in rare instances.

Partisans usually sleep in forests, in temporary bunkers which they improvise of tree trunks and branches, in caves, or in hills. Wherever they are strong enough to engage the enemy in more open and direct combat, they are quartered in villages or towns whose population they take under their protection. In such situations friendly planes fly in supplies to the partisans and take back the wounded for medical treatment or hospitalization.

World War II brought death to 40 to 50 million people. Included in this staggering number were six million Jews. If I focus my attention here on the Jews, it is not because their blood is any redder than that of the others, but because most of them perished not in battle but as the result of a cold-blooded process of extermination inspired by the insane racist theory of the Nazis. I'm not going to re-examine all the forms of mass murder employed by the bestial Nazis. This has been done, and much more still has to be done, in order to convey to the people of America a true picture in all its gruesome dimensions, of the incredible brutalities visited upon the Jews by the Hitlerite madmen, with whom we lived under the same God's sky.

Nor is it my purpose to recapitulate here the story of the one and a half million Jews who fought under the flags of the various Allied armies, except to set down the statistical record for those who may not be familiar with the facts:

600,000 Jewish soldiers fought in the armies of the Soviet Union;

500,000 Jewish soldiers fought in the armies of the United States;

75,000 Jewish soldiers fought in the armies of Great Britain;

30,000 Jewish soldiers fought in the armies of Palestine (now Israel);

30,000 Jewish soldiers fought in the armies of Poland;

24,000 Jewish soldiers fought in the armies of Yugoslavia;

100,000 Jewish soldiers fought in the armies of France;

200,000 Jewish soldiers fought in the armies of Canada, South Africa, Australia, New Zealand and other countries.

* * *

The question has frequently been asked with great amazement: How could you Jews allow yourselves to be destroyed like that? The answer to these well-meaning people is that the Jews were not the only ones who "allowed" themselves to be destroyed. At the moment, it is not important to know just what was the ratio or percentage of those who thus "allowed" themselves to be exterminated in any particular nation. And why talk about a civilian population which had a naturally large proportion of elderly persons and children, when at the same time whole armies of well-trained soldiers were also annihilated? The fact is, the Nazi forces smashed one army after another, and succeeded in occupying almost all of Europe and parts of Africa.

In the Katin forest, not far from the city of Smolensk in White Russia, some five thousand Polish soldiers were murdered. They were shot in the head, hands tied, and laid in the pits in their military garb. In 1943 the Germans trumped up charges that it was done by the Bolsheviks, in 1941 before they were driven out of the area, and the Bolsheviks said that it was done by the Nazis. One thing is clear, that soldiers and many officers of yesterday's Polish army were murdered not on the battlefield but in a forest, with only one bullet in the head. They didn't fight back, either.

In these circumstances, it should be obvious why a civilian population was unable to offer more effective physical resistance to a powerful and ruthless army. But this is precisely the reason for my decision to present to the wide reading public the facts concerning *one* remarkable chapter, one striking exception about which the American people are still not well-informed, though twenty-three years have elapsed since the end of World War II.

It should be stressed that the notion that Jews, as Jews, failed to offer resistance to the Nazis is completely unfounded and erroneous. On the contrary, Jews were active everywhere in the vanguard of the partisan movement, delivering powerful

19

blows against the Nazis and contributing in no small way to the collapse and defeat of the Third Reich's armed might.

At this point a word must be said about expressions of partisan jargon which are found in the text and which need to be explained. For instance the reader will frequently come across references to units and divisions bearing purely Russian names—e.g., *Voroshilov Brigade*—which may create the impression that those divisions consisted only of Russian fighters, whereas in reality they were composed wholly or in large part of Jews. After a beginning was made by the Jews from the nearby small towns and villages and they were ready fighting units, they were incorporated into the general Soviet partisan movement and adopted pure Soviet names.

Another instance was that of the city of Orsha, on the White Russian front, where a Lithuanian army brigade took part in the fighting. The German command found out about it and in an Order of the Day warned the soldiers in that sector that in spite of its name, the Lithuanian brigade actually consisted entirely of Jews, and this was the reason for the brigade's exceptionally tough and stubborn stand. There was truth in this. The Lithuanian brigade was recruited from among Lithuanian Jews who had fled to Russia when the Nazi armies marched into their country. The same was true of the Latvian brigade which was made up almost entirely of Jewish volunteers. Also the Polish Kosciuszko brigade in Russia was heavy composed of Jews.

The strongest partisan movement was in Eastern Europe. Effective partisan activities existed also in Yugoslavia, France, Greece, Italy and other countries. Everywhere Jews were to be found either as leaders or as active participants.

Unfortunately, the Jewish partisans had to contend in many instances not only against the German army and its Gestapo, but also against the dregs of the population. Thus, for example, there were individuals who, in return for a kilo of sugar given them by the Nazis, acted as the informers from whom the Germans learned where unarmed Jews were hiding. When the partisans found out about such informers—which happened innumerable times—the traitors were executed; when their bodies were found, there was always a note saying: "He was shot for betraying a Jew." Consequently, many civilians refused the Nazi gift of sugar, even though this article in wartime was regarded as a veritable fortune.

There were also cases of anti-Semitism and hooliganism within the ranks of the partisans. Wherever these manifestations cropped up, the guilty ones were given a warning that a repetition would bring merciless punishment. Short shrift was made of those who failed to take heed.

When the German army was at last defeated, its soldiers surrendered at the various fronts either to the regular armed forces of the Allies or, here and there, to the partisans. It was a never-to-be-forgotten spectacle to see the former Nazi "heroes" quake in their boots on learning, as they did in many cases, that their captors were Jews. With their hands up and mortal fear in their eyes, these members of Hitler's "superior race" begged the Jews for mercy. The picture of post-war Germany, broken and in ruins, was not pretty. The wives and daughters of the *herrenvolk* sold themselves for a crumb of bread or half a cigarette. The country became one huge brothel and even the men crawled on their hands and knees for a handout from the Americans and other allied troops.

For the crimes that the Germans committed on the Polish territory, the Germans who remained in Poland after the war, had to wear armbands, for a time, like the Jews had to wear while under the Nazi rule, and they had to walk in the gutter and not on the sidewalk. They walked like this with shame and they did not resist.

Any one who was in Germany at the time, was certainly debunked of the idea that the Jews "allowed" themselves to be killed. It is simply that when the German army was at the height of its success, destroying everything in its path, populations of many countries, including the Jews, were helpless since they were unarmed and unorganized. The moment groups of partisans sprang up and began to harass the Nazi forces from positions in the hills and forests, the Hitlerian heroes became frightened and did everything they could to avoid taking on the partisans in a fight. Instead, they sent the S.S. divisions which they organized from the local population to take the risk of engaging the Jews. It can truly be said that the Jewish partisans put the fear of God in the heart of every Nazi soldier.

This book makes no attempt to analyze the political colorations of the various partisan groups. My aim is to depict the role of the Jews in the partisan war against Germany, but I am fully cognizant and appreciative of the part played by the partisans of all nations who fought heroically against the Brown occupation. Although Jews in many cases served as the spark plug in organizing partisan groups, there were certainly a tremendous number of non-Jews who joined the movement and gave their lives on the altar of freedom. With some minor exceptions, we were allied, just as on a large scale the mighty America was allied with the nations of Europe, and all together deserve credit at the hands of history for the great victory over the dark forces of Nazi Germany.

Because so little is known by the world about the Jewish role in the gallant struggle against Hitlerite barbarism, this book seeks to fill the lacuna by presenting some historic facts for the record.

I make no pretense that this material is exhaustive, but I do feel that I am offering an opportunity here for a wide American audience to become better acquainted with what happened.

I. K.

Part I

Background

WHY VILNA IS CALLED THE "JERUSALEM OF LITHUANIA"*

IN the course of our many years of wandering through strange lands, Jewish history records that when we settled anywhere for many centuries, we usually added the name of "Jerusalem" to the cities of our sojourn. We have an example of this in ancient history, about 150 years after the destruction of the Second Temple. Pumpaditha, the city where the *Mishna* was concluded, was called the "Jerusalem of Babylonia."

In more recent history, 800 years later, we had a "Jerusalem of France" in the city of Troyes, which contains the last resting place of *Rashi.*

This was also true of Germany. We had a "Jerusalem of

---

*Written by the prominent writer A. J. Grodzenski for the "Wilner Almanach."

The "Almanach" was initiated by me, and my father's printing and publishing enterprises, were the co-publishers, with the daily Yiddish evening newspaper "Ownt Kurier."

This "Almanach" is now a very rare publication, because it was published shortly before the war (1939), and only a few copies were circulated throughout the world.

Germany" in the city of Wurms, also known as Vermua in ancient times. Wurms was also called "New Jerusalem" in Hebrew.

Four hundred years ago, Toledo was called the "Jerusalem of Spain."

Prague, the city made famous by *Maharal* and the *Golem*, now under the Czech regime, was once called the "Jerusalem of Bohemia."

Lublin, the city of the "Council of the Four Lands" and of the *Maharal*, was called the "Jerusalem of Poland."

It is noteworthy that not one of the above mentioned "Jerusalems" was as popular in the Jewish world, as was the "Jerusalem of Lithuania," which was the name given to Vilna.

All the aforementioned cities, which bore the added appellation "Jerusalem," lost this identity long ago. (Only Vilna was privileged to carry the nickname "Jerusalem of Lithuania" until the outbreak of World War II—I.K.) We no longer had a Jerusalem of Poland, France, Germany, Holland, or Italy. Even though Padua in Italy, Frankfurt in Germany and Amsterdam in Holland played a vital role in the Jewish world, and were famous for their scholars, Gaonic Rabbis, Talmudical Academies, etc., none of these cities was any longer honored by the Jewish people with the added title of "Jerusalem."

Why, then, was Vilna crowned with the holiest name in Jewish history, and why was Vilna singled out for this honor until its final hour?

It is not easy to answer this question, even though the name "Jerusalem" is self-explanatory. The name Jerusalem does not necessarily have the connotation of the capital of an independent Jewish state in Israel. It is also connected with a psychological concept of a holy city of piety, Torah-learning and scholarship. This concept was later brought along by the Jews in their wanderings all over the diaspora. It is understandable, then, that any other city designated as "Jerusalem" had to be characterized by the same standards of piety, Torah-learning and scholarship. We find that very few cities could live up to the high standards set by the holy city in Israel.

At the end of the 16th and the beginning of the 17th century, these concepts found their highest expression in the Lithuanian city of Vilna. Of course, it took generations of Torah study and great scholarship before this unknown city set in Lithuanian pasture lands attained the moral right in exile to inherit the name of Jerusalem.

One must be familiar with the history of the old Jewish Vilna to understand why she richly deserved the appellation. Of course, it would be worth while to consider at length the process which led to the adoption of the name of "Jerusalem of Lithuania." But this is not our purpose. I shall only cite a few appropriate legends. It was not by accident that she acquired the name.

One legend tells us that Napoleon had something to do with it. In 1812, when Napoleon was in Vilna, he found so many Jewish scholars possessed of Jewish piety and strict Jewish consciousness, that he was very much impressed and he called Vilna the "Jerusalem of Lithuania." (Since then the name stuck, until the final destruction of the city.—I.K.) This is only a legend since it is unlikely that a non-Jew like Napoleon could estimate Vilna's Judaism and bestow the title "Jerusalem of Lithuania." The fact is that Vilna carried the title a few centuries before Napoleon.

A second legend also throws light upon the fact that Vilna was designated as the "Jerusalem of Lithuania" a few centuries earlier: During the 17th century, in the period of the formation of the "Council of the Four Lands," Vilna was refused membership, because she was considered a city of illiterates and boors not worthy of being included in the organization. The repeated appeals of Vilna Jewry were of no avail and the many well-substantiated petitions did not convince the council that Vilna was not a backward city. Vilna sent many emissaries and delegations to the Council, to prove that Vilna was in reality a city

25

of learning and outstanding scholars. It was all in vain. Vilna was not accepted into the "Council of the Four Lands."

Once, when there was an important convention of the Council in the city of Grodno, a large parchment scroll was received from Vilna. It was written in Torah script and signed by the entire Vilna rabbinate. The letter indicated that Vilna had 333 Jews who knew the six tractates of the Talmud by heart. Included were the names and addresses of all the 333 scholars. The number 333 is equivalent to the Hebrew numerical acronym "Snow."

This declaration fell like a cold snow upon the heads of the Council. Finally, one of the leading scholars of the day rose to his feet, raised his hands and called out with wonder in his eyes:

"To think there are *Sheleg*—333 Jews in one city who know the entire Talmud by heart! And we were unaware of that! Why, this is equivalent to 'Jerusalem in the diaspora'!"

Since then the city of Vilna was known as the "Jerusalem of Lithuania."

This last legend is close to historical fact. It is true that the city of Vilna was not accepted into the Council for a long time, and that she did a great deal of lobbying to get in. It is also a fact, that Vilna was in actuality a city of scholars, of Jewish literary giants and Talmudic experts.

Between 1620-1648, Vilna was famous for scores of outstanding Jewish personalities who were renowned in the world of Jewish scholarship. A few of these were: Rabbi Moses Lima, author of "Chelkas Michokayk"—a Portion of the Law; Rabbi Ephraim Kohen, author of "Sha'ar Ephraim"—The Gate of Ephraim; Rabbi Aaron Samuel Koidenower, author of "Birkat Hazevach"—The Blessing of the Offering; and Rabbi Hillel, known by the acronym "Shach" (for Sifray Kohen), author of "Beth Hillel"—the House of Hillel. There were many other scholars and great personalities.

Vilna issued many outstanding publications on Talmudic

themes which were spread throughout the diaspora. She trained rabbis who occupied pulpits throughout all Europe. Then, more then ever, Vilna was compared to the Jerusalem of Israel. The famous quotation of Isaiah "that from Zion will issue Torah" was rephrased to read "from Vilna will issue Torah."

Vilna really produced the greatest experts in knowledge of Torah, who spread their learning throughout many lands— to Germany, Austria, Holland and Turkey. That, too, added strength to the name of "Jerusalem of Lithuania."

More and more glory was added to the name as time went by. No other city could equal Vilna in Torah, wisdom, scope and piety. For 240 years the golden chain of Jewish learning was forged link by link until it reached its climax in the Gaon of Vilna (1720-1797) who took first place among all his rabbinical contemporaries.

With the advent of the Gaon of Vilna, the city matured and was most deserving of the name "Jerusalem of Lithuania."

However, the golden chain of learning was not destroyed and after the death of the Gaon it was continued in later scholarly personalities, among them "Chayay Adam" and his confreres.

*　　*　　*

The Soviet news agency *Nowosci*, circulated a report that in January 1966, there was a big festival in connection with the tenth anniversary of an amateur theater in Vilna.

In the ten years that the theater existed, 200,000 people went to its performances. Vilna now contains a quarter of a million people, of whom 15,000 are Jewish. Most of them returned from Russia where they were during the war, after they retreated with the Soviet armies, due to the German invasion. Other Jewish inhabitants of Vilna are those who came from many small cities surrounding it. Jewish people are very rarely found in these small towns.

Vilna is now one of the very few cities in Russia where Jewish life is still in existence, and therefore the Vilna style is in small part prolonged.

Dr. Jacob Wigodski was the main Jewish spokesman even before the first World War. In World War II, at the age of 86 he was a preacher of disobedience against the Nazis. Wigodski was arrested and incarcerated for a while in the Lukiszki prison where he suffered inhuman treatment like the other thousands of prisoners. In prison he agitated for the destruction of the money and other valuables in the possession of the inmates. He was sent with all the others to Ponary, to his doom.

Dr. Wigodski was at one time a Parliament senator.

Polish President Ignacy Moscicki with a group of generals on a visit to the Vilna Synagogue. Present are the leaders of the Jewish community.

DANZIG — WORLD WAR II

AFTER Poland freed herself from the yoke of Czarist Russia, after she became fully independent in World War I, she liberated the city of Danzig which was situated near the Baltic Sea. Many nationality groups were in Danzig: Germans, Poles, Jews, etc., with a population of more then a quarter of a million.

According to the Versailles Treaty, Danzig was to be a free city, and administered by the Poles. German citizens could enter and leave Danzig on their German passports and they did not need any special visas from the Polish government. They could also import and export merchandise from Danzig without payment of any duties.

When Nazi Germany embarked upon her expansionist policies, after the capture of the Saar Basin, Austria, Sudetenland, she also demanded a "corridor" on the way from Germany to Danzig. Such a "corridor" would cut through Polish territory.

In general, Poland and Germany were on good terms, then. Important government officials used to visit each other and go hunting together. But these cordial relations did not deter Nazi Germany from demanding that Poland open a corridor through her territory for a free passage to Danzig, for her armed forces.

Naturally, Poland would not agree to any such policy and Hitler's hordes fell upon Poland on September 1, 1939* with fearful ferocity. Thus it came about that the flames of World War II were kindled, at a cost of about 40-50 million dead and about the same number wounded and crippled.

In the Hitler-Stalin treaty of 1939, Vilna was allotted to the Soviet sphere of influence and thus it came about that Vilna was taken over by the Soviets and not by the Germans.

*The Polish president, Professor Ignacy Moscicki, issued a manifesto to the Polish people in which he declared that "the eternal enemy of Poland—Germany—has suddenly attacked Poland . . ."

After the Soviet powers stayed in Vilna from September to October, 1939, they handed Vilna over to independent Lithuania, during the presidency of Antanas Smetona, in keeping with the terms of a treaty with Lithuania.

Poland and Lithuania were at sword's point with each other. General Lucian Zeligowski in October 1920, tore Vilna away from Lithuania and proclaimed it a "Middle Lithuania." Later, in March 1922, it was incorporated into Poland. There were no diplomatic relations between Poland and Lithuania, until the year 1938.

Lithuania always regarded Vilna as her capital city, despite the fact that she had designated Kovno as a temporary capital.

According to a treaty between Russia and Lithuania, Soviet Russia was permitted to have certain military bases in Lithuania, for the duration of the war. She designated New Wilejka, 10 kilometers from the city of Vilna, as one of those bases.

Because they were overwhelmed with joy that Vilna became the capital of Lithuania again, all sorts of hoodlums made a pogrom upon the Jews, which lasted for several days.

Things got out of hand. Jewish leaders appealed to the government at Kovno to intervene and stop the pogrom. But the government did not comply effectively, most probably because it did not have powers to act, in those first days, or it did not have any intention to stop the pogrom. So the Jewish leaders had to turn to the Soviet garrison at New Wilejka for help. The Soviet military leaders replied that they were in the vicinity only as guests, and their status did not permit them to interfere in the internal affairs of Lithuania.

When the pogroms were not stopped, and losses in Jewish life and property kept on mounting, a delegation was dispatched for the second time to the general of the garrison. Again they pleaded for some defense for the Jewish citizens of Vilna. The general acceded to their request. (Most probably he had received instructions from Moscow in the interim.) He consented to send some forty tanks into the city. In so doing, he dampened the hotheads among the independent Lithuanians and the disillusioned Poles. When things returned to normal and the seat of Lithuanian government was transferred from Kovno to Vilna, then living conditions and the attitudes toward all the citizenry changed for the better. This change was of benefit to the Jewish citizens as well, and the Jews enjoyed cordial relations with the government.

A great mass of refugees started to stream out of Poland when she was trampled under by the German war-machine. The refugees were Polish as well as Jewish. Many paid with their lives in the attempt to cross the border from occupied Poland into Lithuania. Thus it came about that about 20,000 Jewish refugees fled to Vilna. They were sustained there by the Jewish community in Vilna and especially by the American Joint Distribution Committee.

On June 5, 1940, Vilna was retaken by Soviet military forces, who administered the city until June 24, 1941, when the Nazi hordes captured Vilna.

German soldiers breaking up barrier at a Polish frontier.

German bombers in action.

Defenders of Gdansk (Danzig) Post Office being led to execution.

600,000 Polish soldiers and officers were taken as war prisoners including 60,000 Jews. Later most Jewish POW's were annihilated by the Nazis.

Warsaw surrendered September 28, after four weeks of bloody fighting.

THE ATTACK ON THE SOVIET UNION

THE news that Germany had attacked the Soviet Union struck us Vilna Jews like a clap of thunder. We immediately took stock of what would await us if the enemy should invade our domain.

As I was trying to manipulate the radio in order to ascertain details of the surprise attack on the Soviet Union, I accidentally overheard Hitler's declaration of war, relayed from Bulgaria. This was taped from the original broadcast to the Bulgarian people, and immediately translated into Bulgarian.

I remarked then and there that this was deviltry. Hitler, in his declaration of war, violently attacked the Jews.

The significance of this was self-evident. Germany had declared open war against the communist regime and Hitler included the Jews in his vituperation. It took no great mind to come to the conclusion that he had lumped the Jews together with the communists and that the Jews were automatically in a state of war with Germany.

Even though the city of Vilna was in a terribly nervous state over the outbreak of war, even though I, myself, had heard Hitler's declaration via radio, somehow I had the feeling that maybe, maybe this was only a grim joke . . .

The day before, as a group of my friends came out of a movie theater after the last showing, we were overwhelmed by the loud noise of a siren. After 15 minutes the alarm ended.

These test alarms then went on continuously. This was the first time the population was disturbed late at night. Everybody understood that air attacks can take place during the night. Therefore, it was quite logical to have these alarms take place during the night, to see how the people would react in the late, dark hours.

Our group which had just came out of a fine movie, was happy that it was such a short alarm. What would we have done if the alarm had sounded for a few hours, and we would have to hide somewhere in a cellar?

34

We went to bed at one in the morning. I heard in my sleep that Germany had attacked the Soviet Union. At first I thought it was only a dream. I opened my eyes and it occurred to me that I was fully awake, and that which I heard was real...

As I said before, the radio soon assured me that it was not a dream. I didn't have to wait long to convince myself that action would follow the words I had heard.

At about 10 A.M., a second alarm sounded. This time it was not a test alarm. Airplanes soon beclouded the sky. They were flying high. Anti-aircraft guns sounded . . . The airplanes disappeared into cloud banks. It looked as if they were afraid of the anti-aircraft artillery. It was only an illusion. Soon the airplanes descended and dropped their bombs. They did not spare any explosives. The airplanes descended still further, directly over the house tops and bestrewed the city with machine gun fire.

Due to the war panic a long line of people queued up on Nowogrudska Street to buy meat and other provisions.

A few airplanes dropped away from their squadron formation right over the heads of the people and machine-gunned many of them.

Hundreds of dead and wounded resulted from the first attack on Vilna. Many houses lay in ruins.

The reports which reached us declared that we Jews of Vilna were to be wiped out. They stated that the Germans had penetrated the boundary line and were advancing rapidly. Calamity-mongers believed that any day now the Germans would take over Vilna.

Small youth groups hastily took counsel with each other. Many decided to retreat with the Red Army. Many military vehicles arrived in the city and they parked at Kijowska Street near Block No. 2, where many families of the officers of the aviation guard lived.

The machines were dusty and muddy, which meant that they had traveled long distances at breakneck speed.

I tried to get information from the drivers, but they were close-mouthed. However, other people had already found out that they had come from border towns; that the Germans had attacked with unprecedented violence, and that Germans were advancing fast, destroying anything and everything in their path.

In the Jewish quarter, all ways and means were discussed. Various reactionary elements soon appeared in the city to wait for the moment when the Germans would take over.

A Polish student passed across my field of vision with a simpering smile on his face. He wore a student cap of pre-war Poland. These hats used to be worn originally in a jaunty manner. Later, when the Soviets took over, these students were forbidden to wear them for they spelled defiance.

At this critical moment some Poles hastened to don these caps, which denoted their inference that Soviet power was ended. They awaited the Germans. In addition, they threw a "knowing" smile in the direction of the gate behind which the majority of the Jews lived. That look left nothing to the imagination.

The Retreat with the Army

Young people hurried silently in the direction of the railroad station tower to load the trains. Others were ready to leave the city by bicycles, on foot, etc.,—all taking off in an easterly direction.

There was pandemonium on the train. Thousands of young men were ready to retreat. I made last-minute preparations, packed my knapsack, and took leave of my family.

The only available places on the train were in the open freight cars where we crowded together for endless hours. Now and then, an airplane flew by directly overhead toward an unknown distant target, lifting itself up higher and higher.

In the beginning, we were sure that it was one of ours, a Soviet plane, because an enemy plane would not fly so low over the railroad tracks and not shoot. But, evidently, the plane had another assignment: to see what was doing on the train. We could see the pilot in his leather cap sticking his head out. And he could distinctly see that the people were running away from the Germans.

After long hours upon our feet in the freight cars, in the company of other refugees, we finally arrived, to our amazement, at our original point of departure. We had not moved at all. These were only maneuvers, and the train was backtracking.

When I went back to the train station, I encountered a good friend of mine, Dr. Meyer Ginzburg, standing alone. He had half a loaf of black bread under his arm, upon which he was munching as if it were pastry. We looked at each other, shook hands and agreed to stay together through thick and thin, until we would reach our goal. That is to say, until we would get to a place which the Germans could not overrun so quickly.

Finally, after sitting on the train for an hour, we felt it lurch forward. After riding a distance of some 20 kilometers, we were attacked by enemy planes. The train stopped in its tracks. Everybody who could do so evacuated it, ran for shelter in a nearby woods and spread out on the earth.

We dragged ourselves from place to place to the accompaniment of flying bullets and exploding bombs. Our makeshift unit suffered scores of casualties. We got in and out of the cars time and again to hide from the deadly onslaught. It was a nightmare. One had a bleeding foot, another had blood running down his back and from other parts of the body.

The wife of a Soviet commander sitting next to me was stone-dead—a bullet pierced her heart. At the next station they took her off together with the rest of the dead.

After many such bombardments, during which we fled to nearby forests, we managed to find our way back to the train to be together again.

But after one particular evacuation, we were separated and could not find each other again. At the time I was inclined to

believe that nothing happened to my fellow passenger because the airplanes flew by without attacking. They were on
their way to bombard Molodeczno, which we soon saw from a
distance. We got lost among the large crowds of people and we
got into different cars.

In the distance we saw Minsk. We found ourselves on the
old Polish-Soviet border near the town Radoszkowicze.

The train stopped. People who were familiar with the
region said that this was the old border. Why did the train
stop? There were no airplanes in sight. Soon everything was
clarified . . .

A certain colonel at the border issued an order that all
non-military personnel were to vacate the transport. They were
forbidden to cross the border.

All those ordered to vacate were thunderstruck. They nearly collapsed. They were between the devil and the deep blue
sea, in a strange environment, with no way out, ahead or behind.

After I lost my previous companion, I joined up with the
journalist Siomka Kagan and his family. Since he was a communist in good standing for many years, he did his best to intervene with the authorities that they allow him and his family
to cross the border. He showed his party-card and reached the
highest official in the echelon. Even though his quest was un-
successful, we both were apprised of the underlying reasons for
the refusal.

Until now, trains had been allowed to cross the border
without interference.

Now it was different, the officers explained to Siomka.
The Germans dropped many parachutists in this section
who formed a fifth column, then entered the transports
and penetrated deep into Soviet Union territory. The Germans
dropped subversives, spies and other disruptive elements of all
nationalities.

We were aware of the truth of this explanation, because

we had seen it all from a distance in the wagons of the train. Many parachutists had dropped down from the planes. In the woods, they discarded their parachutes and mixed with the masses of refugees. Many were caught by us. They usually dressed in tatters, and posed as poor refugees. Furthermore, the official explained, this was an order from his higher-ups.

The reason for exclusion was a weighty one, even though it went against us. Siomka's pleading and his reference to his past accomplishments were of no avail. He argued that going back or remaining on the spot was fraught with great danger. The Germans would reach Minsk at any moment.

As he relayed the conversation to me, Siomka mentioned the officer making this statement: "Who tells you to fall into German hands? Fight against them . . . "

When he told me this, we looked into each other's eyes. We surely had the same thoughts then. That officer was an anti-Semite. He was part of a mighty military force and he had the gall to leave in haste and delegate a journalist to obstruct the onward march of the Germans.

I would have been lost in thoughts for a long time, if an acquaintance of Siomka had not descended upon us and assured us that the officer who rejected us was not an anti-Semite, but a Jew. He had known him in Vilna and they had met on many occasions.

The order applied to everybody alike—to the young, to the older people, to Siomka the communist and to hundreds of others like myself. With broken hearts we watched the train and the people disappear in the distance without us.

To console ourselves, we went into a nearby wooded area and ate whatever we had. We analyzed our situation and listened to each other's conclusions.

Siomka could not forgive the officer. I had little to add to the discussion. If a man like Siomka, with such a loyal communist record who was at one time a fugitive from the Polish police at the time communism was illegal in pre-war Vilna

—if such as he was excluded from communist Russia, what could I say? An order was an order, I thought.

As I was eating, I was moved to speak to Siomka and remark how valuable his experience in the forest had been. He had learned a lot when he spent some time with gypsies when he had been sent as a journalist by the Vilna daily, *Wilner Tog*, to live with them and gather material for some articles. Sarcastically, he replied that he did not like life in the forest then, but now it was much different. There was shooting on all sides . . .

During an idle moment, I tried to delve into the turn of events. We had met up with a high officer in the Russian army, who was not an anti-Semite, but a Jew. What did he mean by, "Who tells you to fall into German hands? Fight against them." These words echoed in my ears all the days of the Nazi occupation. At the time, this was only a rhetorical phrase, for there was no question of standing up against the German Wehrmacht. The mightiest had to retreat in the face of their Blitzkrieg. But the ringing words had a very vital message.

Siomka and his family decided to stay in Molodeczno with relatives, because his mother-in-law could not undertake a return march of about 150 kilometers.

The entire rejected group gradually started to return to their points of departure.

The way back was a terrible nightmare. We spent the night in the woods near the border. There we saw from a distance of 20 kilometers the conflagration of Minsk which burned with a hellish fire. At dawn, we saw the tanks of the enemy.

Our first meeting with the enemy wasn't anything like what we imagined it would be. The Germans did not pay any attention to us and allowed us to proceed on our way back.

A spark of hope buoyed us up. Maybe we would get back to Vilna after all—to our families, our homes—where 90% of the Jewish population was left. There was no report at the time that the Germans had exterminated all Jews.

40

We would all be together. It's a city full of Jews. We'll see . . . Of the thousands of wayfarers who started back to Vilna on foot, only a few hundred arrived.

In contrast to our first uneventful meeting with the Germans, when nothing was done in the way of murder, we were later to learn who they were and what they could do.

Our path was strewn with Jewish corpses.

An order was issued in the surrounding cities, that no one was to be found in the woods. Anyone encroaching upon the woods, was to be shot at sight. Large groups could not walk together. If anybody carried weapons, all Jews in the group would be shot.

There were walking groups of 5, 10, or 50 and more, for not everybody was aware of the order of some insignificant German officer. It was a chaotic walk. Strangers and friends strode along together.

The surrounding peasants began to waylay and rob us.

If any wire or antenna of a passing German tank was torn, that was reason enough for shooting an innocent passer-by—for the crime of a torn wire.

I had occasion to trudge along with all kinds of people and groups. Some faltered and could not keep up with the set pace; they dropped out along the way. It was necessary to change the component members of a group quite often.

In this way, I met up with a sturdy refugee from Lodz, his wife and ten-year-old child. We became friends and walked quite a distance together.

Once we had to resort to a peasant for some food, when a large detachment of military tanks descended upon us. Mercilessly, they besieged the entire village including the peasant huts and they confiscated milk, eggs and other edibles.

We realized that we had better hit the road as fast as possible—away from the village. At the same time, we stood in mortal fear of the two-footed and eight-wheeled beasts of prey.

My fellow-walker, a man with a fine head of gray hair, and

I found ourselves at the entrance of a house where there was a German officer. We asked him whether we could walk through, and he motioned to us through a window that we should go through a field. As soon as we crossed over onto a highway, where a long line of tanks and heavy artillery was parked, a squadron of planes appeared. We did not pay any particular attention to them, because we believed they were German planes. This was no novelty to us.

From a distance we heard a command to halt. We stopped in our tracks. A German soldier with a pistol in hand ran over to us and shouted: "Why did you cross over the open field with airplanes flying overhead?"

In self-defense we said that the planes suddenly appeared from out of the woods and by coincidence they got us in the open field. There was no place to hide.

"Who gave you permission to wander about while our tanks were standing here?"

"A German officer," we answered.

"That very officer ordered me to bring you back. You will be shot as spies."

After we heard the accusation, we considered ourselves dead ducks. This would really have been the case, if not for an unexpected rescue. It was a radio-command by the general in charge, that everybody was to man the tanks which soon began to move, leaving us a few meters behind. That saved our lives from being spectacularly snuffed out.

Another incident occurred when we joined another group of people. A German guard posted on a little bridge ordered us to break it up. "Divide into two groups." The order was carried out. We divided ourselves up into groups of seven. We didn't realize the purpose of his order.

The six people with whom I found myself, were commanded by the officer to march on. He kept the second group of seven near himself. After we walked away some 20 meters we paused. We indicated that we were waiting for our friends, and he should release them.

The officer, noticing our hesitation, yelled that we should go on. The others had to stay behind, for a time. Then he gave a few consecutive shots in the air with his automatic as a warning to us that we should take our leave.

We went on for a few paces and stopped again to wait for the others.

To our horror, we saw this scene: the German officer ordered them to line up at attention and then he fired his automatic at them, and killed them all.

We were rooted to the spot. The Germans did not shoot at us. Our group entered a wooded area and discussed the horrible episode. We reached the unanimous conclusion that none of us would reach our goal. That is, no one would get to his home town alive, for every step was fraught with danger. We decided to attach ourselves to larger groups—to the extent of a few hundred people. If anybody would dare play the same "tricks" on us, we would act in self-defense. Naturally, we meant individual adversaries.

Again we separated and fell apart, until we dragged ourselves to the city of Smorgony—90 kilometers from Vilna. Before we had a chance to enter the city, we were overtaken by a mob of peasants. For a few days previously, they had noticed that Jews were returning to Smorgony with knapsacks and hand baggage. They set themselves to rob, beat up and kill the refugees, if they couldn't rob them.

Since we were about equal in number, we engaged them in a hand-to-hand battle.

As a result, a few Jews were killed; some received deep knife wounds; others got off with a good pummeling. I was one of those who was punched. We got off relatively easy. The peasants were armed with butcher knives, scythes, iron bars and we had only our bare fists . . . Soon more peasants entered into the fray, and we thought we would never come out alive.

After we broke through Smorgony, in the section where no Germans were quartered, we walked about 50 kilometers. We proceeded further to avoid being in the vicinity of the city. Nobody was permitted to sleep over in the woods. That was certain death. So we gathered our strength and we made 20 kilometers more until we got to the city of Oszmiana.

In Smorgony we did not find any Jews, for they had fled to the surrounding wooded areas in the morning, leaving behind all their worldly goods. In Oszmiana, on the other hand, we found the Jews in their places of residence.

After spending the night in Oszmiana, we went on our way and arrived at Vilna in the afternoon. There we found out that on the perimeter of the city there stood a strong guard with tanks and machine guns. They captured all Jews returning to the city.

After we had gone through such a dangerous journey we faced the possibility of falling into the bloody hands of the Germans. Their contention was that we had attempted to retreat with the Red Army.

Now it was clear that we could not go in groups at all. We had to go individually, each man for himself. Maybe one would succeed in breaking through.

I found out later that many of those who had braved the dangers of the road with me, were captured when they attempted to enter the city. Inside the city they were under strict surveillance. After that they were brought to a concentration camp near Minsk where they were later exterminated.

I succeeded in entering the city by means of a milk truck, for a fee to the driver, who was a man of principles. Like many others before him, he could have taken my money and handed me over to the Germans. This non-Jewish driver saved me from doom.

When I was inside on Berlinska Street, I learned that men were being kidnapped in the street. I managed to go through a few court yards and reached the house of my sister's girl friend. They had a big orchard near the house where I found the entire Nemzer family. There they felt safer than in the house. The orchard was partially hidden by trees and bushes and fences, through which one could flee in case of danger.

I greeted the family heartily and then I took advantage of the fruits of the orchard. From my sister's friend I learned that all was in order in my own household, and that my family was sorry that I had left them.

I fixed myself up, dusted off my clothes and relieved my hunger. Then my sister's friend offered to accompany me home. (Women could go through the street undisturbed in those days and I accepted her kind offer.)

I came home without incident.

I found the entire family around the table eating lunch. They were deliriously happy at my return—especially my mother.

"Come eat with us, my son," my mother said. "I just thought about you. God knows where you roam and whether you have anything to eat as we have here. Take something, don't worry. Whatever happens to all the Jews, will happen to the individual Jew. Meanwhile, eat your fill . . ."

The elderly generation still remembered the famous speech of 1917 which General Ludendorff had delivered in *Yiddish* to "my dear Jews in Poland."

Back in Vilna

That same day I was fully informed how conditions were in the city and how the Germans were carrying on. I learned:

That large sections of the population—Lithuanians, as well as the Poles—warmly welcomed the Germans;

That the Germans, in the first days of the invasion, did not particularly concern themselves with the Jews;

That on the third day after the German army goose-stepped into Vilna, the Gestapo set about its bloody work;

That Gestapo-men in small taxis, like motorcycles, drove over to Jewish houses and arrested people at random on the pretext that they found a list somewhere showing they belonged to some kind of party or social institution;

That the Gestapo had already organized a Lithuanian "Ipatingo" (Elite-Guard), whose aim was to terrorize and kill Jews;

That hundreds of men were snatched away for hard labor outside of the city and the majority of these men had not as yet returned home;

That in the time of my absence from the city, a squadron of Soviet airplanes arrived and destroyed the greater part of the air base in Porubanek. Quite a few Jews who were dragged there to do forced labor, perished;

That my family heard that somebody saw me in Porubanek. As a consequence, they sent a good old friend, a non-Jewish woman, to look over the dead to see if I was among them. Later I was told by that Christian woman that she could not find me among the corpses . . .

All the Jewish business concerns were closed. People used the provisions they had on hand. Then they just resigned themselves and waited for the black day to come. That was the state of affairs during the five days I was absent from the city.

The day after I reached Vilna, I went over to a friend of mine, who was my closest neighbor. He was also the most suitable person with whom to discuss plans for action.

He was called Boria (Dov) Szneider, a man of high ideals. He told me that he also tried to run away, but he could not get any transportation. After he had gone a few kilometers on foot, he came to the conclusion that it was useless to go on, because the Germans would catch up with him before he could make 50 kilometers. Therefore he had turned back.

I told him of my own experiences, with the comment that we would perish at the hands of the Germans in one way or another, if we would not fight back.

Dov was of the same opinion, that the "fuhrer's" speeches

were not empty words; that we were on the brink of liquidation.

We discussed the matter for hours and we came to the conclusion that as long as we were not united in a ghetto, in a compact unit, it was impossible to do anything. First of all, men were not allowed to go freely into the streets. That completely disrupted any contact with friends. We decided that as soon as we would be herded into the ghetto, we would somehow take matters in hand.

It took over a month before we were driven into the ghetto.

Each one of us was anxiously awaiting the moment when we would find ourselves in the ghetto. We were in a state of nervous tension from the fear of a most certain rap on the door, which would mean a visit by the so-called "Snatchers."

We were tired of the numerous and conflicting ordinances and restrictions which were poured upon our heads.

First, came the order for the confiscation of all weapons. Before this was carried out, the order came to give up all radios, bicycles, etc. Then came the third order for the donning of round, yellow patches, 10 inches in diameter. The letter, "J" for Jews, was to be imprinted on the patch. In a few days, the patches were abolished and changed to something else: a smaller "Shield of David." Following these ordinances, came the astounding "Nowogrudska provocation." Hundreds of able-bodied Jewish men were taken as hostages for the "crime" that a German had been shot in Nowogrudska Street. There was an added penalty: a fine of one million R-Marks had to be paid by the community. This money was collected and brought to the German makeshift court by Jewish representatives called "Judenrat." As a reward for the latter's prompt and accurate service, the Germans arrested this temporary "Judenrat," which consisted of some 15 persons, and had them all executed.

The Jews could not even greet an Aryan. Then came the Straszuna Street incident. They trumped up the charge that two minor officials were shot. For that the entire population of Straszuna Street—men, women, children, old folks—without any exception, were dragged out in the middle of the night and taken to an unknown destination.

The Jews of Vilna had to bear all of this during the first days of the Nazi occupation.

It was clear that it was impossible to live in this atmosphere of continuous threat to life, limb and sanity. It would be better to be driven into a ghetto. Maybe such incidents would not occur.

We heard that Warsaw had such a ghetto for the past two years and life went on regardless. We had never had anything like this. True, it would be terribly hard to live. But every step was dangerous outside. Perhaps that would not be so in the ghetto.

This was the train of thought in the mind of every rational Jew. This was the reasoning of the majority. Perhaps in the ghetto they would avoid the dread and fear of the "Snatchers."

Nobody knew what happened to the Jews who were snatched away. Hundreds who were captured on the streets were gone for days on end; others came back after a short while. They had been forced to do hard, unnecessary and back-breaking work and were beaten mercilessly.

Men avoided the streets.

The snatchers got 10 rubles* a head and that gave them the incentive to raid homes. Men had to hide wherever they could, in order to escape the bandits, who operated in broad daylight.

A woman who delivered milk to us and to all others in our courtyard, told us that early one morning, when all traffic was still forbidden in the city, she witnessed how a group of men were led under heavy guard into the Ponary woods. The guards carried bare bayonets. She told us further that she had not gone more than a few steps, when she heard the crack of bullets and piercing human screams.

*10 Rubles = 1 Reichsmark.

I and some of my neighbors in the courtyard, understood exactly what happened. The doubters in the neighborhood, on the other hand, did not believe the tale of the milkmaid. Some accused her of exaggeration and of latent anti-Semitism. Perhaps she had wanted it to be so . . .

The news brought by the milkmaid spread quickly throughout the city.

Hardly anybody believed that all the missing able-bodied men who were snatched away would be dispatched without rhyme or reason in the woods of Ponary.

But they didn't have to wait long. Confirmations came from other Christian witnesses. Despite that, it still was incredible to many.

The snatchers still continued their dirty work. Those Jews who had to go to designated jobs received special passes. This meant that the snatchers were to let them alone, for these workers were assigned to military duties.

Passes were only in the possession of a small number of Jews. The snatchers had a wide field to choose from outside of these passholders.

Suddenly, there was a rise in demand for work which provided these passes, in order to avoid being snatched.

For a few days, the snatchers honored the passes; then they got orders not to honor them any more.

This was only a rule on the part of the Germans to get the Jews into their net. They freely captured great numbers of Jews who returned from their jobs. Later, it was decreed that the passes should be honored again if they had a special stamp. Those without the stamp were not honored. This was done in order to cause confusion, so that people should not know what to do and how to act.

The Snatchers

The snatchers became more and more aggressive. It was only known that the captured men were brought to the Gestapo.

After a while they took large groups of men in the direction of Pohulanka Street behind the white pillars.

Wives and sisters tried to follow their men to see where they were taken. They brought back the report that they had followed their men up to the white pillars of Pohulanka Street. There they were ordered to return back on their heels and not go behind the pillars, on pain of being instantly shot.

The rest of the story can be easily surmised. The way led to the Ponary. That meant that the milkmaid spoke the truth, that the men were led to their death.

This was borne out by the fact that in the following days the snatchers went after the old and the sick men.

Everybody grumbled that the snatching was not for forced labor. There was no doubt that the men were led to their destruction. But the majority of the Jews still did not believe their ears.

In that period the Germans wanted to keep their systematic executions a secret from the surrounding populace and from the Jews as well. In spite of this the more alert elements among the Jews of Vilna caught wind of what was being done to their fellow-Jews.

Little by little, the veil was lifted concerning the Straszuna Street incident, where young and old were driven out in their underwear and slippers. It was clear that the people were not led to any "labor camp," as they tried to convince us, but to their doom.

In such circumstances, the Jews had no other choice but to wish to be brought to the ghetto. Ten thousand of our brothers and sisters disappeared without a trace during the month of terror. Everybody expected the same fate.

Of course, it stands to reason, that such a ceaseless pogrom caused the Jews to long for the day when they would be driven into the ghetto. They sincerely believed it was the only solution. Perhaps there would be work to do; the people would live together and such atrocities would not take place.

German notice in three languages.

NOTICE

Last Sunday afternoon, German soldiers were fired upon from ambush.

Two of the cowardly bandits were recognized. They were Jews.

The attackers paid with their lives. They were shot immediately.

In order to prevent the occurence in the future of such hostile acts, new, stronger measures have been ordered. The responsibility lies with the Jewish community.

First, all Jews of both sexes are forbidden, from this day on, to leave their homes from 3 o'clock in the afternoon until 10 o'clock in the morning. Exceptions will be only those Jews and Jewesses who have a clear work order.

The above order is for the security of the population and for the safety of their lives. It is the duty of every right-thinking citizen to co-operate and aid in the preservation of order.

THE MILITARY HEAD OF THE CITY OF VILNA
(*signed*) HINGST

Vilna, September 1st, 1941

51

GHETTO DOCUMENT

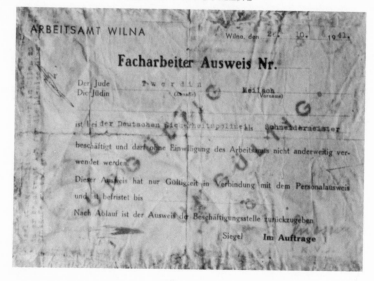

Selection at the gate of the Ghetto

Part II

Preparation For Resistance

DRIVEN INTO THE GHETTO

THE long anticipated moment came at dawn, September 6, 1941. The Jews were awakened early in the morning by long whistles and yells from those who came to force us into the ghetto.

At first, no one knew exactly what was going on. Soon it became clear that the time had come to go. That day, traffic was stopped for non-Jews.

All the military and police forces of the Germans and the Lithuanians were mobilized. Germans and Lithuanians were stationed in every courtyard and they commanded the Jews to evacuate their homes in 15 minutes.

It was self-evident that 15 minutes were not sufficient for the aged and the children to get ready. It was impossible to get dressed and take along the bare necessities.

This was in great contrast to the city of Kovno. There the Jewish population was given a couple of days to move into the ghetto, with a chance to transfer their household goods

MAP OF THE VILNA GHETTOS

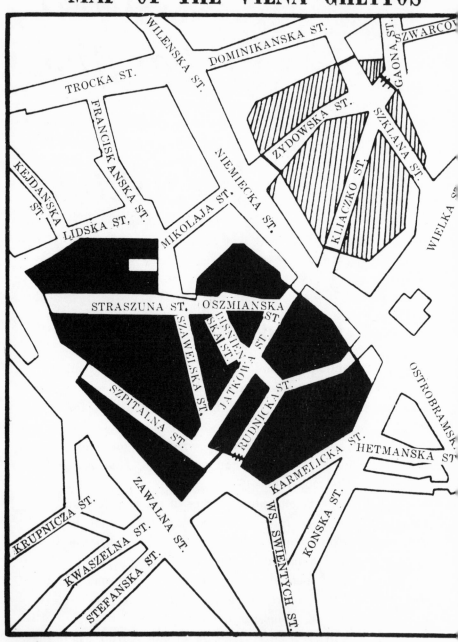

 1st Ghetto—September 6, 1941—September 23, 1943

2nd Ghetto—September 6, 1941—October 28, 1941[1]

in wagons and carts. In Vilna they only allowed us 15 minutes to get dressed and get packed. Each person could take only that which he could carry. Being awakened from a deep sleep and rudely driven into the ghetto did not make for organized thinking. The Jews had to get dressed, and grab haphazardly in the little time allowed them. As a result, homes were left in a panic, and when they reached the ghetto they lacked basic necessities. For example, some grabbed a few colored cloth napkins and no sheets; or they grabbed a basket of raw potatoes and they lacked cooking facilities. They left loaves of bread behind; the children's diapers were forgotten. All these little things made life miserable in the ghetto from the moment they arrived.

It was a hot summer day when thousands of Jews from all streets and side lanes of Vilna were driven in the direction of the ghetto. It looked like the old pictures of the exodus from Egypt.

Those who wanted to rescue as much of their clothing as possible, put on more than one costume in addition to summer and winter coats. Whatever they could or could not carry was taken along.

When they were driven out into the unbearable heat, they got too weak to carry things. Many of the people dropped their bundles and later found themselves with superfluous clothes and without food.

The path to the ghetto was strewn with thousands of bundles which the Jews had to drop because they could not carry them any longer.

The German military trucks followed the columns and picked up everything and took it for themselves.

Thus it came about that there was a food shortage and hunger in the ghetto. Jews had to share the little they had with each other the first few days.

When we were driven into the ghetto, they were completing the wooden gate that separated it from the city.

When we crossed the threshold of the ghetto, we all breathed easier. Now we were free of the escort of the Germans and the Lithuanians.

The feeling that we came into our own, and we left our oppressors outside, gave us some consolation.

Among Jews

My family, as well as all the others, began to free themselves of their baggage. I had succeeeded in dragging the sack of provisions—the most vital bundle of all—to our destination.

Wiping off my perspiration, I tossed the sack to other members of my family and I rushed outdoors to find my friends.

This emergency had unwittingly united us. Previously it was impossible to meet with them. By coincidence, I came upon my colleague Boria Szneider in all the confusion. He had also relegated his baggage to members of his family. Here we were out of danger. We went to the end of the ghetto on Szpitalna Street, in order to discuss further steps to take.

We decided to look for Boria Friedman, whom we wanted to take into our plans.

We were lucky. With the help of others, we found Friedman without too much difficulty.

During this period, it was a great problem to find people. It often happened that a member of the family got lost and a search went on for days without success. That was because people seized upon any empty available spot. Some 50,000 Jews were crowded into a few streets. There were no means of locating any individual in the initial period. That is why we were so lucky that my group found each other without too much difficulty.

This time, our trio sought a small, ruined alcove away from the noise and confusion, for our meeting. We didn't have to talk too much. Each one of us had seen, heard and experienced a great deal.

Boria Szneider suggested we should co-opt Rivka Karpinkes to our initiative group. We quickly agreed to this, knowing her courage. She used to visit Menachem Begin, the former leader of Betar in Poland, when he was in the Lukiszki prison, held as a political prisoner because of his anti-communist stand, after he came with the stream of refugees from Warsaw to Vilna. It is needless to point out that to visit such a prisoner was risky; we knew we could rely on Rivka as a member of our planning group.

We all agreed that we had to proceed immediately to organize a self-defense unit. The decision was unanimously adopted.

In the meantime, the members of my family sought and found a corner of the earth upon which to lie down. We were pressed together like sardines.

At the next day's meeting, we learned from Friedman that the ghetto was to be divided. The first section would consist of the following streets: Rudnicka, Jatkowa, Dzisnienski, Szawelska, Oszmianska, Straszuna, Szpitalna. The second ghetto would have these streets: Zydowska, Klaczko, Szklana, Gaona. The two sections would be separated and would have no connection with each other.

This was the first big blow. Our forces would be divided.

Pola Deiches, one of our first underground co-workers.

That meant we could not reckon with the friends we had counted upon. Communication was broken and we could not contact each other. Then we had to concern ourselves only with comrades in our part of the ghetto.

Our mission was extremely difficult, because of the initial confusion in the ghetto during the first few weeks. Yet we did break through and we organized contact with friends.

The ghetto had unbearable conditions. Hunger stalked. The gates opened and thousands of Jews were let out for various labor assignments in the city, which relieved the situation somewhat. Those who went to work ate somewhere, sometimes the Germans gave them a bit of soup, or they could buy something from nearby Christians.

We decided that Friedman should get work in some newly established Jewish institution. We assisted him in carrying out the idea. We already had one of us planted there and we would eventually find out what was brewing in regard to the ghetto.

We also decided that our friend Rivka Karpinkes should be placed in a newly created teashop, so that our membership should be able to take advantage of some of the warm meals which would be served there. Here we were not successful in our first attempt because of the members of the "Judenrat." They preferred to have their own relatives and friends in such an institution as a teashop.

Thus we kept on working tirelessly to organize a *foundation* for a big movement.

Those who thought they would find peace in the ghetto were mistaken.

In a few days we learned that here and there a group of Jews, returning from work, were abducted and left no traces.

Before we were able to accomplish anything concrete in the period of confusion, we were shocked by the news that on the 28th, 29th, and 30th of October, 1941, the entire second ghetto with some 20,000 Jews was liquidated under the supervision of the Gestapo officer Horst Schweinenberg.

It developed that the residents of the Kalwariska section of Vilna were not driven to the ghetto, but directly to the Lukiszki prison under cover of night. After staying there a couple of days, they were led to the Ponary woods and shot.

This was also the fate of those in the ghetto on Licka Street. A little later the Germans decided that Licka Street should be outside the ghetto, and the people who were already living in the houses on that street were not led to a nearby ghetto street, but to the prison. The giant courtyard was over-filled with Jews—old, young, men, women and children. When the Germans evacuated the prison, they conducted a registration of skilled professional workers.

That the Germans were well trained in the art of mass murder can be borne out by this fact: before they led all the Jews in the prison to their death, they freed a few hundred professionals like engineers, technicians and the like. They were given to understand that nothing would happen to professionals. That was substantiated by the fact that they were freed after they were incarcerated in the prison. Of course, these tricks made an impression on some Jews.

Those who returned from the prison told shocking stories about the conditions under which they were forced to live while in the prison. They were given no food. People perished there of hunger and thirst. Hundreds of valuable fur coats were piled up at the entrance of the lavatory, to cover the dirt piled up to the knee, and for people to step all over them. Great sums of money were offered for ameliorating the pains of death. All sorts of valuables were given as bribes. The picture was horrifying.

As stated above, the liquidation of the second ghetto followed soon thereafter. A second mass murder took place on Yom Kippur, when five thousand Jews met their doom.

After the Yom Kippur holocaust, the District Commissioner

announced that those with professional certificates could go to work undisturbed.

The first live witnesses to the mass murders were those Jews who miraculously rescued themselves from the lime pit graves of Ponary.

They told that they were brought to the Ponary woods under a heavy guard. As they penetrated deeper into the woods they came to a tower. Heavy barbed wire surrounded it. They were led inside and driven to mass graves lined with lime. They were commanded to undress and were told that those who would give up their money and jewels would not be shot.

The murderers took away all valuables and after their victims were systematically robbed, they opened up a hurricane of machine-gun-fire and the poor Jews fell dead and half-dead into the open graves.

When all were executed, the murderers went around to check whether any of their victims stuck their heads out of the lime. If so, they dispatched them individually.

The very few who saved themselves by a miracle told this story.

After all these incidents during the first months of the Nazi occupation, there was no doubt that the Brown Beast had every intention of exterminating all Jews—without exception.

Under such circumstances and in the face of a permanent genocide action in which the Nazis engaged, it was impossible to concentrate on any sort of resistance action on our part. You spoke to a man and the next moment he was killed in some devious way. And that meant starting all over again.

After a few weeks of comparative "quiet" a new slaughter plan awaited the ghetto.

Yellow Passes

The German Labor Division began to distribute the above-mentioned yellow passes. At first, people did not pay much attention to them. Previously, various passes were given out, and when a collective action was taken by the Nazis, these passes had no value.

The news spread that this time the Germans would "honor" the yellow passes.

In the meantime, the yellow passes were distributed among three thousand Jews who had the right to support their families.

Those who acquired the passes, with or without effort, had something in hand that was supposed to be privileged.

Only those with white or yellow passes could go to their jobs in the city.

It was obvious that more than half of the ghetto was to be deported, if only three thousand passes were issued.

On October 24, 1941, it was announced that all passes were annulled except the yellow passes. At 8 A.M. the next day, all the possessors of the yellow passes had to leave the ghetto for 3 days and take their families along to their places of work. All others had to remain in the ghetto. Even a blind person could see what that meant. The announcement was made just as it was getting dark the day before, on October 23rd.

This was the first time the ghetto had the dubious advantage of having an entire night to think about the prospect of mass extinction the next morning.

The ghetto was in an uproar. It was like being on top of a volcano. The ghetto divided into two parts: one part had to be ready to die the next morning and the other part got a temporary parole which was not very reliable.

People ran helter-skelter in the ghetto like maniacs. They made last-minute preparations to hide in disguised hideouts; others offered large sums of money to have a child registered on the pass of one who had no children or only one child. The yellow passes were good for a family of four. There was an ugly trade in human lives.

It was impossible to leave the ghetto, because the guard had been strengthened. Secondly, there was no place to go. The hour was getting late. Nobody was allowed on the street, even outside the ghetto, because of martial law. The average person saw no sense in risking his life beforehand.

The Judenrat had a limited number of yellow passes at its disposal which were not yet given out.

Many who were employed in the ghetto institutions did not receive the yellow passes, because the Jewish Gestapo agent Dessler, sold them for thousands of Marks to fellow-Jews who wanted to save themselves. The streets were pitch dark because military orders forbade any lights.

People ran around in the darkest hours of the night as if going to say "Lamentations," with candles in hand. Some ran to relatives, acquaintances, or to a hiding place; others tried to add their own names to somebody else's yellow pass.

The Judenrat was besieged by thousands of Jews who tried to register for going out of the ghetto with the yellow passes. Almost none of my friends had a pass. Death threatened all of us.

We held an emergency meeting. We decided to urge everybody to scatter, to go out on their own. Unfortunately, the most vital part of our youth suffered the same fate as all other Jews who had no yellow pass.

My quartet did not get the yellow pass. Even though Boria Friedman had a high-ranking job in the Judenrat, he could not get it either, in time.

Then and there, Szneider and I decided to get out of the ghetto somehow under cover of night even though we might perish in the attempt.

My family was all prepared to go into the disguised hideaway where they had withstood all previous actions.

I was given the job of camouflaging it as best I could. I thought that my family and neighbors, 32 souls in all, had a good chance of coming through the threatened danger alive.

"So, good night."

"Till we meet again," I called out to those behind the trapdoor. I received the same answer.

My mother insisted that I should also enter the trapdoor. I answered that I could not go into the safest trapdoor. I must be free to move about . . .

My family knew that it was not in my makeup to go into hiding when there were other alternatives.

Woronowa

What the other alternative was going to be, I myself did not know. But, when I went down to the dark, narrow ghetto streets, I saw a German military truck pull in and stop a few buildings from the ghetto gates.

A German soldier came out from behind the wheel and met with a Jew, who was working in his detachment as a forced laborer.

In seconds, the truck was loaded with people who knew the pre-arranged escape. One of the men was missing. As I was standing near the truck, a friend of mine beckoned me to board it. Then the truck left the ghetto immediately.

When I had the ghetto gates behind me, I felt relieved of some of my tensions. We left during the night while the city was under martial law. This meant that only military personnel could move. We arrived safely at Woronowa, a small city that was 60 kilometers from Vilna, and was considered a part of White Russia. Woronowa was, in those days, more or less safe for Jews. They did not know of mass-murder at the time, in spite of the fact that Ponary was close to them.

After being in Woronowa a week or so, all the Vilna Jews, consisting of several hundred persons, were picked up and herded into the movie house, where all were burnt alive along with the building.

I was staying with the Levin family in Woronowa. My friend, Shimon Levin, lived and worked in Vilna, and was a former corporal in the Polish army. He was captured by the

Russians and became a prisoner of war. Minutes before the Nazis herded all the Vilna Jews into the movie house, the Levins found out and warned me. Thus I was able to hide, seconds before the Nazis came for me.

A few days later I escaped from Woronowa and made my way back to Vilna ghetto. If I had to describe the entire journey from place to place, I would have to repeat many of the same villainous events that I experienced on my way from Minsk to Vilna.

Months later, the same fate overtook the few thousand Jews residing in Woronowa, and they perished in various ways.

Back in the Vilna ghetto, I learned that about 10,000 people perished on October 23, 24, 25, 1941 in the actions of the yellow certificates. My family and the others who were with them in the hideout, survived, and they were glad to see me again after my ordeal in Woronowa.

I heard from my family, that during my absence, Dov Szneider came to them continuously to find out about my whereabouts. But all they could do was to hope for the best, and they were not able to tell him anything about me, since the time I closed them all in their hideout.

I found Dov immediately, and I learned how he and his family survived in their hideout.

Family members of the bearers of the Yellow Certificates had these blue cards.

The Story of the Jewish United Partisan Organization in Vilna

We then started our talks on the organization of an underground which would be capable of repaying the Germans and their helpers.

A little while later, from a labor-camp of Resza, a village 10 kilometers from Vilna, came Joseph Glazman, the former head of the Youth Zionist Revisionist Organization "Betar," in Lithuania, and we immediately put him in charge of all the groundwork. Glazman became the speaker of our group, and he retained this office until the last days of the ghetto's existence.

EXECUTIVE COMMITTEE OF JEWISH STUDENT ORGANIZATION

Sitting from right: A. Harlig, Kacenelenbogen (*chairman*), Prof. Rudnicki (*curator*), J. Manela and A. Tajc. *Standing from right*: L. Adler, A. Gutman, L. Kaplanowicz, L. Lisak and (x) Boria Szneider.

Boria Friedman

From left: Rivka Karpinkes, Isaac Kowalski,
Fejgele Milstein

LIFE IN A "STABILIZED" GHETTO

WITH the establishment of the larger Ghetto No. 1 engineer Anatol Frid, an assimilated Jew, was selected as the head of the ghetto Judenrat. Members of the Jewish Socialist Bund, such as attorney Grisha Jaszunski (later belonged to the same fighting group of 5, that I belonged to), and A. Fiszman, became members of the new Judenrat. Engineer Guchman (non-partisan) and attorney Sh. Milkanowicki (General Zionists), also became members. Jaszunski was in charge of the commissary post, while Herman Kruk (Bund), headed the cultural department. Simultaneously, Jacob Gens became police commissioner of the ghetto, appointed by the Germans. He was a former Lithuanian army-captain.

A "Judenaelteste" (Jewish Elder) was created on July 12, 1942, with Jacob Gens in total power. Later Gens added many other people, among them such as Salek Dessler, who became a dangerous Gestapo-man and Joseph Glazman who became a pillar of the United Partisan Organization. Gens nominated Jaszunski as the head of the cultural department, who with extraordinary vigor established two Yiddish and one Hebrew school, arranged concerts and subsidized a theater. With lectures and courses he tried to start a "Renaissance" in the tragic ghetto atmosphere. Consequently, there arose Hebrew and Yiddish writers, clubs, and even a "Ghetto University," the dean of which was Zelig Hirsh Kalmanowicz. The University offered courses in philosophy, social sciences, linguistics, natural history, mathematics, physics and chemistry. Various Zionist groups in Vilna centralized this Hebrew cultural work by inaugurating the *Brith Ivrith* (Hebrew Association). Many other Hebrew institutions, such as a repertory theater, attracted ghetto audiences. Cemach Finkelstein edited the "Ghetto News," which was typed in Yiddish.

Now culturally on foot, many other problems had to be tackled. The "Social Self-Help" Committee rendered valuable service to help alleviate hunger and distress. Aside from relief contributions, the self-taxed Jews supplied funds to aid voluntary charity institutions, orphanages and nurseries. The Judenrat's "Social Relief Department" aided the ghetto people with its feeding kitchens and health and sanitation departments. Physicians of the ghetto offered free medical service. "Quick Help" located at Straszuna 6, was on hand with day and night ambulance service. Lectures on health hazards kept the entire ghetto in incomparable diligence.

Almost overnight a miracle transpired, brought about by these men and women. Through home industry, factories and laboratories were able to exist. Vitamins, soap, sacharrine tablets, artificial honey pastries, dentifrices and even cosmetics were made available to the ghetto people.

With the price of bread reaching 30 rubles a kilo, a wage of 300 rubles a month was hardly suitable. With organized food distribution, work cooperatives, and food smuggling and stealing from the German military units, mass starvation was prevented. The main savior, though, was production. For raising employment, plants for carpentry, locksmithing, tinsmithing, tanning, shoe making, appliance making, etc., were established. Consequently, smaller businesses, such as shoe repairing, tailoring, hosiery, etc., evolved. This routine continued unbothered for almost a year, until the first three months in 1943, when the Nazis decided gradually to seize and liquidate the ghetto.

Kittel

Bekanntmachung

Gemäss einer Anordnung des Herrn Gebietskommissars Wilna-Stadt sind sämtliche Juden verpflichtet, im Ghetto zu wohnen. Trotz dieser Anordnung kommt es immer wieder vor, dass Juden von ihrer Arbeitsstätte nicht zurückkehren, sondern bei dem Arbeitgeber übernachten. Einzelne Personen der einheimischen Bevölkerung gehen zum Teil so weit, dass sie Juden geheim aufnehmen und verbergen.

Ich fordere daher alle Einwohner Wilnas auf, alle Juden und Halbjuden, gleich ob getauft oder nicht getauft, welche sich noch ausserhalb des Ghettos befinden, bei dem zuständigen Polizeirevier zu melden.

Wird nach dem 30. 10. 1941 ein Jude ausserhalb des Ghettos in einer Wohnung angetroffen, so erfolgt strengste Bestrafung der Wohnungsinhaber.

Wilna, den 29. Oktober 1941.

Der Gebietskommissar der Stadt Wilna,
I. A. Murer

Order from Franz Murer about the "responsibility" not to hide Jews.

Vilna, 15 October, 1941

DISTRICT COMMISSAR IN THE CITY OF VILNA
IN THE REICHS COMMISSARIAT, OSTLAND
No. M/K

To the Municipal Administration of Vilna
Messrs Burogas
Vilna

Subject: Collection of Taxes in the Ghetto

The Jewish Council is authorized to mobilize the necessary means to conduct the affairs of the Ghetto, by imposing taxes. First of all I authorize a tax of 10% of the gross wages of the working Jewish population. The collection will be implemented by the Jewish Council in the Ghetto. It is not desirable that a large administrative staff be set up for managing the Ghetto affairs.

District Commissar of the City of Vilna
I. A., *Adjutant*
(——) BUROGAS
Spokesman on Jewish Affairs, Administration of the Vilna Municipality

Franz Murer

Martin Weiss

A. The German Government

Circular No. 1

To all the Establishments and Officers in the City of Vilna

Subject: Payment of wages to the Jewish labor force.

1. Beginning 10 October 1941 wages are to be paid to the Jewish working force. The scale of wages will be:

a) To male workers, age 16-60—0.20 Reichsmark per hour

b) To female workers—0.15 Reichsmark per hour

c) Young workers, below 16—0.10 Reichsmark per hour

These wage scales apply only to private employers. German civilian services, Wehrmacht services and the municipal administration of Vilna will pay half the above amounts. Private employers must pay half of the above scale to the Jews while the second half will be paid to the district commissary. In order to maintain the level of the technical skills of the Jewish workers, it is desirable that the employers provide hot soup at noon. For this purpose it is possible to deduct 0.30 Rmks of the daily wages paid to the Jews.

2. Before paying the wages to the Jews, the wage list is to be presented to the District Commissary; half of the wages is to be paid in there. All establishments and officers that employ Jews must advise at once in writing how many Jews are employed by them.

In case the wage money is withdrawn from the Government of Lithuania Bank, the half of the wages due to District Commissariat may be paid there. The amount paid must be made known to the District Commissariat in writing. A separate wage report for Jews must be kept and must be designated as such.

3. Jewish manpower can be requested only through the Vilna Labor Office.

The labor office provides Jewish labor only in groups of ten or more. Only in special cases is it possible to provide individual Jewish workers. These Jews must prove their identity through special identity papers issued by the labor office.

4. These Jews must go to their work via the shortest way, in a group, and they must return the same way.

It is forbidden to leave the place of work without permission.

Jews who run around the city alone will be arrested.

The employer must see to it that the Jews do not leave the place of work. If he cannot do this, he will no longer get Jewish workers.

By dusk, the Jews must return to the Ghetto in a group.

—ROSS
In Charge of Trade Unions War Administration Council
Vilna, October 15, 1941

NAZI GREETINGS . . .

"We greet all our customers and friends upon the occasion of Christmas and New Years of 1942. We hope that the coming year will bring success and a lasting peace."

—THE STATE PUBLICATION IN KOVNO AND ITS
BRANCH OFFICES IN VILNA AND ITS ENVIRONS.
Kovno, December 1941

Jacob Gens

Anatol Frid

Salek Dessler

Part III
U. P. O.
(United Partisan Organization)

THE ORGANIZATION OF THE U. P. O.

L IKE myself and my circle, that consisted of Zionist-Revisionists, other individuals tried to make contact, each with his comrades of his particular party, with the aim to resist the Germans.

This way contact was made in the ranks of Hashomer Hazair, General Zionists, Achdut Hoavoda, Bund and the Communists.

The Hashomer Hazair had some good contacts with idealistic youth, like the non-Jew Heniek, who came as a courier from Hechalutz in Warsaw in the beginning of November 1941, and met with Edek Boraks and Aba Kowner in a monastery where they were hiding in those days.

In the middle of November 1941, Heniek returned to Warsaw and brought the first news about the mass-murder. He met in the city, and not in the ghetto, with Frumka Plotnicki and Cywia Lubetkin. The latter forwarded the news to the ghetto, where it made a tragic impact.

The Warsaw ghetto was in existence for about two years and they still didn't experience mass-killings. Even Jews in the ghetto questioned the existence of Ponary.

Yitzhak Cukerman sent a message about the underground

Mordechei Tenenbaum-Tamarow

Moshe Balasz

Rushka Zilber

Sara Zilber

Tamara Szneiderman

Frumka Plotnicki

Arie Wilner

Schlomo Entin

Andzej Labedz

Tosia Altman

Edek Boraks

Chajka Grosman

activities of the Hechalutz in Warsaw vicinity and made contact with his party comrades in Vilna.

In December 1941, Israel Kempner and Yehuda Pinczewski, like Szlomo Entin and Edek Boraks a little earlier, brought the terrible news about the massacres in Vilna. "Jerusalem of Lithuania," as she was known in the Diaspora, was also chosen by the Third Reich to be the *first* for the "Final Solution" of the Jews.

Pinczewski and Kempner met in the summer of 1942 with the President of the Revisionist movement in Poland, Dr. David Wdowinski in a folk-kitchen in Warsaw ghetto. Through him they warned the Warsaw ghetto leadership about the oncoming great danger. They also confirmed Ze'ev (Vladimir) Jabotinsky's death in the summer of 1940 in New York, since even the leadership in the ghetto wasn't sure whether the sad news was true.

Dr. David Wdowinski, who at this time was already the commander in chief of the Resistance Organization Irgun Zwai L'umi in Warsaw, aroused the ghetto leadership and this later led to founding an organization for the ghetto uprising.

In a second gathering Edek Boraks, Szlomo Entin and Chajka Grosman met with the civic leaders Dr. Emanuel Ringelblum, David Guzik, Menachem Kirszenbaum, I. Sak, Morgenstern, Choleva, Dr. Nathan Ek, Yitzhak Cukerman and others.

Szlomo Entin and Edek Boraks returned to Vilna.

Mordechai Tennenbaum, Frumka Plotnicki, Cwi Mersik, Bela Chazan, Liona Kaziborowska, Sara and Reizel Zilber, Tamara Szneiderman, Tosia Lichtensztein, Szapiro, Lajzerowicz and some others were the couriers of the U. P. O. in Vilna and they visited other ghettos under great danger in Poland and Lithuania, agitating for an armed resistance.

Many contacts were made even before the U. P. O. was officially established.

In January 23, 1942, in a small room, a group of the

leaders of the resistance held a meeting, consisting of: Joseph Glazman (Revisionist), Itzik Wittenberg (Communist), Aba Kowner (Hashomer Hatzair), Abrasha Chwojnik (Bund), Nisl Resnik (General Zionist), Major Isidor Frucht (non-Aligned) and Chiena Borowski (Communist). Later were also added Jacob Kaplan (Communist) and Liowa Ziskowicz (Revisionist).

The operation-command consisted of Itzik Wittenberg (Leon) as commander, Joseph Glazman (Abraham) and Aba Kowner (Uri) as members of the high command.

Frumka Plotnicki brought from Warsaw Joint Distribution Committee an amount of money and news about the Treblinka gas chambers.

Beside those and others, there were Christian couriers who helped in the preparation for an armed struggle against the Nazis.

The newly organized high command immediately found itself facing a big dilemma: To fight the Nazis inside the ghetto or furnish the fighters with weapons and send them to the forests where they would fight the Nazis from the woods.

It was agreed that the U.P.O. members would fight in the ghetto and after destroying the ghetto buildings and the ammunition-depots in the city itself, we would retreat to the forest, where we would continue the battle against the Nazis.

The tragic events that happened to our commander (this chapter is separately described in the book), and with the establishment of Scheinbaum-Ester-group, the high-command was forced to revise the before agreed tactic and after thinking it over, decided to move our battle-positions to the forests in the vicinity of Vilna where Soviet partisans were frequently seen.

GHETTO DOCUMENT

COMMAND OF THE U.P.O.

Joseph Glazman

Itzik Wittenberg

Abrasha Chwojnik

Nisl Resnik

Aba Kowner

A resemblance of Sonia Madejsker and Itzik Wittenberg, in a conspirative basement room. (Published in *Sovietish Heimland* in Moscow February 1968).

OUR FIRST PROCLAMATION

LET US NOT GO LIKE SHEEP TO SLAUGHTER!

"Jewish youth, do not place your confidence in those who lead you to annihilation. Of eighty thousand Jews in the 'Jerusalem of Lithuania' only twenty thousand survive. Before our eyes have been torn from us our parents, our brothers and our sisters.

" — — — Where are the hundreds of Jews who were taken away for work by the Lithuanian kidnappers?

" — — — Where are the naked women and the children, who were taken from us during the awful night of the provocation?

" — — — Where are the Yom Kippur Jews?

" — — — And where are our brothers of Ghetto II?

"Whoever has been taken beyond the Ghetto gate will never return.

"All the Gestapo roads lead to Ponary. And Ponary is death.

"Those who waver! Cast aside your illusions: your children, wives and husbands are no more alive.

"Ponary is not a concentration camp. There they were all shot!

"Hitler aims to destroy *all* the Jews of Europe. It is the lot of the Jews of Lithuania to be the first in line.

"Let us not go like sheep to the slaughter.

"True, we are weak and without a protector, but the only answer to the murderers is—revolt!

"Brothers! Better to fall as free fighters than to live at the mercy of the murderers.

"Let us revolt! We shall fight until our last breath!"

January 1, 1942, Vilna, in the Ghetto

BATTLE REGULATIONS OF THE
U. P. O. (United Partisans Organization)

I. GENERAL

1) The order of battle that we are about to set forth is the test of physical and moral values of the U. P. O.-men, and of the individual capacity of each fighter to stand firm.

2) We shall be entering combat after nerve-wracking strains, in an atmosphere of panic, after harsh defeats that may befall the U. P. O. even before the battle begins.

3) The U. P. O. fighter is obliged not to lose his clarity of thought under difficult battle conditions, and not to recoil from danger.

4) Every unit commander and every individual fighter must prepare for the battle by adjusting to the conditions at hand and the realities of the approaching combat, in order to avoid surprise and not be broken in spirit, so that a person, who has never fired a weapon in his life, will not be frightened by his own shots.

5) This will be achieved by constant individual practice and study, that will picture beforehand in detail all possible situations that might arise during the moment of battle.

II. FIGHTING-ORGANIZATION

6) The U. P. O. is divided into two battalions.

7) Each battalion consists of six to eight units.

8) Each unit consists of three groups.

9) Each group consists of five fighters.

10) With each group there is a group-commander.

11) With each unit there is a unit-commander.

12) With each battalion there is a battalion-commander, a member of the command staff.

13) Each battalion has a reserve battalion at the disposal of the command.

14) Each commander has at his disposal a courier, who is used in an emergency.

15) The highest order is the order of the U. P. O. commander.

16) The reserve courier has to be well briefed and has to be used only when the regular staff courier has been killed.

17) Couriers have to know every battalion-commander and all the mechanism of the group and unit-commander. They have to be informed about duties and functions of the units and battalions.

83

III. MOBILIZATION

18) The mobilization is a pre-condition for battle.

19) The U. P. O. mobilization will be arranged
    a)   According to orders of the Command
    b)   According to automatic mobilization

20) The mobilization will be under a pass-word (mob. call).

21) The pass-word is, "Liza calls!"

22) Upon hearing the pass-word the commander is obliged to mobilize his unit immediately and report at once to the mobilization point.

23) Every fighter must report at once to the mobilization point, as soon as he gets the pass-word (regardless of who brings it).

24) The mobilization is at 31 Niemiecka Street.

25) If together with the mobilization call no other place is designated the mobilization point remains 31 Niemiecka Street.

26) Under all circumstances, one has to report to the M.P. using all exit combinations. In case of any resistance, one has to tear himself away and rush (cold weapons) to the M.P.

27) Come to the M.P. at any cost.

28) On coming to the M.P. each fighter has to find his own commander (and not reverse).

29) If he cannot find his own group-commander, the fighter has to report to the unit commander of a second group in his unit.

COMPOSITION OF TWO BATTALIONS

30) *First Battalion*—Commander Abraham (Joseph Glazman), first unit-commander Szmulke (Kaplinski), second unit-commander Aizik. Group 5 Chaim. Group 19 Goldman. Group 6 Aizik. Third Unit-Commander Baruch (Goldstein). Group 3 Abraham. Group 19 Witka. Group 2 Boruch. Fourth unit-Commander Gordon Lejb. Group 10 Baruch (Boria Szneider). Group 22 Gordon Hirsh.

31) *Second Battalion.* Commander Uri (Aba Kowner). Group 20 Widucki. Group Yismoel. Seventh unit. Commander Raff (Jaszka Raff). Group 13 Isaac Rogalin. Group 14 Rewski. Group 15 Isaac Lam. Eighth unit. Commander Hersh. Group 11 Pine. Group 12 Hersh. Group 10 Cepelewicz.

32) In the event that the command has been silenced by unforeseen factors, the U. P. O. organization must mobilize itself automatically.

33) Under what conditions shall there be automatic mobilization? When the Ghetto is suddenly faced with danger, when there is panic

among the people, accompanied by flight to the "Malinas." This would be called an emergency situation.

34) In this case, every U. P. O. fighter must report without waiting for an order of mobilization or a command.

35) By the same token, all difficulties must be conquered. Break through to the mobilization point, to work as decided in the instructions 26, 27, 28, 29, 30, and 31. Any other behavior, for example, to fall into panic, to run away to the family in a "Malina," is treason.

36) The flight of a U. P. O. member to the "Malina" will be considered in all situations and circumstances as desertion from the battlefield during war—as treason.

37) After coming to the mobilization point as a result of automatic mobilization, and in the case of not finding the commander, put on an emblem of the U. P. O. and organize a group on your own.

IV. INDEPENDENT ACTION

38) Every unit, commander, or fighter, could be cut off from the center during battle without being able to get directives from the command staff.

39) It is therefore imperative that the units, commanders and individual fighters should operate during the battle in an independent way with individual initiative.

40) Everybody is obliged to be in contact with the center, if possible: the fighter with the group, the group with the unit, the unit with the battalion.

41) Every unit must seek out the command and establish contact at any price.

42) In the event that the command staff is captured, a substitute command will take over the U. P. O. and work according to prearranged plans.

43) The substitute command will be chosen in advance.

44) The pass-word of the reserve staff is "Leon is in the hospital." The answer of the U. P. O.-fighter is "I'm his brother."

45) If separated from the center during a battle, the unit commander leads his unit independently into the fight.

46) If torn from the unit, each group-commander leads his group to battle.

47) If torn from the the group, each fighter battles independently.

48) Each commander upon seeing that his group or individual fighters were left without a contact, is obliged on his own initiative to unite and organize a possibly greater group to lead them to the battle.

49) Every soldier left alone has to activate groups of people and take charge of them as a commander and lead them to the battle.

50) The battle is to be waged with the full complement of fighters, without regard to the amount of weapons at hand.

51) When there are no hot weapons (firearms), the fight is to go on with cold weapons (knives, sticks, etc.)

52) The fight is to go on even without any weapons at all.

53) Fight also without arms.

54) To leave the battlefield is treason.

55) Only by an order of his commander can the fighter leave the battlefield.

56) Every individual U. P. O. member has to place himself in a fighting collective.

57) Each U. P. O. member is to display courage during the hour of danger, to inspire the maximum number of comrades to heroic deeds in combat.

58) The signal to start the battle has to be:

    a) An order from the command,

    b) Direct danger of a threatening liquidation.

59) If the commander of a unit is missing from the ranks, then one of the fighters has to substitute for him.

60) If a group commander is missing then every soldier has to be prepared to take over the leadership of his group.

61) If lacking an order from a higher unit, the commander is not entitled to be passive during the battle.

62) During the battle, the fighter has to be constantly prepared to render help to a wounded member, by handing him grenades, hatchets and shovels, etc.

63) Automatic weapons consume a great deal of ammunition which cannot be replaced during combat. Therefore each fighter is to economize as much as possible, to aim well and thoughtfully. A shot should be fired at the right moment after proper consideration.

64) It is forbidden to waste a single bullet.

65) The U. P. O.-soldier has to fulfill his battle mission with initiative, with cleverness. He has to fool the enemy.

66) The U. P. O.-soldier has to know to make precise decisions and then carry them out.

67) During a battle, the group-commander stays at the head of his group.

68) The unit-commander should be right behind his unit in time of battle.

69) The battalion-commander should be in a designated position at the time of offensive or defensive action.

70) The orders of the commander have to be clear and short, without commentary, so that the fighter is able to understand his duties. The order has to be logical.

71) To avoid misunderstanding it is the commander's duty to repeat orders if the fighting is to continue.

V. WEAPONS

72) The arming of the units shall be in accordance with their goals and capacities.

73) Every battalion will have a reserve group of U. P. O., a group of grenadiers, and a group that has automatic weapons.

74) It is essential that the acquisition of weapons shall take place during battle in the form of spoils taken from the enemy.

75) Those, for whom no guns are available, must immediately organize and conscript iron staves, knives, shovels, etc.

76) Weapons may be taken from ghetto-stores, workshops, or schools: take away everything that can be used as a cold weapon,

77) Every fighter when he is wounded and is not able to participate in battle must surrender his weapons and ammunition to another fighter.

78) When a comrade is killed his weapon and ammunition are to be taken away immediately.

79) [Paragraph 79 is missing].

80) The substitute command has to be informed of all important matters of the command.

81) The high command has to know all the sub-commanders.

82) In case the work of the command is obstructed, then the substitue command has to contact the courier or the substitute courier.

83) If the command is captured because of unforeseen circumstances, the substitute commana will assume charge of the organization and conduct its work properly.

84) The fighters first duty is to establish contact with the arrested commanders.

85) If the command is imprisoned due to extraordinary circumstances on the eve of battle, then the substitute command has to mobilize the organization and to assign a unit to special duties.

86) If the command is locked up by the Gestapo and all attempts at rescue fail—the battle is to start at once independently, to bring the U. P. O. into the battle.

Leo (Itzik Wittenberg), *Commander*
Abraham (Joseph Glazman)
Uri (Aba Kowner)
Moshe (Abrasha Chwojnik)
Chaim (Nisl Resnik)

April 4, 1943 in the Vilna Ghetto   *Members of the Command*

EXPLANATORY COMMENTS

While studying the Orders of Battle, questions of fundamental importance were asked in some units. Some of these questions were based on doubts, and had their origin in weakness and inadequate preparation to accept the real facts of the war. For this reason the command found it necessary, without connecting it to any of the units in particular, to give a full reply, as follows:

1) How shall the organization act in case there is a partial destruction of the Ghetto?

2) What shall the fighter do, in the event that he remains alone in the battle without any hope or capacity to continue his fight against the superior force of the enemy?

3) Should one go immediately to the forest?

4) What is the aim of the battle? (the ultimate goal?)

5) Is it permissible to hide in the "Malina?"

ANSWERS:

A. How shall the organization act in case there is a partial destruction?

1) The U. P. O. organization will enter the battle when there is danger that the entire Ghetto is to be destroyed.

2) It may be that there will be partial "actions" in the Ghetto, of a local nature, that will cost the lives of individuals, tens or hundreds.

3) Our view is that *all* Jewish lives are valuable and should be defended and they should not be abandoned to the murderers without resistance.

4) However, the U. P. O., which is not a large military force that can start an open battle with the enemy, will not start a fight to save the life of an individual Jew.

5) U. P. O., which is the vanguard of the Jewish community that still survives (not only in Vilna) can, *by premature action* bring about its own destruction and thus leave the Ghetto without the U. P. O. itself.

6) Such tactics would be quixotic, a kind of suicide. In addition, the Jewish community would view us as provocateurs and we would become involved in a civil war.

7) But just as premature action would be considered light-minded, so would action that occurs *too late* be viewed as a crime.

8) U. P. O. will enter into action when it is estimated that the beginning of the end has come.

9) The time of the action will be decided by the command, in keeping with its estimate of the situation and the information it has in hand.

10) Our inadequate equipment explains why the U. P. O. cannot act at all times. But this situation does not justify the avoidance of battle when it is clear that danger threatens the existence of the entire Ghetto. In such an hour, we must fight with all the weapons we have, even with a lack of weapons, with our bare hands.

B.   What shall the fighter do, when he is left to fight alone, without any chance or ability to continue his fight against a superior foe?

11) In such a situation, *which is the result of a battle, the individual may and should retreat.*

12) If there are any other survivors of fighting units, the individual fighter must slash a way to them, as fast as possible, to their fighting units, and join them.

13) If no others of the fighting units have survived, the single fighter is to try to save his life by whatever means possible.

14) Despite its preparedness to fall in battle, it is not the aim of the U. P. O. to fall during the last stand of the Ghetto.

15) *The aim of the U. P. O. is defense, combat, rescue.*

16) The aim of U. P. O. is to stand up, to resist to the end of the battle.

17) This does not mean that a person who sees the unequal forces and the scarcity of arms in his hands should give up in advance.

18) Non-participation in the battle during combat for any reason (shortage of arms, lack of chances, and so on) is like *treason.*

The Ghetto Prison.

C. Should one go to the forest immediately?

19) No. The desire to go to the forest immediately shows a lack of understanding of the U. P. O. ideas.

20) The idea of the Jewish partisan organization is a national and social one: to organize the struggle of the Jews and to defend our lives and honor.

21) Going to the forest at this time can be interpreted as a request for *individual refuge,* to save oneself, just as the hiding place at "Malina" means one seeks to save himself as an individual.

22) We shall go to the forest only as a *result* of battle. After we accomplish our mission we shall take with us a large number of Jews, as many as possible, and plunge into the forest, where we can continue our struggle with the conqueror and murderer, as an integral part of the general Partisan movement.

23) Only as a result of combat and thanks to our resistance shall we be able to save masses of Jews.

D. Is it permissible to hide in the "Malina?"

24) No. The answer to this question is given most emphatically in the Orders. Going to the "Malina" under any circumstances, is—*Treason.*

"Remember: until the last breath—our first proclamation read. That was many long days ago. Two years of bloody conflict. We shall continue until the last breath! And perhaps—until light."

"But we did not fight for the sake of life alone, but in order to give meaning to life that has lost its meaning.

"And those who shall remain alive, whether they know it or not, their lives shall be sanctified by this death.

"An outcry such as has never been heard before, comes to us from this soil: Continue!"

German police line up Jews against a wall

PARTISAN HYMN

Words: Hirsh Glik   *English Translation*: Esther Zweig

Do not say that you are
   headed for the end,
When leaden skies above you
   threateningly bend,
The hour we longed for
   days on end will soon appear,
Our steps will sound like
   drums announcing we are here.

From lands of flowering palms,
   from distant lands of snow,
We gather here with all our
   pain, with all our woe,
And where our blood was
   spilled and sacrificed in vain,
Brave men will rise and
   carry on in our name.

This Song is written with our
   blood and not with lead,
It's not a song of summer-
   birds that have no dread,
Mid crumbling walls
   a people took their final stand,
They sang this song
   with levelled guns in every hand.

PARTIZANER LIED
(*Yiddish*)

Zog nit kainmol az du gaist
   dem letztn veg,
Ven himlen bleiene farshteln
   bloiye teg,
Veil kumen vet noch undzer
   oisgebenkte sho,
Es vet a poik ton undzer trot,
   mir zeinen do.

Fun grinem palmen land biz
   veisn land fun shnai
mir kumen on mit undzer
   pein, mit undzer vai,
Un vu gefaln iz a shpritz fun
   undzer blut,
Shprotzn vet dort undzer
   gvure, undzer mut.

Es vet die morgn-zun bagildn
   undz dem heint,
Der shvartzer nechtn vet
   farshvindn mitn feint,
Nor oib farzamen vet die zun
   in dem cayor
Vie a parol zol gain dos lied
   fun dor tzu dor.

Dos lied geshribn iz mit blut
   un nit mit blei,
S'iz nit a lied fun zumer-foigl
   oif der frei,
S'ota folk tzvishn falndike vent
Dos lied gezungen mit naganes
   in die hent.

Derfar zog kainmol az du gaist
   dem letztn veg,
Ven himlen bleiene farshteln
   bloiye teg,
Veil kumen vet noch undzer
   oisgebenkte sho,
Es vet a poik ton undzer trot,
   mir zeinen do.

PARTISAN HYMN

This song was written by the U. P. O. member, Hirsh Glik who was later killed. He predicted, that "as a password this song would go from generation to generation."

Today the song is sung throughout the Jewish world and has been translated into many languages.

I knew the composer of the song personally and I did not foresee that his "Do Not Say" would become a song which would truly never be forgotten.

Stairs to the YIVO interior. The map in the background.

Szmerke Kaczerginski sorts books. In the back of these piles was our temporary hiding place of weapons brought to us by our weapon delivery partisans. Later, after work, Kaczerginski, Michal Kowner and myself used to smuggle the weapons into the ghetto.

93

ON ROSSA STREET. Here were selected all Jewish books of Lithuania
that were sent to the paper factory in Wilejka.
The Germans did not manage to carry away all the books which were left
on the platforms of the Vilna railroad station. When Vilna was liberated,
on the same spot as in the photograph where the German officer was
standing when he shipped the books to the Institute for Investigation of
the Jewish Question in Frankfurt, about June 1943, I stood a year later
as director of the Polygraph Trust in Vilna and through a favor I secured
the use of a truck which was used for an entire day to cart the books
over to secure buildings. This way I prevented the books from being
taken away for various uses. Shown in the doorway in the picture are
Brigadier Cemach Zawelson and his brigade as they worked during
German occupation.

Liza Magun

Michal Kowner

Julian Jankauskas

THE NAZI "CULTURE CORPS"

PARALLEL with the Nazi efforts to exterminate the Jews was the German drive directed at wiping out the Jewish cultural treasures. With this aim in mind, a group of "experts" from the staff of Alfred von Rosenberg arrived in Vilna and launched this sinister project.

By the entrance of the YIVO at Wiwulska 18, there was a huge painted map, captioned "YIVO and Its Contacts in the World." The Germans covered this sign with one saying: "Deutschland wird leben und deshalb wird Deutschland siegen" (Germany will live and therefore Germany will win).

The group consisted mainly of educated officials, many with doctorates and several of whom knew Hebrew, Talmud and other scholarly Jewish disciplines. They were led by one Mueller and the group included Dr. Johan Paul, who knew Hebrew from his studies at the Hebrew University in Jerusalem. He was the director of the Frankfurt Museum for Middle East Research. He was also a contributor to the notorious "Der Stuermer."

Others in the group included Dr. Gotthard, Dr. Wolf, and Willy Shaeffer. They wore yellow-green uniforms and red arm-bands with swastikas.

In addition to these, there was one Sparkas, of Polish Lithuanian descent, who became sort of a "superintendent" over the buildings of the YIVO.

The group arrived in Vilna as early as 1942.

The Rosenberg staff ordered the Jewish Labor Office in the ghetto to make available to them a group of Jews who knew Hebrew and Yiddish, to perform certain tasks for them. Such a group was recruited.

Two of them, Professor Noah Prilutzky and the writer, A. Y. Goldsmith, were in the Lukiszki Prison at that time. When Dr. Gotthard was informed of this, he arranged for them to be brought every day to the University Library on Sigmuntovska

Street, where the headquarters of the Rosenberg staff was located and they were assigned specific research tasks.

Others in the Jewish work force assigned to the project included: Zalman Kalmanowicz, the philologist; Herman Kruk, the librarian; and a number of poets, artists and writers including Leib Scheftel, Dr. Leon Bernstein, Dr. Zemach Feinstein, Rachel Krinski, Abraham Suckewer, Szmerke Kaczerginski, Michal Kowner, Ita Olkienicki, Naomi Markeles and others.

Meanwhile, Joseph Glazman had told me about the Nazi unit working at the former YIVO building and of the fact that a Jewish labor force had also been working there for some time. He said that the U.P.O. staff felt that it would be advisable if I were to start working there also, at least for a brief time, to see if we could use the building for our purposes. The next day I was assigned to the Jewish labor force where I "worked" for three months.

Among other tasks, my real work consisted of searching for books on explosives which were hard to find. I managed to find several such valuable books which our experts were able to use for making the first home-made hand grenades and other explosive devices.

I also reported to the staff that, since the building was located in a quiet area far from the center of the city, we could set up a storage place for badly needed equipment.

At first one of the Germans would spend time in one of the rooms doing "research work," but after a while he began coming for only a short time each day. It turned out that most of the time we were on our own without any Nazi supervision at all. It was an ideal place for us to bring the arms we received and store them among the piles of books.

After work, Michal Kowner, Szmerke Kaczerginski and I would smuggle the arms into the ghetto. We were assisted in this by those who brought us the weapons—mainly our "Aryan" U.P.O. members.

It was while doing this that I first got to know the partisan Julian Jankauskas, a non-Jew, and Lisa Magun, who was living in Vilna with forged Aryan identity papers. When the police authorities announced that new identity cards would be issued, Lisa decided to go to police headquarters to exchange her false papers for legitimate ones. The police discovered the forgery, however, and she was arrested.

The U.P.O. staff tried everything to secure her release from Lukiszki Prison since she was one of the most important of the liaison personnel and she knew many of our secrets. The U.P.O. staff succeeded in bribing an important Lithuanian police officer and he tried to help her. Later, however, he got word to the U.P.O. that he had seen her dossier with the fatal "X" marked at the top, indicating that she was marked for death by the Gestapo and was beyond any help.

She managed to smuggle a message out of the prison to let us know that she knew there was no hope but that we should not worry—she would take all U.P.O. secrets with her to her grave. She wished us all success and died at the hands of the Nazis.

In honor of her heroism, the U.P.O. designated as their password in the event of a general partisan mobilization, the words: "Lisa calls."

Although I left my job at YIVO to go to work in a German printing press, at the war's end fate ordained that I should be one of the first to be instrumental in saving thousands of books and manuscripts at YIVO and at other Jewish libraries, which would otherwise have been shipped to the paper factory in Wilejka near Vilna.

The sacred and secular books, manuscripts and other materials were at a railroad siding awaiting shipment to Wilejka, where the Nazis planned to destroy them. The literature was soaking in the rain when the Russians liberated Vilna. The treasure was in danger of being sold as wrapping paper for herring.

As one who was in the printing field immediately after the

war, I took the initiative, saved the material and sent it for safekeeping to various libraries in the city.

In addition to the so-called "intellectual brigade," there was a "physical brigade" headed by Cemach Zawelson, an energetic young man with a fluent knowledge of the German language. The brigade consisted of 20 men, which, along with the other group of 20 brought to 40 the number of Jews working in the building.

One day I happened to overhear Zawelson mention in a conversation with his co-workers that they were to visit the Printer's Shul on Szklanna Street. I immediately asked to go along in order to get a last look at the place.

This was the shul where my father served as head *gabai* for many years and he supported the synagogue generously even later when he could not afford to.

It was a small shul accommodating about 100 worshipers located in an old, dark courtyard. Inside, however, it was one of the most beautiful synagogues in the city. On the walls were large murals depicting the twelve tribes. Such murals could be found only in the Painter's Shul.

It was in the Printer's Shul that my Bar Mitzva was held and that of my older brothers. Because every ghetto Jew felt, whether he liked it or not, that he could die at any moment, I was struck with the impulse of visiting the shul where I used to pray with my father on the festivals (my mother would attend the large Choir Shul which is still standing) and which was associated with so many of my youthful memories.

So it was, that I entered the shul with the members of the brigade. Everything was as it was before. Nothing was disturbed. The Vilna printers who used to fill the shul on the High Holy Days were no longer around, except for a few who were still alive, and with Glazman's help, I was able to get 14 certificates from the ghetto authorities that protected them from destruction.

What convinced them was my argument that, if there was

to be a new world after this world, Jewish printers would be needed to perpetuate the story of what happened to the Jewish community of Vilna. Knowing that Jacob Gens, who was in charge of the ghetto, was partial to history, Glazman convinced him to issue 14 permits which I was able to distribute to the printers who were still around.

Despite the fact that all the Jewish type in my father's and brother's shop and of all other Jewish plants in Vilna, had been shipped to Germany, to be melted down for bombs.

When the brigade opened the Holy Ark and began carrying out the Torah scrolls, the ornaments and other religious articles, I was standing at the same seat I occupied in the years I attended the shul. I felt as though I were at a funeral with the remains being carried out of my home.

While it was confidential and I did not know it at the time, I later learned that the brigadier Zawelson also belonged to the U.P.O. and that he took the Torah scrolls and other things to the YIVO building where the religious articles of all Vilna synagogues were collected. The silver ornaments, however, were smuggled into the ghetto and given to the U.P.O. staff. They melted them down and sold the silver to buy weapons.

When I returned to the ghetto, I told my father where I had been. He turned pale and began to weep when he heard it. I tried to comfort him, however, by telling him that nearly all the silver articles that he had so generously donated to the synagogue were now in the ghetto in good, Jewish hands and that the fruits of his labor would buy bullets that, sooner or later, would find their way into Nazi flesh.

This is how a family sentiment developed.

Later, a Pole, Konstanti Gruzovski, who took part in executions of Jews and who had killed Prof. Noah Prilutzky, one of the founders and leaders of YIVO, was captured and brought to trial in the Pomeranian town of Koshalin. He was found guilty and sentenced to death and the sentence was immediately carried out.

100

He was one of the few who paid with his life for the destruction of Jewish life and cultural treasures.

One of the apartments that belonged to the U.P.O. In this place we had a little party in honor of our first clandestine publication. On the stairs is Berl Szereszyniewski who used to live with his wife Rosa in this apartment. Itzik Wittenberg was hiding for a while in this place. Picture taken after the war.

Montage of the Polish-German newspaper *Goniec Codzienny* and some
clips in Lithuanian and German languages of anti-Jewish character.

A SECRET PRESS IS ESTABLISHED

DURING the first weeks of the German occupation of Vilna, not a single newspaper appeared in the city. People did not know what was going on at the fronts or in the world at large. Particularly isolated from the world were the Jews, whose radios had been confiscated immediately after the Germans arrived. It was therefore quite natural that all kinds of rumors should spread about conditions at the front, and these were hopelessly contradictory. In this chaotic period, people were satisfied that a Polish-German newspaper began to appear, *Goniec Codzienny* (Daily Courier). The entire population of Vilna waited impatiently for this newspaper. The Jews, who in those days were not yet forced into the ghetto, also awaited the Polish paper. The Jews knew that only official reports were being printed, but they tried to read between the lines in order to form some kind of a real picture of the situation on the battlefront. It is understandable that in those terrible conditions, in days "without law and without judges" for Jews, they were deathly afraid; in that psychological state of fear, every event or report evoked countless explanations and conjectures. So, for example, the Jews concluded, several weeks after the occupation of the city, that the Red Army had launched a massive counter attack and was nearing Vilna. Where did this news come from? At that moment some large explosions were heard in the city, and this was interpreted to mean that the Soviet troops were shooting. Later it turned out that the detonations were the work of the Germans, who were getting rid of unuseable explosives.

In this atmosphere of rumors and conjectures, Jews were happy to have a printed word about what was happening on the battlefield.

In one of its first editorials about Jews to appear in the Polish-German newspaper, we read the following: "Jews may be beaten even after they have fainted and lie on the ground."

Such "pearls" were published in the newspaper quite often, since the German authorities set as their immediate goal the poisoning of the minds of the Christian population. Their influence was very great.

From time to time the Polish-German and Lithuanian newspapers printed pictures of corpses with the explanations that these were bodies of Lithuanians and Poles whom the Jews murdered when the Soviet forces left Vilna.

A fire burned in one's heart—how to answer these repulsive creatures? How to tell the broad masses that which they were not told? I was tortured by such thoughts ever since I got to know the Germans at first hand.

However, on September 6, 1941, we were driven into two separate ghettos. It was impossible to execute the plan to keep the population informed about conditions at the front, and particularly about the post-war prospects. The Jews were literally lying in the streets, with no place to rest their heads. Naturally it was their first concern to find sleeping places for themselves and their families.

The Jews of the ghetto were being seized and abducted. You could talk to some people and decide where to meet, but in a few hours these people would be kidnapped by the day-robbers. It was impossible to get anything organized.

It was clear that under such conditions it was impossible to plan such a dangerous and difficult work as publishing, and we had to wait for a propitious moment.

The favorable moment came on January 23, 1942, when the United Partisan Organization was formed in the ghetto. This was a unification of all important Jewish parties which had existed in the pre-war era.

At one of the meetings of U.P.O. command in May 1942, I submitted my project to organize a secret press that would print a newspaper for the non-Jewish population. Every member of the command weighed the suggestion carefully, knowing that this involved great dangers, not only for the individuals who would deal with the project, but for the existence of the entire ghetto. But because of the extraordinary importance of the matter, after devoting several meetings to it, the command decided to set up the secret press. I was empowered to go ahead.

The main question was: where to get type, printing presses, etc. One way was to smuggle into a German print shop and take out what was needed. How could this be done? First of all, I decided to call on an old friend, a Lithuanian who headed the German government press, *Aushra,* to let me work in the plant.

One evening I left the ghetto without wearing the yellow patches, and went to the private home of this director. I made my way safely through the city. Entering the courtyard, I rang the bell. The door opened and there was the director himself. He was confused and surprised by my "visit." Putting a finger to his mouth, a signal to be quiet, because he had the kind of company in the house who should not be permitted to see a Jewish face, he hid me in a nearby small room and went back to his guests. I kept my "blazer" ready, in case it turned out that he had fooled me into a trap. I stood there for more than an hour, in the dark room. Countless thoughts ran through my mind. Did he leave by the back door for the police? This frequently happened when a Jew came to a Christian home. Did he intend to turn me in?

At last the tension broke. I heard the guests getting ready to leave. Finally I heard them say, "Good night."

The door of my hideout opened and the director invited me into the guest room. He locked the door with bolt and chain, and led me into the largest room of the house. I went to the point: "I have come to you with a request—since I am doing hard labor for the Germans (truthfully, I was doing forced labor in the YIVO building, where the bigwigs of the Nazi staff held forth, and I happened to have an easy, interesting job sorting out the archives of YIVO)—I would very much like to get some work in your printing plant. You know that I am an expert and am anxious to work at this trade."

The director opened up a pair of eyes, "Yes, but it is impossible. Under present conditions no Jew can work in a German print shop. Here in Lithuania there has never been such a case."

"Nu," I said calmly, "this will be the first case. You have good connections with the German labor office and you can somehow arrange for me to be employed by you."

Wrinkling his brow, he said to me, "Good, we shall see. I shall try to arrange it. Come to me between 8 and 8:15 tomorrow morning, and I shall give you the answer of the German employment office."

Thanking him politely, I left his house satisfied.

The next day, punctually at the prescribed hour, I came to the director. This time his wife opened the door. She said that he was waiting for me. This first welcome made me feel good. On greeting the director, he squeezed my hand and said, "I succeeded. I thought up a practical reason which they accepted. I told my foreman that we needed a specialist for the speed press and there was one in the ghetto, a former employee of mine. I wanted to get him some easier work. Then I dictated a letter to the German labor office, stating that since the machine did not have the right technical care, there was a danger that the daily Polish-German newspaper, which was being published by the Propaganda Ministry, would not be able to appear regularly, but this could be avoided if the labor office would allow us to hire for this work a Jew who was living in the ghetto."

Getting such a letter from Director Skemas, they immediately made an exception and allowed him to engage the Jew, whose name and address had been supplied. The German labor office commanded the ghetto labor office to release me for work in the *Aushra* press.

Things moved swiftly. I got the necessary permit the next

day, with a pass that allowed me to go alone to and from work, by way of the gutter and not the sidewalk, of course.

After working a few days, during which time I made myself known to many of the Christian workers (some of whom I had known before) I proceeded to my real objective, for which I had come. The first phase was to steal type and deliver it to the right place. It was arranged that at lunch time, when the exits of the print shop were opened, someone would be waiting to take the goods from me at the opposite side of the building.

In order to minimize the dangers the command decided that the press must be located outside the ghetto. It was therefore established on the property of a Christian, who was an honest Polish patriot. It was so conspiratorial that only a few members of the command were allowed to know this location and who would be the links to me.

Joseph Glazman informed me that I would have to maintain contact with Sonia Madejsker, an extremely courageous and devoted comrade. It was she who brought me into first contact with the aforementioned Christian, whose name was Jan Pszewalski.

From the day that I met him, we had almost daily contact for over a year. He showed exceptional devotion and great courage by helping to organize the secret press.

Promptly at twelve, just as the door was opened, I carried out unnoticed, in all my pockets and in a lunch pail which was supposed to contain my food, the material which I handed over to the man, who was Jan Pszewalski. Simultaneously, he handed me an exact duplicate of the pail and I hurried to disappear into the printing plant where I was among the last to finish my lunch.

This went on for a long time. Every day, different materials were stolen out for the secret press. In order to speed up the process, it was decided that a second expedition would be made at five o'clock in the afternoon. More than three months later we had assembled enough type to be able to print a small newspaper in the Polish language. But type alone is not enough for the job, we had to have some kind of a press.

The first problem was to get to the machinery department of the print shop. My job was in the typesetting department. Any attempt by me to sneak into the press room would have aroused suspicion and have spoiled the whole plan. But there was no alternative. The risk had to be taken.

Using all sorts of maneuvers, such as volunteering to fix a broken machine, or replace a sick pressman, I succeeded in getting into the machine room. There happened to be a small, worn out hand press that was not in use. In the course of a few days I took it apart and gave it piecemeal to Jan.

Equipped with everything that an underground press needs: type, press, ink, paper, etc., we prepared to issue the first number of the Polish newspaper, *Sztandar Wolnosci* (Freedom Flag) and in Lithuanian *Tevynes Frontas* (the Fatherland Front).

After a day's work at the German press, I spent a whole night with Jan to put out this paper. We used his home, at Zamkowa Street 15. Sparks would fly from my eyes as I worked for the Germans by day and against them by night. I could not endure this pace very long, so I began to teach Jan the trade. He was a very capable fellow and caught on quickly, since he knew a little bit about printing from before. He became so expert that I could release myself from the work and rely upon him entirely. I also taught his wife so that she could help him. As the issues of the paper appeared, all I had to do was lay out the pages, but eventually I did not have to do even that. Husband and wife did it themselves.

The first edition made a terrific impression. Here was an illegal Polish-language paper that appeared under the very nose of the Gestapo, castigating them and their leader, Hitler, and telling the masses about things which the oppressor would rather suppress!

108

The Gestapo tried every trick to uncover the press, but without success.

A most interesting reaction to the appearance of our newspaper was that of the illegal Polish nationalist paper, *Niepodleglosc* (Independence). Instead of greeting the new underground paper, it sought to tear it apart. It came out with several theories, including the idea that our paper was financed by Moscow, that a press had been dropped by airplane somewhere, because here such a thing was impossible. The proof, they said, was that they who had the backing of the entire Polish people, were having great difficulties establishing an underground press.

In honor of the appearance of our first edition, the U.P.O. command decided to throw a little party. The participants were Itzik Wittenberg, Joseph Glazman, Aba Kowner, Sonia Madejsker, Chiena Borowski, Berl and Rosa Szereszyniewski and myself.

Word got around next day that the first edition had been received in hundreds of Christian homes either through the post office or by special messengers. In our printing plant also there was whispering about this daring event.

The work went on systematically; it was not long before the secret press had a full set of letters, so that printing could also be done in Lithuanian and German. Proclamations in various languages appeared, in rapid succession. The Gestapo hunt for the press continued unabated, but they could find no clues. The more stubborn their hunt, the more stubborn was our effort to put out more proclamations which would unmask the inhuman deeds of the Nazi occupiers against all sectors of the population. We did not stress in particular the persecution of the Jews because that would have created the opposite reaction to the one we sought. We appeared as Polish patriots and told what the Germans were doing to the Polish people, including what was being done to exterminate the Jews. We advocated that it was the Polish patriotic duty to help save Jews and give them the maximum protection. Whoever betrayed the Jews to the Gestapo was committing a national betrayal. The other Polish underground paper did not write this way. On the contrary, it was glad to be rid of the "Jewish problem" which had bothered them so much before the war.

Our proclamations were published over the signature of the Association of Polish Patriots.

Our paper had a noticeable influence among the Polish people, who assumed that this friendly attitude to the Jews was the official policy of the Polish underground. They never dreamed that the paper came to light because of the initiative of a Jew and that it was published almost entirely by Jews. Aside from the command staff, contributors to the paper included Dr. Gordon and Sonia Madejsker.

The secret publications of the nationalist Poles warned that our newspaper was counterfeit and its contents should be ignored. But their message did not get across everywhere. It is most likely that the few Jews who did hide out and were saved, would have shared the fate of millions of their brothers and sisters if some of our counter-propaganda had not made an impact on some Poles.

When the press was working in the city at capacity, day and night, I decided, naturally with the approval of the command staff, to set up another press which would be held in reserve. This was necessary for two reasons: In case there was a breakdown or exposure, which could happen at any moment; and also, to utilize the fact that I was still working in the German press, because one could not tell what unforeseen circumstances would arise that would force me to leave that post.

The second printing press, which was quickly prepared, was in the ghetto itself, in a small camouflaged place. We could allow ourselves such a risky venture because the Jewish partisans in the Vilna ghetto had by then become strongly organized and were able to execute highly conspiratorial projects.

ORDINANCE NO. 22

Issued by the Police Chief of the Vilna Ghetto, December 1, 1941.

1) Be it known that any person found in the ghetto without the Mogen David (the yellow badge) firmly affixed on all four sides to his sleeve, will be fined 5 rubles.

2) It is strictly forbidden to gather in groups in the streets of the ghetto. If this order is disregarded, the offender will be fined 3 rubles.

3) It is strictly forbidden to go out of the ghetto gates without the yellow pass or the special permission of the Police Chief.

4) Any attempt to sneak through the ghetto gates will draw a fine of 10 rubles.   (*Signed*) Police Chief, December 6, 1941

ORDINANCE NO. 26

Issued by the Police Chief of the Vilna Ghetto, December 18, 1941.

I hereby order all the residents of the ghetto to live in the houses assigned to them by the housing authority. Those who will be found in unauthorized houses will be punished severely—even to the extent of being sent out of the ghetto entirely.   Chief of Police

ANNOUNCEMENT   NO. 30

Issued by the Police Chief of Vilna Ghetto, January 5, 1942.

On January 3, 1942, I jailed 2 residents for spreading false rumors and creating panic among the populace.

I herewith give warning that anyone committing similar offences will be severely punished.   Chief of Police

In April, 1942, Murer sent the following memorandum to the Jewish Chief of Police.

1) The Jewish Chief of Police, Yakov Gens (together with his police staff) is responsible for keeping order in the ghetto.

2) It is the duty of above-named police to keep order in the ghetto; to carry out the orders of the district commissioner and to watch that the labor force march in columns to their assigned places of work.

3) The guards at the gate must see that no food is smuggled in.

4) If these orders are not carried out, the Jewish Police Chief will suffer the death penalty.

ANNOUNCEMENT OF THE SOCIAL WELFARE OFFICE

Vilna, 15 April, 1942

Announcement To Owners of Yellow Certificates

This is to announce that the validity of the *yellow* certificates will expire on 30 April 1942, and by that day they will be exchanged for new certificates.

The new certificates will be issued for an unlimited period and will bear the signature of the Government Commander Wagner.

Exchange of the yellow certificates for new ones will be made by the liaison man, A. Braude.

Possessors of the new certificates will be obliged to:

1) Carry the certificate with them at all times;

2) Accept at once the proposed work;

3) Not to change the place of work without permission;

4) Obey at all times the instructions of the Social Welfare office of the Labor Department in the Ghetto, whose authority is enforced by the Social Welfare office.

5) In the event the possessor of the certificate is released from his place of work, he must immediately inform the Labor Department in the Ghetto about it;

6) All changes of address must be given *immediately* to the Labor Department in the Ghetto.

A person having in his possession a new certificate, *and is engaged in a job,* must *immediately* (the day after getting it) have it signed at his place of work and show it immediately afterward to the Labor Department of the Ghetto, so that it may be recorded in the files.

Failure to follow the above instructions will lead to punishment.

In this connection, in the event a certificate is lost or disappears by any other means, no duplicate will be given to the loser.

District Commissar of Vilna, Social Welfare Office

(*signed*) Wagner
(*signed*) Government Commander
(*signed*) Labor Office, Vilna

112

PURCHASE OF HORSES FOR THE GHETTO PERMITTED

The District Commissar of the City of Vilna has permitted the head of the Ghetto to purchase two additional horses for the needs of the Vilna Ghetto. Also, a washing machine has been promised for the new laundry.

THE GERMAN LABOR OFFICE

Conducts a monthly inspection of the Labor Department of the Ghetto and investigates its activities.

("Ghetto News" No. 30)

NOTIFICATION TO DEBTORS OUTSIDE THE COUNTRY

The Ghetto head issued the following announcement:

I have received from the District Commissar of the City of Vilna a letter, in which he writes:

"Re the collection of debts from Jews, especially from those living abroad, it has been clarified that a large portion of the money demanded of Jews has not been collected. This is particularly true of debtors living in Germany, Latvia, Esthonia, friendly and neutral nations, as well as those in the lands of the enemy which have been conquered by the German army. I request you to conduct an investigation and bring me the results in the form of lists, showing the names of the debtors and creditors, the amount due and the basis of the claim. In addition, indicate the *valuta* of each claim. As for German debtors, for example, the claim will be registered in Reichsmarks, dollars, etc. I request that the results of the investigation be submitted to me within eight days."

Interested parties must present the necessary details to the police office by 25 July this year, at 12 noon.

Moshe Brause   Witka Kempner

Izke Mackiewicz as Kericenko

THE FIRST DIVERSION

THE resistance headquarters decided to carry out its first diversionary action in Vilna in the beginning of June, 1942.

A partisan, Witka Kempner, was sent out on a three-day reconnaissance mission. It was her task to find out the most suitable and effective place, time and method for such an action. Witka dyed her blonde hair still lighter and left the ghetto. The few people who knew of her assignment were, it must be admitted, extremely nervous. Everyone realized the tremendous risk to which the entire ghetto was subjected in case a single ghetto resident was caught with a mine in hand. However, the risk had to be taken.

Moshe Brause, a former Lithuanian officer, who was one of the very few Jews who had attained officer rank in the small Lithuanian army of the prewar period, was one of three persons entrusted with carrying out this diversionary action. The other two were Witka Kempner and Izke Mackewicz.

Moshe Brause had previously been ordered by the U.P.O. to become a member of the ghetto police. As a vice-commissar, with his police armband on his sleeve, he escorted the other two out of the ghetto gates, supposedly taking them to a forced labor assignment for a German unit. When they had gone some distance away from the ghetto, all three removed their yellow patches; Brause also took off his police armband. Then they set off for the township of Wilejka, some eight kilometers from Vilna.

At that time there were as yet no sabotage partisan units in the area, and this was the first effort of its kind.

After they waited in hiding for two or three hours, the favorable moment arrived, with the approach of a large transport train rushing soldiers to the front. When the transport came near enough to the partisan ambush, Moshe Brause pulled the cord which set off a tremendous explosion, derailing and turning over dozens of cars.

The three partisans saw a huge burst of fire from exploding

ammunition and heard the screams of wounded German soldiers.

Brause and the others kissed and embraced with joy and quickly withdrew deeper into the woods. Soon after that they returned to the ghetto by roundabout ways.

Our scout learned later from nearby peasants that more than two hundred German soldiers had been killed, and an even larger number were wounded in the first sabotage action carried out by the members of the U.P.O.—Jews confined in the Vilna ghetto.

Tin-plate number the Jews of the ghetto had to wear. On the plate are the letters "W" for Wilna (English Vilna), "G" for Ghetto, (W) Wife. The letter (M) would be for Men, and 8501 was his registration number.

BLACK FLAGS

FROM time to time I used to notice German soldiers wearing black armbands. The more I saw these black armbands, the more I realized that Germans die, too, and not necessarily a natural death. The fact that very young Germans wore the bands was a sign for me that members of their families perished in the massive allied bombardments, or that they were mourning the death of a father or brother who fell at the front.

One day, as I came home to the ghetto from my work in the city printing shop, I noticed that every other soldier wore a black armband. At first I could not understand the significance of it, because on my previous walks from work I used to meet only a few soldiers with armbands. On that day there were very few without them. As I thought the matter over in my mind on my way home, I recalled that at the printing shop there was talk about the Germans' projected observance of a mourning period because of a defeat in Stalingrad.

We knew that there was fierce fighting going on for weeks in Stalingrad (now Volgagrad). Because we were isolated in the ghetto, we did not know the extent of their terrible defeat.

When I reached the corner of the ghetto, one block away from the Lithuanian 1st Police Precinct, to which the ghetto belonged, I observed a black flag fluttering at half mast. Then I understood that the sudden increase of the black armbands was connected with the great losses they probably had suffered there at Stalingrad.

As I entered the ghetto I spoke to many Jews who worked in various work units. They told me that there was a mixed reaction to the bad reports for the Germans. Some officers flew into a rage at the news of the defeat and whipped the Jewish slave laborers mercilessly; others for the first time muttered. "We are undone," under their breath. Those who had the premonition that they were undone at the fronts were right.

The mourning for the Germans lasted three days.

COUNTERFEIT DOCUMENTS

A T that time—about January 1943—the situation in Vilna city became complicated. Anyone, man, woman, who did not have documents exempting him from deportation, was in danger of being shipped off to Germany as a slave laborer. This threatened the existence of our printing project, as the few Christians who helped us could no longer come into the city. Also, our Jewish "Aryans," who went on various missions, could no longer appear on the streets without the proper papers, showing that they were exempted from the shipments to Germany.

They were looking for non-Jews even in the ghetto. The streets in the city were surrounded by army-units that had installed machine-guns and small tanks in many places.

About 500 men and women were arrested, including the Archbishop Reines and many priests and nuns.

In the technological high school on Zarecza Street and in a laboratory on Nowogrodska Street they conducted a pogrom against Christian students.

In order to get out of this pickle, we had to engage in a new enterprise: the production of false documents.

I had been at the printing plant a half year and had become quite friendly with the Christian workers. Our informal relations enabled me to work in different departments, where it would be possible for me to smuggle out authentic documents which were printed there.

This venture required the maximum of caution for it had to be done under the very nose of the worker who happened at the moment to be printing the job.

How could one get into that department?

I worked on the second floor, in the typesetting department, while the presses were on the first floor, which I seldom visited, because it was not in my assigned area. One day I came early, on purpose, before the others had arrived to work, and sneaked into the press room. I saw some type locked up, in forms, ready to print. It was an important German proclamation. I pulled out one letter. When the press started to run, I casually walked over, picked up a sheet and read it. Then I showed to the pressman the error that I had "discovered." The foreman thanked me for the discovery, and the worker who had to make the correction was reprimanded sharply. He made excuses that he did not know the German language well and therefore the error was most natural . . .

That was exactly what I aimed at, and I grabbed the opportunity, suggesting that it would be easy for me to catch the mistakes before press time. On the spur of the moment I got the foreman's approval. "I've got them where I want them," I thought to myself.

From then on, all I had to do was go in to look for typographical errors in the room where there were printed blanks of important documents. I kept an eye open for those which were useful for our purposes and purloined as many as needed. This had to be done while the presses were running, before they could be counted and packaged, and when the pressman stepped out of sight for a moment. These chances were rare. Usually, when I came downstairs "officially" to inspect the sheets, the pressman would be at his post, and I could make no move. I kept dashing up and down, from first to second floor and back. A correction that could have been made in five minutes would take me an hour. To explain my slowness, I would say that I could not find justifier (most of the type was set by hand type), and there was danger the type would break during the press run. I had to think up all kinds of alibis to cover my dilatoriness. I kept up this game until I got the forms and documents that I wanted, which I hid in a prepared envelope that I stacked away in the typesetting department where I worked.

I did not work in this manner very long. It required split-second timing. Sometimes, it had to be done when the pressman turned his back for a moment to say something to another worker nearby, and I had to grab my quarry practically by reaching over his shoulder. Each such "grab" made my heart throb wildly. Running up the stairs to my own department, I would glance back to see if I was being chased, whether someone else had noticed my act. I knew that if this continued much longer, I would collapse. I therefore decided to approach the director for permission to work in the printing department, at a press. My argument was that he had informed the German labor office that I would be working as a pressman, and here I was a typesetter. He could have some unpleasantness . . . The director immediately agreed, because some of the workers had to go on vacation and he did not have any replacement for them.

Thenceforth I began a new life. I could easily, and with minimal risk, get anything that was printed in the plant. After being in the press department a short while, about three months, I had a fine collection of all kinds of blanks, certificates, labor permits, and similar papers from German institutions, such as the commissaries, labor office, and even from the S.S. and the Gestapo.

Having a full set of these documents, all I needed was a sample of the original rubber stamps of the various offices. After more tricks and maneuvers I succeeded in getting the samples, from which I was able to make the stamps in the ghetto. Thus, we had everything essential for the production of documents that our people could use.

Nionia Telerant

Po przeciwuni... ... angieb.

Śmierć hitlerowskim okupantom!

OBYWATELE!

Aby ratować się od ... ni był re klęski, wróg przygotowuje powszechną mobilizację na naszej ziemi. Hitler zapowiedział w swojej odezwie, że nie będzie żałował życia i krwi ludów okupowanych wtedy, gdy żołnierze niemieccy leją krew na frontach. Możemy być pewni, że zechce on dotrzymać swojej zapowedzi.

Dać się zmobilizować do szeregów armii niemieckiej, to znaczy dla nas bić się przeciwko- naszym braciom, którzy walczą za naszą wolność i niepodległość na wszystkich frontach wojny, to znaczy bić się przeciwko własnej Ojczyźnie.

Armija Czerwona, gromiąc hordy hitlerowskich ludożerców, postawiła sobie za zadanie nie wypuścić z kraju ani jednego żywego niemieckiego żolnierza. Bądźmy pewni, że zadanie to zostanie wykonane. Być przebranym w mundur niemiecki na froncie wschodnim oznacza teraz pewną haniebną i okrutna śmierć.

Wszyscy, którzy mogą podlegać mobilizacji, powinni już dzisiaj przygotować się do uniknięcia tego. Łączcie się w mniejsze grupy, i przygotowujcie broń, odpowiednią odzież, wybierajcie sobie doświadczonych przywódców i w razie ogłoszenia mobilizacji, otrzymania wezwania, lub wieści o brance, obławach, uciekajcie masowo do lasów, kierując się na wschód, gdzie znajdziecie swoich braci—partyzantów, niszczących wroga na tyłach. Pora roku wkrótce będzie odpowiednią.

W razie, gdy mimo wszystko uda się wrogowi wcielić was do swoich szeregów, czy to na froncie, czy na tyłach, powinniście szkodzić mu wszelkimi możliwymi sposobami: psuć i niszczyć materiał wojenny, strzelać do oficerów i hitlerowców, a przy pierwszej okazji uciekajcie do lasów i łączcie się z partyzantami, lub przechodźcie grupami i pojedyńczo, z bronią, na stronę Armii Czerwonej. Lepiej jest nawet zginąć w walce z wrogiem, niż zginąć jako jego niewolnik.

Precz z niemiecką okupacją!

ZWIĄZEK WALKI CZYNNEJ
Z HITLEROWSKĄ OKUPACJĄ

One of our clandestine publications in Polish language (translation on next page).

After reading—pass on to someone else!

Death to the Hitlerite occupation!

CITIZENS!

Aiming to survive, the enemy has prepared a general mobilization on our soil. Hitler has proclaimed that he will not spare the lives and blood of the occupied nations, while blood of German soldiers is being shed at the front. We can be sure he will try to keep his promise.

Whoever lets himself be mobilized to the German army, means that he will fight against your brother, who is fighting for your liberty and sovereignty on all battle fields, and against your own country.

The Red Army attacks the Hitlerite cannibal hordes, undertaking not to let one German soldier escape alive. Let us be sure that this aim will be accomplished. To be dressed in a German uniform on the Eastern front invites a sure shambles and dreadful death.

All of you who may be drafted, must immediately make ready to dodge the draft. Unite yourselves in small groups, and collect arms, the right clothes; chose an experienced leader, and in case of mobilization, or a call up or news of raids, run in force to the woods, go to the East, where your brothers the partisans are stationed and are striking the enemy in the rear. The season soon will be ideal.

In case the enemy manages to put you in his lines on the front or in the rear, your duty is to sabotage with all available means and at the first opportunity to run away to the woods and unite with the partisans, or come over in groups or individually, with your arms, to the side of the Red Army.

It is better to die in battle with the enemy than to die as his slave.

Away with the German occupation!

ORGANIZATION IN ACTIVE FIGHT
AGAINST HITLERISTIC OCCUPATION

WE NEED MONEY

THE clearer it became that the ghetto would not last long, the more we realized that everything was chaotic and lawless, that we would not escape the fangs of death, the more did the average Jew in the ghetto take long risks. He began to steal from the Germans, anything and everything, from food to military goods, shoes, clothes, paint, buttons, tin or whatever was handy. Those who worked as glaziers or locksmiths would put pieces of tin, wood, glass into the toolkits they were allowed to carry. They would buy food from the nearby Christians, paying exorbitant prices.

There was one thing that the Jews did not collect: weapons. They shied away from arms, in order to avoid any suspicion. The Germans did use Jewish labor brigades at their munitions deports, to detonate defective bombs and do other dangerous jobs. More than one Jew died while handling such explosives at Burbishok, but the average Jew did not dream of stealing or buying any weapons. This was done by the people of the United Partisan Organization.

But when the hope of being saved from death in the ghetto grew dimmer, when the Jews began to realize that they had nothing to lose, the number of individuals who began to risk their lives by stealing even weapons, began to grow. Some took the loot for themselves, in case they would have to make use of it. Some included the arms in their "business" deals. However, there were not many who cared to engage in that brand of trade in the ghetto, but if anyone did want to buy a "thing," he would have to pay plenty for it.

The percentage of arms smugglers grew larger and larger.

Ordinary Jews, of course, did not know about this new branch of commerce in the ghetto. But our intelligence service knew exactly who was bringing in the weapons, because about ninety percent of the smugglers were talked into going for the material and later were bought out by our people.

It was rather peculiar that precisely at the time when more arms were being smuggled into the ghetto, that that item became more expensive. Revolvers, which once cost 1,500 or 2,000 marks, soared to 10,000 or 15,000 marks when they became plentiful. This upswing in prices caused difficulties for the U.P.O. Until this point, the chief source of funds for the U.P.O. had been the second ghetto, which had been liquidated. The Jewish police used to send groups of policemen to the second ghetto to gather up what the Germans and Lithuanians had left behind.

Since Joseph Glazman, who was one of the most important leaders of the police force, was also vice commander of the U.P.O., he set up a group of police who were also members of the secret organization. They were separated from the general police expedition, and their main job was to ferret out hidden treasures that had belonged to the exterminated Jews of the second ghetto. Everything that they found went into the treasury of the U.P.O. and served as the basis of its financial structure.

But as the scope of the organization broadened and as the price of weapons began to reach fantastic levels, the financial condition of the U.P.O. became more critical. New sources of money on a large scale did not appear. The high command therefore decided to make a collection among its own membership. The goal was one hundred thousand marks. Everyone had to give until it hurt, hurt hard. The drive yielded twice as much as expected.

For the moment, this sum was adequate. But after several large purchases of arms, the treasury was empty again. To make an external fund collection to bring in larger sums was impossible, for this was a conspiracy only for comrades.

How were we to get out of the dilemma? Money, a lot of money, was needed. Every minute that went by without buying arms was endangering our work. I hit upon an idea, which at first frightened me. Nevertheless, I went to Glazman and told

124

him of my plan. At first he was shocked by it, but then agreed to present it to the command group.

The core of my plan was that the U.P.O. would print counterfeit ration cards, which could bring in a million marks a month.

After long hesitation, the U.P.O. leaders adopted my proposal. It was decided, in order to reduce the chances of failure, to print enough ration cards to bring in only a quarter of a million marks.

I laughed . . . They were bargaining with me for less . . .

There was no need for lengthy discussions. It was clear: money! Money in the hands of the U.P.O. meant ammunition, guns, revolvers, grenades and so on. Money in our hands meant death for those who were killing us.

I was authorized to go ahead with the matter. Comrade Murawczyk was assigned to help me. He was a chemist and knew inks. He also had at his disposal a small room, which belonged to the organization, where I could eventually work during the day rather than my constant night work in the secret room were we had our caches with ammunition and arms.

We went up to Murawczyk's apartment. In the first room was a family from Kovno with whom he lived in the friendliest

Murawczyk

of terms. I examined the second, small room and decided that it would do for the production of the ration cards.

We began to transfer parts of the hand press. In and out. In and out. The people in the front room paid no attention.

On the third trip, I noticed that someone familiar was seated at the table. It was one of the ghetto administrators who knew me as "one of those." When I left, he asked the family whom I had come to see, and the Kovno people told him that I came to their neighbor Murawczyk. The ghetto official told them all about me, that I belonged to the armed secret organization in the ghetto and that I was not visiting just socially.

Terror seized the elderly woman and her household.

When we arrived for the third time, lugging a heavy "cannon" on our shoulders, they all rose, and we saw at once that they knew our secret.

The Kovno family, which had treated my colleague as a son, poured out their bitterness after I had left Murawczyk's room.

"We know everything. That comrade of yours, whom we never saw before today, and who has come here three times, belongs to 'those.' And we understand it now, you also belong to them. This would not bother us so much if you did not bring a cannon into the house." And with these words the old lady burst into tears.

I had not finished eating when my collaborator showed up at my place and told me what happened. With the same expenses, we took our load back to where it had been before.

When the family saw that the room was again open and that there was nothing in it, they began to breathe more freely and could not stop thanking their neighbor for removing the "cannon."

As a result, I had to work nights again at my place where we kept our main firearms at the arsenal.

In the meantime, a special group had been formed to use

Brot 25 Woche	Brot 26 Woche	Brot 27 Woche	Brot 28 Woche	Der Ghettoverstaher und Chef der Judenpolizei	Fleisch 28 Woche	Fleisch 27 Woche	Fleisch 26 Woche	Fleisch 25 Woche
Mehl 25 Woche	Mehl 26 Woche	Mehl 27 Woche	Mehl 28 Woche	**BROTKARTE**	Butter 28 Woche	Butter 27 Woche	Butter 26 Woche	Butter 25 Woche
Zucker 25 Woche	Zucker 26 Woche	Zucker 27 Woche	Zucker 28 Woche	1 Pers.	X 28 Woche	X 27 Woche	X 26 Woche	X 25 Woche
Salz 25 Woche	Salz 26 Woche	Salz 27 Woche	Salz 28 Woche	für die Zeit vom 2.7.1943 bis 30.7	Y 28 Woche	Y 27 Woche	Y 26 Woche	Y 25 Woche
Graupen 25 Woche	Graupen 26 Woche	Graupen 27 Woche	Graupen 28 Woche	(Zuname und Vorname)	Gemüse 28 Woche	Gemüse 27 Woche	Gemüse 26 Woche	Gemüse .25 Woche
Kartoffel 25 Woche	Kartoffel 26 Woche	Kartoffel 27 Woche	Kartoffel 28 Woche	(Adresse)	R 28 Woche	T 27 Woche	U 26 Woche	W 25 Woche
				(Unterschrift des Kartenausgebers)				

Druck „Ausdruy" Wilna, 1741-5063

Bread card

the ration cards to obtain the goods and sell them. This group
was headed by the lawyer, Abrasha Chwojnik, a U.P.O. staff-
member who did a superb job of organization.

Hundreds of pounds of goodies were redeemed with the
counterfeit cards. A quarter of a million marks soon filled up
the U.P.O. treasury. The organization was on its feet again. A
monthly income of such dimensions was not to be sneezed at!
And if need be, there would be more. It depended on us alone...

Impatiently, we who knew about the cards waited for the
first of the month, when we would be able to bring in fresh
money, which was needed so urgently.

* * *

On the broad Wielka and Sawicz Street, there was a Polish
print shop. The owner, Donbrowski, together with his partner,
used to print various anti-Semitic publications in pre-war Vilna.
They themselves were members of the Endeks, an anti-Semitic
party.

When the Gestapo looked for our secret press, they made
a search of Donbrowski's shop. They were astonished to find in
the place signs of counterfeit ration cards which the two partners had printed in order to enrich themselves. They were arrested and hanged in public in front of the cathedral.

127

ON JULY 15, 1942, the following announcement appeared in the Vilna Ghetto:

"Attention:

"At the command of the District Commissar of Vilna on the 12th of July, 1942, I assumed, as head of the Ghetto and as chief of police, all responsibility for the Ghetto.

"The basis of the existence of the Ghetto is disciplined work and order. Every resident of the Ghetto who is capable of working, is one of the pillars upon whom our existence rests. There is no room amongst us for those who hate work and by devious ways engage in various crimes.

"Out of conviction that all the residents of the Ghetto will understand the spirit of my words, I have commanded the release of all who are in the Ghetto jail and I hereby proclaim a general amnesty. I have in this manner given the transgressors of yesterday a chance to improve their ways and to resume a straight way of life for their own sake. But let no one think that, in time of necessity, I shall refrain from taking strong measures against criminal elements.

"I hope that all residents of the Ghetto, without exception, will support this proclamation.

"HEAD OF THE GHETTO AND CHIEF OF POLICE

(*Signed*) GENS"

THE MOST EXTRAORDINARY PUNISHMENT FOR DESERTING THE GHETTO

Six Jews ran away from the Bialewaker Concentration Camp. The German command decreed to shoot 10 Jews in the same Camp for each runaway; that is, 60 adults (not counting children). The punishment was meted out. Sixty adults and seven children were shot in the above prison camp.

A similar punishment awaits the population of the Vilna Ghetto should a similar thing occur here.

I greet all the ghetto residents on the New Year. I wish everybody health, tranquility and a happy future.

JACOB GENS, Ghetto Representative and Chief of Police.
Rosh Hashana, Vilna Ghetto, September 12, 1942

Niusia Lubocki-Dlugi

Chaim Lazar

THEY WANT TO GET RID OF US...

I WORKED until two o'clock in the morning at the secret press in the ghetto. At six o'clock, the command's liaison, Raszke Markowicz, came to awaken me from sleep. She told me that today there would be a major roundup of the Jewish police and many who were busy in the ghetto proper would be sent to work at the airfield at Porubanek. Raszke also said that the ghetto police would issue cards with a special stamp for those who are exempt from work at Porubanek, because they are working for the ghetto administration.

It was clear, that unless quick action was taken aforehand, it would be simply impossible to conduct certain underground work in the ghetto.

A few minutes later, we were both in the street. We went up to her room which was occupied by friends. I was shown a genuine card.

I examined it closely and was satisfied that I could duplicate it without trouble. In the meantime, the people with the keys to our largest and most important arsenal where we kept the press, were aroused from their sleep. I crawled in and in about an hour had a hundred cards ready.

In order not to arouse the suspicion of the Jewish police, the U.P.O. command decided that several of its members would go to the special job at Porubanek. One of them was Miriam Ganionska, who was already half-exposed. By this means, sand was thrown in the eyes of Gens and Dessler, the Jewish rulers of the ghetto. There was a strict control throughout the entire ghetto, and our comrades, overtly at least, behaved according to the rules.

*　　*　　*

In those days Niusia Lubocki and Chaim Lazar came over to my room with a message from the high command, that I

130

was next on the list of the ghetto police and that they were going to arrest me. Therefore I would have to leave the apartment immediately and sleep some place else until further notice.

I left my room together with the two messengers and hid for several days in one of our partisan houses till I got word that the danger was over, and I could go back to my old living place.

David Swirski

Raszke Markowicz

SUICIDE AND MURDER IN THE GHETTO

PSYCHOLOGISTS all over the world, after World War II, concerned themselves with the relative percentage of murder and suicide which occurred amid the terrible conditions in the ghettos in general. Oddly enough, they came to the conclusion that it was almost zero.

During the entire period of the Vilna ghetto, there were only a few suicides. These were much less in number than normally occurred in the pre-war period.

The first case which came to my notice was the well known dermatologist Gersz Gerszuni who committed suicide in the courtyard of the Judenrat at the age of 80. Before he died, he cried out that he was worthy of the ghetto agonies he suffered, because he had many opportunities in previous years to go to Eretz Israel and he passed them up. Therefore he deserved his fate in the ghetto.

A second case was a young, seemingly healthy and pretty girl. She attempted to commit suicide by setting fire to her clothes with matches on a deserted place near an unused kosher abattoir. But the fire was put out. In the process, her hands were badly hurt. When several other ghetto residents and I ran over to see what happened, I saw a few Jewish ghetto policemen holding her firmly in their arms as she grappled with them and screamed, "Let me die!" They took her to the hospital where her life was saved. Later she perished with thousands of others in the Nazi holocaust.

A third case, with entirely different motives, happened with one of my good friends, Grisza Krawczynski. This is his story:

Grisza Krawczynski arrived from Poland in the company of a stream of refugees. He was one of the first members of the U.P.O. He was a police sergeant in the ghetto. When the ghetto police began to pursue our members, he was put under investigation. During one tense moment of interrogation, he inadvertently mentioned something about a revolver. The police hammered away at him and wanted to know his contacts, etc. Under the impression that he had revealed too much, after he was set free from the investigation he attempted suicide by hanging himself. But he was rescued.

When the chief of staff of the U.P.O. found out the reason for his attempted suicide, he summoned Krawczynski and told him that he was not under any suspicion; that he had the same confidence and trust in him as heretofore.

Shortly after, I met Krawczynski in the street. I approached him, greeted him and engaged him in conversation. Then he assured me how extremely happy he was that people like myself who were aware of what went on previously still spoke to him and were as friendly to him as I was.

I tried to convince him that he should abandon the thought that he had voluntarily or involuntarily said anything out of the way. I also told him that with his devoted campaign for the idea of providing armed resistance against the enemy he would find peace of mind. At the same time, he would be performing an important service for the U.P.O.

In spite of all the consolations given by me and many of his closest co-workers, he did not recover sufficiently to free himself from his guilt complex. Two weeks after his first attempt, he succeeded in committing suicide.

Besides these few suicides there was a murder in the ghetto in June, 1942. The motive was robbery. The underworld gang of 5 who committed the murder consisted of two brothers, Isaac and Eliahu Geiwusz, Leib Grodzenski, Yankel Polianski and Hirsz Wituchowski. They attacked a former Yeshiva student, Josef Gersztein, with the object of robbing him of money he made by doing business in the ghetto. They lured him into a cellar at No. 1 Szawelska Street and there murdered him.

Later, it came out that this same gang had also killed a

ghetto Jew by the name of Herzl Lides with the aim of robbing him. They buried him in a cellar at Straszuna Street No. 9,

According to a verdict issued by a ghetto court, another name was added to the five gangsters. It was the name of Jankel Avidon. He was confined to the ghetto jail for an attempt to stab Jankel Grienfeld, a ghetto policeman. This Avidon was a squealer to the Gestapo and worked behind the backs of the Jewish police. Therefore, the Jewish police wanted to get rid of him.

The residents of the ghetto approved of the verdict of the ghetto court to hang the above characters.

SPEECH AT THE EXECUTION BY GENS

'To the Police and the Jewish Council (Judenrat):

Out of 75,000 Vilna Jews only 16,000 remain. These 16,000 must be worthy, honest and industrious people. Anyone who refuses to be in that category, may expect the same end which awaits the condemned men today. We shall punish every offender and execute him with our own hands.

Today we carry out the execution of 6 Jewish murderers who killed fellow Jews. The sentence will be carried out by the Jewish Police who guard the ghetto and who will continue to do so. The police must carry out this death sentence as a duty.

We begin.

Dr. Gersz Gerszuni

134

LET HIM DIE A "NATURAL DEATH"

I KNEW that some of the Poles, who belonged to the secret A. K. (Armia Krajowa) Land Army organization, had asked their higher authorities about what kind of relations they should have with "the Jew" in the printing plant, and they were told: let him die a "natural death . . ."

I knew many of the workers before the war when they were employed by the only really democratic Polish newspaper *Curier Powszechny*, (Universal Courier) edited by Boleslaw Wit-Swiencicki, and printed in our plant.

There were those who had a good word for me, which made the others follow suit. Seeing that the Lithuanian administrators of the shop were behaving politely toward me, the Poles wanted to outdo the Lithuanians and treated me even more politely. Be that as it may, I was able to make use of their nationalistic "politics."

I had to sweat out my eight hours in the print shop, and later, even ten hours, a day. Then I worked late almost every night, sometimes until dawn, in the ghetto press. This sleepless regime drained me of my strength. Instead of arriving promptly at eight in the morning, I used to come at nine. I began to do this after I had accidentally come late once. I then made up the excuse that there was a very long line at the ghetto gate which took two hours to go through, as the exit was strictly controlled. The manager accepted this explanation as a fact (as it frequently happened) and said that it didn't matter. After getting such an answer my tardiness became a habit. For me this extra hour was invaluable.

This one hour, of course, did not make up my loss of sleep. I went around the shop with glassy eyes, which still begged for slumber. Once, during the day, I hid among the tens of rolls of paper for the rotary presses, which were stored in a special room. There I stretched out for a half hour, but slept for three. When I went back up, no one said anything about it.

The burden of my work in the ghetto grew heavier. It got so bad that the German press was my resting place. After saying hello to the managers of the plant, I would head for my hideout among the paper rolls and sleep till noon.

The whole game was played with sign language. The foreman of the typesetting section, the highly enlightened and liberal Christian, Pashkewitz, was fully aware of my sleeping till noon, but he kept quiet.

So that they would not take my sleepiness for "Jewish laziness," I tried one day to explain to Pashkewitz my living conditions in the ghetto. I told him that I was living in a small room together with many other people, including little children, who cried all night. The heat was unbearable and I could barely fall asleep. The elderly Christian told me that I was doing well by sleeping a bit in the shop . . . After hearing this, my daily nap before noon became a regular feature of my "work" program. Soon, many of the workers knew of the terrible living conditions in the ghetto and that I had to have some additional sleeping time in the shop.

After the noon break, I would get to work with a vengeance. I would run from one circle to another. I would take apart the Polish-German newspaper, *Goniec Codzienny*. Ninety percent of the time in the afternoon was used for our needs . . .

A group of Jewish Partisans in the Rudnicki forest.

A BROKEN FINGER

THE Gestapo also had its men in the ghetto itself. One of them was Berke Rosenthal, the former publisher of the pre-war Vilna evening newspaper, *Der Ownt Curier.* I knew him well.

When Rosenthal used to meet me in the ghetto, he would grab hold of me and try to talk. I already knew who he was, having been warned by Glazman.

No matter what we discussed, he would inevitably come up with an innocent question: what are my relations with Glazman? By then he knew partially that a secret organization was in existence and he wanted to know my link with it. I assured him that some time ago Glazman and I had been friends, but later we had quarreled. Berke believed this. Unfortunately, however, that very night, when the ghetto was asleep, he spotted Glazman and myself as we were walking, deep in conversation.

For security reasons, the command staff decided that I should stop going to work for a while. I bandaged a finger with a stick, to simulate a broken bone.

Before we concluded that his "job" was other than to trail me, it took a month. According to the law, one had to

Children
Partisans

bring a doctor's confirmation of illness, but I could not get one. Chiena Borowski, who was one of our most effective U.P.O. workers, worked in a ghetto clinic and even she could not get an excuse slip. I had to arrange for one myself . . .

A GESTAPO AGENT INSIDE

THE only man in the printing plant with whom I had no contact was a young Lithuanian, who worked in the seal department. This was not because I did not want to be friendly with him, but because he did not even acknowledge any of my greetings. I avoided meeting him. I was pleased that he was in a different room, which one could enter only with a special permit. I suspected that he was a Gestapo agent, and soon enough my suspicion was confirmed.

A party was held in the shop, and almost all the workers attended. Among the missing was this young, unfriendly Lithuanian. Around midnight, the door opened and in swaggered this Lithuanian, dressed in junior officer's uniform of the S.D. I was told about this incident soon thereafter.

Partisans are mining a track.

Then I was satisfied that I knew what he was. An exposed S.D. can be handled more easily. Nevertheless, his being in the printing plant was a great danger for me, and as was later demonstrated, also for the Poles.

I would greet him in the morning even though he never replied. It was evident that some of the Poles were interested in getting rid of the bird, too. They saw to it that word got to the S.D. that he had come drunk to a shop party and thus besmirched his uniform.

The rat was removed by the S.D. from the shop, not because he had besmirched the uniform, but because he had put it on when he had no right to do so.

138

Simon Wiesenthal

Dr. Mark Dworzecki

ANTON SCHMIDT

I WAS initiated into the secret that the U.P.O. was in contact with a German sergeant of the military police in Vilna who was friendly toward the Jews and hated the Nazis.

To hear such a thing within the ghetto walls was no small thing. It was balm to our hearts, a reassurance that the word "human" was not yet totally dead.

One day I met the sergeant myself. He was a man of medium height, with the regular iron helmet on his head and the usual badge slung across his chest, which meant that he was a member of the military police.

At one of our secret meetings I asked him whether he could obtain for me certain printing inks and paper. He told me that he could supply me with paint used for military trucks; as for paper, all he could get was printed military blanks. He added with a smile that I would have to get the kind of ink and the kind of paper from other sources.

*   *   *

On subsequent occasions, I heard from various U.P.O. members who had contact with Schmidt how dedicated he was to the idea of fighting Hitlerism.

Anton Schmidt was tireless. He placed his military truck at our disposal. Whenever it was necessary to go on dangerous missions in the province, he transported our people himself. When he was asked why he was doing all this at the risk of his life, he would answer, "I'll outlive them. They won't take me alive! . . . "

One day I proposed at our headquarters that Anton Schmidt should be warned to be more careful. I said that, after leaving secret staff meetings, he often stopped in the ghetto streets, talking and laughing with U.P.O. members, treating them to cigarettes, and behaving in obviously friendly fashion. (It must be remembered that entry into the ghetto was strictly forbidden to Germans, even of the highest rank, unless they were on some "official" business.)

I was told by the leadership that it was aware of this and had already spoken to him about it, but he shrugged it off, saying: "I am Anton Schmidt, M.P. in the accursed German army . . ."

* * *

Suddenly Anton Schmidt disappeared. For many weeks he had not been in contact with our members, and we had begun to be concerned. At best, we supposed that he had unexpectedly been sent to the front and had not had time enough to inform us. One thing we knew: we had lost an important ally in the resistance against Hitlerism.

Time went by. After the war, we learned that the Gestapo discovered his activities in Vilna and shot him.

* * *

It was only in 1966, when I began to prepare my final manuscript for publication in English, that I came across a press report on the case. The indefatigable Simon Wiesenthal, whose home I visited in 1945 when passing through Linz, in Austria, learned that a court martial had sentenced Schmidt to death in Vilna in 1942, and that the sentence was immediately executed.

Simon Wiesenthal quotes from a letter which Anton Schmidt sent to to his family before his death. He wrote:

"Every man must die once. One can die as a hangman, or as a man dedicated to helping others. I die for helping other men."

The report continues that Wiesenthal, who was one of the most active members of the group which found the Vilna hangman Franz Murer, Adolph Eichmann, Franz Stangl and others, had sought out Schmidt's family in Austria. (When we were in Vilna, I had assumed that Schmidt was a Sudeten German). He arranged through the Vienna documentation center, which he directs, for several members of Schmidt's family to come to

Vilna to visit his grave. This visit took place late in 1965. It has been proposed that a street in Israel be named for Schmidt.

* * *

Upon the invitation of *Yad Veshem*, Schmidt's widow and daughter will plant a tree in Schmidt's name in the alley of *Hasidei Umot Haolam* on the Mountain of Memories.

Dr. Mark Dworzecki, one of the first to write about my part in the underground movement, spent the summer of 1965 in Vienna. He came to do further research about the parts that Vilna and Estonia played in the struggle and annihilation of the Jews. In Vienna he met Schmidt's widow, Stephanie, and her daughter. They showed Dr. Dworzecki the letter, partially quoted above and informed him that both were mistreated by their surrounding neighbors until the end of the war.

Right after her husband was executed in April 1942, the Gestapo sent Mrs. Schmidt his bullet-ridden shirt.

Adolf Eichmann SS-Obergrupenfuhrer Himmler's plenipotentiary for the liquidation of Jews in Europe. He was caught in Buenos Aires on May 11, 1960 by Israelis. He was hanged May 31, 1962 in Israel.

A GESTAPO OFFICER SAVES ME...

ONE day I was busily engaged in breaking up the type and looking for the letters that I needed for "myself." Instinctively I felt that someone was standing at my side. I raised my head—and almost blacked out. There was a uniformed Gestapo officer, a captain, and the whole printing plant was full of Gestapo and their civilian agents.

I lowered my eyes and began to fiddle with the type. As I worked, my mind burned with only one thought: is this the end? There was not the slightest way out.

The sudden inspection took place at the end of the working day, when all the documents, including blank S.D. forms, had been taken out of their hiding places, and were sitting near my working place, ready to be smuggled out to the ghetto. At the stone where I was working, I worked feverishly. The Gestapo captain stood there for fifteen minutes, without moving. He looked at the motion of my hands. Boldly I ventured to take a few steps to get something. The captain followed my move. I went back to work, and the "beloved guest" picked up a batch of type which I had just transferred from another spot. But the type, which had been tied well, came apart and scattered all over.

I sprang forward and put on a serious face. For the first time the captain spoke to me. He asked, "Why did the type fall apart in my hands and not in yours? I have caused a great deal of damage, *nicht wahr?*"

"No, no, it doesn't matter," I replied. "I'll fix it up right away."

I began to pick up the scattered type. The captain stood and watched with great interest.

The others turned the shop upside down. They made nothing out of everything and everyone. But me, the little Jew who wore a yellow star even at work, I was disturbed, because the chief of the operation himself was standing by me.

143

I was about to finish, and was hoping that he would somehow spill something again, so that he could continue to stand by me, without talking or doing anything. Just then, I had to get some material that was near the window, I took a quick look outside and was upset by what I saw. The yard was full of Gestapo, armed with long weapons.

An officer approached the captain, saluted and reported that the inspection had been completed. Something had been discovered.

"Take that one with you. The second one, arrest him when he comes at five o'clock afternoon and bring him to me."

"Line up everyone in the yard and I'll be right down."

With a click of the heels the officer went away. He had burned holes in me with his eyes during the entire interview. Certainly, he must have thought that I was the only one who had not been examined . . . He was soon followed by the captain who took small steps.

When he got several yards from me, I lifted my head and watched him depart.

All the Christians were pale and nervous. Their eyes were full of terror. Each one had been thoroughly grilled. They were so worried about themselves that they did not notice whether I had been examined or not. They only saw that the head of the investigation had been standing next to me.

I immediately stashed the documents away and went peacefully back to the ghetto.

Next day, when I came to work exactly on time, the techni-

cal manager came up and told me that the officer, who was in the administration, had made a big fuss about stolen authentic German documents that were being used. Such documents were being printed right here. A counterfeit form had turned up in the district commissary. It had the swastika seal on it. Besides, a new Polish paper was appearing, whose type must have come from one of the city printing plants.

The first accusations had no connection with us, because in those days we did not issue that kind of blank. Later I found out that it was the work of the Poles, who belonged to the niepodleglosc-school (independent organization).

As a final word, the officer stated that if the source of the secret press was not uncovered, all the technical foremen of the Vilna printing plants would be arrested.

The printers tried to calm him with the reassurances that this was only an empty threat and that they would not do it. If anything did happen, someone said, we would all stop working (there were also such naive persons among the Poles). What connection did we have with a secret press?

The agents had "found" that one of the photo-cuts, which lay near the department where the newspaper *Goniec Cadzienny* was printed, had been captioned, The German Terror. Those heading the department were immediately arrested.

This matter was reported at once to the newspaper's editor, who had been appointed by the Germans. He explained that there had been a mistake, that there should have been quotation marks around the caption and that would mean the false propaganda about the German terror. After the editor explained that in reality this was printed a long time ago in a story about the Bolshevik terror, the compositors who were arrested were freed. They returned the next day to their work in the printing shop, but the workers, all of us, had been thoroughly frightened.

JAN PSZEWALSKI

FOR months my meetings with Jan Pszewalski clicked like a clock. He failed to come only once. I went out of the printing plant, looked around, but did not see him. All our workers had already left the narrow Donbrowski Street, but I still wandered about. I waited until a half hour after work, standing like on a burning piece of coal, impatiently.

The plant director stood at the exit gate. Seeing that I had quite a package under my arm, he asked me, apparently without any special meaning, what I was carrying. I told him that it was old papers that we used to start the oven fires with. He accepted this explanation, but in truth I had a printing roller in the bundle.

Since I had no choice, I went to the ghetto. It happened that that day I was loaded down with a heavy package in which there was a part of a hand press for Pszewalski. I went armed with iron and tin. The road to the ghetto was not a short one and I did not know how I would manage to get there. As luck would have it, my trouser belt tore when it caught on an iron hook as I went along the crowded Zawalna Street. I could have sunken into the ground to avoid the looks of the passersby. It was a miracle that I made it to the ghetto.

Sonia Madejsker, who was the liaison between me and Pszewalski, told me the next day that he could not come because he thought that he was being trailed. Later, it turned out that his suspicion was well founded.

In a few days we resumed our rendezvous, and I passed on to him a lot of important materials so that our secret press could go on working.

Pszewalski, a short time later, when we were already in the forest, came to a conference of the brigade staff in the Rudnicki forest. I met him and we had a very friendly chat and immediately after the meeting went back to the city. A few days later, walking along the streets, he was arrested. His wife was informed of this at once and escaped from her home, coming to the Rudnicki forest where she remained until liberation.

Jan Pszewalski was tortured to death in the cellars of the Gestapo.

*   *   *

In 1966 Wanda Pszewalski came from Poland to visit Israel and was met with great honor by high government officials and former partisans. She was awarded distinguished medals for her work in the underground press.

Natek Ring

Miriam Ganionska

THE INTELLIGENCE UNIT

O NE day in March 1942 I was summoned by Joseph Glazman, who informed me that, like every other underground organization, the U.P.O. had formed an intelligence unit under his leadership. He also told me that I was assigned to this service and would henceforth be directly under his command in all matters pertaining to it. He said that Miriam Ganionska and Miriam Bernstein would work side by side with me.

The appointment to such duty took me by surprise. But, of course, I accepted it as a military order.

Glazman told me that my first assignment was of extraordinary importance for the entire future of the U.P.O. Warning me to listen carefully, he said that a group of well-meaning young people was about to form a second fighting organization. If they should succeed in this attempt, they would undoubtedly apply themselves to procuring arms for underground activity; if this should go on without control by the U.P.O., it might lead to a catastrophe both for the U.P.O. and for the ghetto as a whole. The U.P.O. could not allow others outside its control to engage in such activities, for a fiasco could have disastrous effects upon our great and holy cause.

It was my task, said Glazman further, to join this group, get information concerning its action, and so on. Everything I learned was to be reported directly and immediately to him, even if it meant waking him in the middle of the night.

*   *   *

Esther Jaffe, whom I knew very well, was one of the leading spirits of the projected organization. I immediately went to see her and we had a talk about a number of topics. I told her that I had been thinking for some time of forming a secret organization to fight against the Nazis independently of the U.P.O.

Esther knew Joseph Glazman well personally. They had been close friends at one time, since she was registered as

148

his wife. The reason for such registrations was that every man who had a so-called "yellow identity card" could protect a wife and two children. Glazman, who was single, utilized this right to protect another person by registering his friend, Esther, as his wife. This was done by hundreds of people who possessed the "yellow identity card." Moreover, Esther Jaffe was one of the first organizers of the U.P.O. Later, however, the U.P.O. leaders suspected that she had, perhaps unwittingly, divulged some information about U.P.O. activities to the vice-police-chief of the ghetto, Salek Dessler. She was therefore gradually eliminated from activities.

Since she was a very energetic woman, she had managed to win the interest of a number of people in forming a new organization.

The U.P.O. was a highly secret organization, which admitted to membership only the most tried and trustworthy members of each party. Besides, the character of the organization was such that the U.P.O. members served only as a *vanguard* for the coming uprising in the ghetto. Hence, stress was made on quality rather than numbers. In addition, the size of the membership was restricted according to the quantity of arms and ammunition that could be obtained. Therefore, a number of people, as trustworthy and deserving as the U.P.O. members, necessarily remained outside the organization.

Esther confided in me that she had gone a long way toward realizing my idea of an independent fighting group. As we said good-bye, she told me that I would hear from her soon.

On the following day we met and she informed me that she had discussed the matter with some of her comrades, and was empowered to invite me to a meeting at No. 6 Rudnicka Street, in one of the rooms occupied by the Judenrat.

At the appointed time I came to the meeting. Among those in attendance, I found Natek Ring, Ilya Scheinbaum, Dr. Leon Bernstein, Shlomo Bard, Janek Faust and Esther Jaffe. The latter introduced me to the group, stressing "the great acquisition" the group was making in accepting me as a member. Since I knew everyone present, and they knew me, my admission was a simple matter.

Natek Ring informed me that, before my arrival at the meeting, it had been decided that I was to be co-opted to the staff, which consisted of the above-mentioned persons. After that we went on to the formal meeting.

Listening to the discussion, I soon discovered that the group had already been active for some weeks and had purchased arms; in fact, they had already suffered a near-disaster during one of the buying transactions, but had managed to escape and so everything had ended well this time.

The chief concern of the group was to obtain arms without discovery, as that could be fatal for the entire ghetto. And this, indeed, was the chief cause for concern on the part of the U.P.O.

At one of the subsequent meetings, Natek Ring reported about a highly confidential talk he had with the chief of the ghetto, Gens. Ring had told Gens about a plan to establish a fighting organization and asked his cooperation in the mattter. Gens had told him that he was a former Lithuanian army captain, married to an Aryan Lithuanian. Members of his wife's family were serving in many important posts in the occupation government and he could indeed render significant help. Besides, he was extremely anxious to see the formation of another organization to counterbalance the U.P.O., since he was absolutely out of contact with the latter and was held in very low repute by it.

Evidently, Gens really wanted to improve his image among the underground youth. However, he was afraid of Dessler. Dessler, he said to Ring, was an out and out Gestapo man, and was sure to learn sooner or later that Gens had been in contact with a clandestine group. Therefore, although he did not have Ring and the others arrested, he categorically refused to have anything to do with the matter.

When Ring reported this conversation and Gen's refusal to help, I spoke up for the first time in criticism of his attempt to talk to the latter on his own initiative, without a previous decision by the entire staff. He defended his action on the ground that he was a close friend of Gens and would stake his head on the promise that nothing would happen to any of us at Gen's hands. We then went on to other matters.

Soon after that Glazman was, naturally, informed about all this. The U.P.O. staff was called together in a special session and decided to take drastic steps toward abolishing the group which endangered the entire activity of the U.P.O.

It was decided that Chiene Borowski, our "ambassador" to the Judenrat, was to visit Dessler and inform him that Gens regarded him as a dangerous Gestapo man. Chiene Borowski knew Dessler well, and was one of the leading members of the U.P.O.

As soon as he heard this, Dessler ran to Gens and told him what he had just heard. Gens naturally called in Ring and told him what had happened. Ring turned pale as a ghost. He began to stutter . . . shocked, he was too short of breath to talk. When he recovered a little, he tried to explain that there must have been some leak, some provocation. Gens shouted: "I will have you shot! I thought you were my friend! I made you commissar of the largest police district, and you have betrayed me! See how smart I was to refuse to have anything to do with you! Get out of here! Get out!"

Ring called a meeting of the staff. I was amazed at all I heard. (Afterwards it transpired that my U.P.O. comrades had sought me in the ghetto in order to inform me of Borowski's visit to Dessler but were unable to find me. The staff felt that this action was essential in order to show the other group that we had our people everywhere and nothing could be concealed from the U.P.O. Everything had happened so quickly that there was no time to warn me beforehand.)

151

Everyone left the meeting in discouragement. Such a fiasco at the very first steps . . .

Three days later a police sergeant and a policeman came to my little room and told me that the police commissar Ring wanted me to come to his office. I went with heavy forebodings. As I entered the police office, Ring slapped me in the face, and then said to the guards: "You can let him go now!"

A few minutes later I was in Glazman's room and re-ported the scene to him. I laughed, but Glazman was very seri-ous. "Go home," he said to me, "and be especially careful now. Our people will guard you . . . "

When I went out of my room into the ghetto streets a half-hour later, I noticed a group of people listening to a man. "Miriam Ganionska," he told them, "the most beautiful girl in the ghetto and the fiancee of Natek Ring had just entered he first police district office, approached Ring, and slapped him, once on the left, and once on the right cheek. Then, with-out a word, she left. Nobody knows what happened. Only an hour ago, they were both seen walking arm in arm along the ghetto streets, and both were very cheerful, altogether unlike anyone else in the ghetto. Not even any of the police know what has happened . . ."

I listened to the story, and continued on my way.

The incident was the sensation of the day. Whenever I met Ring after that in the narrow ghetto streets, he always hur-riedly crossed to the other side.

Miriam Ganionska broke off all relations with Ring.

*   *   *

However, our attempt at "subversion" did not succeed. The wish of the U.P.O. to prevent the emergence of separate secret groups was of no avail. The group became still more persistent and zealous in pursuing its work.

The U.P.O. realized that the situation and the time did not allow disruption of the group and, after lengthy negotiations, finally incorporated it within itself. The new unit proved most useful and well-armed. Later, one of its members—Lole War-szawczyk—who died a hero's death was posthumously awarded the highest Soviet order that of a hero of the Soviet Union, for his diversion work when he destroyed 15 military trains.

*   *   *

Ring, with a well-armed group, was one of the first to come to the Rudnicki wilderness, to which we had withdrawn from the dying ghetto, making it our new fighting center. Ring easily adapted himself to the conditions of the forest and was one of the most fearless partisans.

*   *   *

One evening I noticed a Russian fellow-partisan wearing a fur hat that looked extremely familiar to me. That morning he had worn a different hat. I asked him where he had gotten such a fine headpiece. A certain man called Ring, I told him, who was stationed several miles away with another unit, had worn just such a hat. The Russian said to me: "Yes, but he will not wear this fur hat any more." With that he left.

I could not puzzle out what his words meant. I thought to myself: perhaps Ring had given it to him, or had bartered it for something. But it was late in the evening and we were getting ready for a night's sleep, and I soon forgot about the matter.

On the following day I met Jewish partisans of the "Revenge" unit, and they told me that Natek Ring and several others had been shot the previous day, and nobody knew exactly why. They had been sentenced by the staff. Now I understood the meaning of the words, "he will not wear it any more."

Later I tried to discover what had happened. It turned out that Ring had left his mother in hiding with non-Jews in the city, and that he had decided, with his friend Micke Lipenholc, to visit her and tell her that he was alive.

However, he had gone without permission of the partisan command. When he returned, he was tried by a secret court and sentenced to death. Such death sentences were carried out by a special unit attached to headquarters. It was thus that my Russian fellow-partisan had inherited his fur hat.

* * *

There was a final epilogue to this story. Natek Ring's mother survived and emigrated to Israel. The last commander of the U.P.O. and later commander of the "Revenge" partisan unit, Aba Kowner, also settled in Israel. The mother had another son in Israel, who had come there prior to the war, and was a prominent citizen. The mother had learned soon after the war, while still in Vilna, that the death sentence had been ratified by Kowner, who had not had the authority, in her opinion, to take such actions. Her second son supported her accusation, and an open scandal broke out in Israel. The newspapers carried the full details of the story.

The mother argued that Natek had been a loyal and devoted son and a good partisan, and that he had gone to see her without realizing that he needed special permission of the partisan command to do so under the conditions of partisan warfare. He had not been in the forest very long and did not know all the rules. Therefore he had not deserved such a grim sentence. Kowner, who had by then became a leading kibbutz member, replied through the press, that under partisan conditions it was not always possible to see into the soul of a man. The fact that he had gone to town armed and in secret could have brought disaster not only to him personally, but to the partisan army as a whole. Since he had gone without the knowledge or permission of his commanders, he might have revealed secrets to the enemy. Besides, he had been a police officer in the ghetto before he joined the underground movement, and such a man could not be given full confidence. True, he had been a good partisan from the first, but it was a dangerous act to go into town for personal reasons, and no one could have been sure of his true motives in going to a place where the Gestapo was master. These and other arguments were used by Kowner in justifying his action. He also pointed out that nothing was

154

done to Micke Lipenholc, Ring's friend who had accompanied him, for he enjoyed full confidence, while Ring did not. Such were the tragic conditions of war.

It took years before the case ceased to be discussed in Israel.

Miriam Bernstein

Micke Lipenholc

Jasha Raff

Baruch Goldstein

From left: Tewke Galpern, Szmerke Kaczerginski are reading a clandestine front-bulletin in a deserted street in Vilna Ghetto.

GHETTO JEWS AS SABOTEURS

JEWS were compelled to do all kinds of difficult and distasteful tasks in the various work units. Among many others was a work unit located in a Vilna suburb called Burbishok.

The environs of Burbishok were converted into a depot for ammunition parts which were brought from or carried to the fighting front. Damaged weapons were taken apart and over-hauled in workshops. Those beyond repair were exploded.

Among the slave laborers was a group of U.P.O. members headed by Boruch Goldstein. He was the one who smuggled out the first revolver from the office of the German commanders and brought it into the ghetto. He had it in his bandaged hands. Later on he brought weapons, among them machine guns, each time under great risk.

The second one to risk his life was Zalman Tiktin. He dragged many weapons into the ghetto. One fatal day, he decided that a piecemeal process was too slow. He wanted to make a big haul at one time. For that purpose he broke the lock of one of the sealed ammunition train cars and helped himself to the weapons. The trouble was that he was observed by the guard, Michalauskas, whose gunshot sounded the alarm. Other German guards ran over and Tiktin was caught under a hail of bullets.

When Tiktin was arrested, he had seven bullets in his stomach and legs. The Nazis interrogated him and tried to find out why he wanted to steal the weapons. His answer was: "For the spilled blood of my near ones."

The captain ordered him removed to a Gestapo hospital to keep him alive for the purpose of pressing out further information under torture. They wanted to know for whom he wanted to steal that large quantity of weapons. Several Jews were ordered to place him in a stretcher and carry him to an ambulance. While he was still possessed of his faculties, he called out to his stretcher-bearers: "Let them go to hell! Comrades, take revenge!"

Zalman Tiktin expired in the hospital shortly thereafter, and he took his secret with him into his grave. The U.P.O. group, of which he was a member, honored their hero who fell in the line of his partisan duties, by naming a revolver in his memory.

The diversive actions of the U.P.O. unit did not end with the death of Zalman Tiktin. There still remained Boruch Goldstein and the Gordon brothers, who carried on their holy missions with more zeal. The quartet had already destroyed 365 cannons, by breaking their locks; 145 zenith guns were demolished; they took out the stems of 90 hand grenades.

Our partisans entrusted the engineer, Ratner, one of the Jews assigned to the munitions depot, with a special job. He was to devise a contraption which would explode a truck full of ammunition on its way to the front. Ratner carried out his mission. He made a time bomb which he put into gasoline reservoirs, and when a particular formation was on its way to Smolensk front, there was a terrific explosion and the entire outfit, with its tanks and ammunition, was destroyed.

This same engineer Ratner once espied a German soldier holding a hand grenade gingerly, as if he didn't quite know what to do with it, and was afraid it would go off any second. Noticing the plight of the soldier, Ratner shouted at a distance: "Throw it away!"—and from afar he indicated the direction. The soldier obeyed. The direction indicated by Ratner was a munition dump. There ensued a terrible cycle of explosions. The entire German encampment was in a turmoil. After the detonations, all attending military personnel were held for questioning as to the facts in the matter. The German soldier took the blame upon himself saying that the grenade began to smoulder in his hand, and in order to rescue himself, he hurled it away. However, he did not say that a Jew egged him on to throw the grenade in the direction of the ammunition dump where the explosion took place.

The Gestapo then arrested the soldier and the Jews got away with it this time although a bit frightened.

Hirsch Lewin, Yitzchak Mackiewicz, Kuperberg, and Weinstein: these derailed a train en route to Ignalina. They worked in a nearby slave labor camp at Bezdan, which was 40 kilometers from the city of Vilna.

Janek Sztul and his buddies, Fritz, Max and Chayim used to assemble bicycles on 4 Zeligowska Street. They worked in a German unit which repaired bicycles. When the bicycles were ready for shipment to the front, they cut the axles during the packing process. Thus they destroyed about 600 bicycles. The same quartet was later assigned to another unit for the repair of tanks. There they used to make holes in the gasoline cases which supplied fuel to the tanks. In so doing thousands of gallons of gasoline ran out. They used to inflict damage on the body of the tanks as well, in many cases, destroying the locks of the cannons.

Zelig Goldberg was an instructor in the Jewish Technion of Vilna, the only one of its kind in pre-war Poland. He was engaged in slave labor as an engineer in the Porubanek Aerodrome. He loosened the screws of vital parts of 50 airplanes sent there for repairs. After he got through with them they were not good for anything.

Molke Chazan, Michal Kowner, Danke Lubocki, Tolye Zabinski carried out a great "appropriations" mission in the German clothing depot. Molke Chazan was dressed up as a German gendarme. He stood at the window of the depot and threw out into a waiting wagon, everything he could lay hands on, such as German military uniforms and coats. The other three folded and packed the stolen clothing into the wagon and drove away with it. A second group of U.P.O. members, who worked as ghetto police, awaited the wagon load and helped smuggle it through the ghetto gates by means of false documents which they showed to the Lithuanian guard. Later, the entire load was stripped of the military stripes and was sold. The money went into our defense fund.

Tevke Galpern had, among other assignments, the task of distributing sacks of letters. These should have been loaded upon a train bound for Germany or the military fronts. Instead, he burned thousands of letters and the German families who should have received them, waited in vain. Thus, he brought about a good deal of demoralization in the German ranks,

Yitzchak Wolozhny worked in a provision camp. He destroyed loads of foodstuffs that were earmarked for the front.

Leibke Distel destroyed many anti-aircraft locks and zenith guns. He was also our most valuable agent for delivering ammunition into the ghetto.

Feldman and Jaszka Raff, who were expert technicians, destroyed many tanks in a German tank-repair-unit. They worked there as slave laborers.

Yitzchok Mackewicz had Tartar identification papers and worked on the railroads as a non-Jew. He spied upon the movements of military units and brought the information to the U.P.O. command. The latter transferred the data to non-Jewish partisans, who made very efficient use of the information.

There were some factories in the ghetto which were appropriated by the Germans for their own use. Our people in the U.P.O. were placed in these factories to produce and repair weapons. The following were engaged in this sort of work: Moshe Szymeliski, Janek Sztul, Szmulke Kaplinski, Mendel Tarle and others. They made hundreds of axes, swords, explosives for hand grenades, iron knuckles and similar items. Our people emptied the contents of electric bulbs and filled them with dynamite. They turned these bulbs into many hundreds of hand grenades. In this manner we built up our arsenal. From practically nothing, we progressed to primitive forms of weapons which gradually developed in power and included such armaments as flame throwers, light bazookas and the like.

Arsenals were found in special armories, cellars, attics, under floorings, in double covers of water pails, in empty vessels, in medicine bottles, etc.

In addition to the sabotage acts committed by members of U.P.O. many other acts of sabotage were carried out by Christian sympathizers. These acts took place as early as the beginning of 1942. That is to say, a few months after the German hordes occupied Vilna.

A few incidents will illustrate this.

A notice appeared one day in the Polish-German newspaper, *Goniec Codzienny*, where I was employed as a laborer, that on Dominikanska Street 11, a fire consumed a factory of surgical instruments. A second news item told about a big fur factory, Kailis, where a few hundred Jews were employed as slave laborers. This factory was outside of the ghetto gates in another part of the city. A big fire broke out, in this factory. One third of the factory and its fur pelts were consumed. These were designated for the freezing army on the eastern front. The Jewish foreman, Glick, was arrested. But the Germans believed that it was not the Jews, but the Christian saboteurs who had committed arson. (Actually it was the work of U.P.O. members.) The Germans soon freed the foreman Glick, because the local newspapers quickly spread the news that the fire was caused by overheated ovens. Thus nobody could accuse anybody of sabotage.

The local German, Polish and Lithuanian press continuously and automatically attributed the larger fires to overheated ovens. Actually, people used to freeze within the city due to a shortage of wood and coal and it was more a question of underheating. But this was a face-saving device of the German propaganda machine to account for the fires that were actually caused by sabotage.

In another instance, in April, 1942, the same newspaper carried an item saying that 16 communist terrorists were shot for acts of sabotage.

About December 1942, the Lithuanian Chief of Police was arrested by a German gendarme, assisted by four Lithuanian policemen. They led him to the Ponary woods, poured benzine all over him and set him on fire. The entire act took one hour. Though I mention this incident here, I admit that it is not entirely clear to me whether it had anything to do with our partisan activity.

There was a jail on the same street where I lived. At this time it was converted into a military jail for Germans and their accomplices.

On December 25, 1942, four o'clock in the morning, disguised "Gestapo" men let out a number of German soldiers from the Stefanska Street jail. After that stricter regulations were put into effect. But I heard no reports regarding the discovery of the men they were searching for . . .

On May 25, 1943, they found a Lithuanian Gestapo agent shot to death on a Vilna Street. During the same period the press reported that the roads leading out of Vilna were strewn with broken glass and nails and that many army trucks bound for the front had their tires cut . . .

The U.P.O. in general was successful in carrying out these acts of sabotage without attracting the attention of the Germans, because the latter could not imagine that the Jews were in any way involved. The Germans knew that we were isolated in a ghetto where we were hard put to sustain our lives . . .

Later the Germans did find out that the Jews were the *main* saboteurs within the city, but the ghetto had already been pinpointed for complete annihilation. Then it did not matter to the Jews whether the Germans would or would not find out about our participation in the general diversionary tactics we used in the city of Vilna and its suburbs.

Father and Son. *From left*:
Mejlech (son) Yirachmiel (father)

From left: Cwi Lewin, Janek Sztul

First Police Station in the Ghetto. *From left*: Janek Faust,
Bernstein, Natek Ring, Joseph Muszkat,

ORPHANS OF THE GHETTO

ONE day Zalman Toker, a mutual friend, came and told me that Joseph Muszkat wished to see me.

I went over and we conversed about general conditions in the ghetto. Then he told me that he wanted to organize the Jewish youth into a Resistance Force in the ghetto.

I knew Muszkat very well since the days he headed a refugee kitchen in Vilna. He held high positions in pre-war Warsaw as the head of Masada, an organization of young Jewish high-school students that was a branch of the Revisionist Party.

This Muszkat was also a brilliant lawyer and orator. With all that I did not quite trust him. At the time he was the nominal substitute for the ghetto Police Chief Gens. In the course of my activity in the special division of the U.P.O. he came up on our agenda more than once and we came to the conclusion that Gens kept him as a front for his police staff and actually gave him no power. He was only given the privilege of wearing a uniform and a chance to exist.

In the ghetto Muszkat took charge of orphaned children and he organized them into a sort of cooperative under his personal supervision. They engaged in transfering products from the main storage center to the various blocs of houses. In this way he relieved the misery of the hungry and became very popular with the children.

We came to the conclusion that Muszkat could bring little use to our organization, but he had enough character not to stand in the way of our resistance activity.

I suggested to him that he discuss his ideas with his colleague, Joseph Glazman, and I felt that with this suggestion our discussion was ended . . .

*   *   *

Zalman Toker was sentenced to death by a partisan court in the Rudnicki forest, because he lost his weapons during the

164

course of the action. It was a brutal verdict against all true justice.

*   *   *

Poland, which since the establishment of Israel had been friendly to it, became hostile to Israel after the Six Day War of June, 1967.

Joseph Muszkat, who was saved from a Nazi concentration camp, settled in Poland and became a prominent editor, lecturer and lawyer. The hostile attitude of Poland to Israel stirred his dormant love for the Jewish homeland and in February 1968, he and his family migrated to Israel, where he became a citizen.

Cooperative of children workers with their leader Joseph Muszkat.

Muszkats Ghetto Children

SOME GHETTO FOLKLORE

A GERMAN asks a Jew to lend him 20 rubles. The Jew immediately takes out the sum of money from his pocket and hands it over to the German. The latter is astounded. "How come? You don't know me and yet you trust me for such a large sum of money?"

"I have the highest confidence in the Germans," answers the Jew. "You took Stalingrad and gave it back. You took Kharkov and gave it back. Therefore, I am sure that you will also return the 20 rubles."

What is the difference between General Rommel and a clock?

A clock goes tick-tock and goes ahead.

Rommel makes tock-tick and retreats.

What is the difference between the Germans and the sun?

The sun rises in the East and sinks in the West.

The Germans rose in the West and sink way down in the East . . .

Why can't there be an understanding between the opposing forces?

Because Hitler says that race will win; Stalin says that the masses will win; and Roosevelt says that cash will win.

Which city is the longest in the world?

Stalingrad, because it took the Germans the longest time to go from the suburbs into the center of the city.

The Jews of the ghetto created a joke:

What is the ghetto? It is the S.S.S.R. — four of the principal streets are: Szawelska, Szpitalna, Straszuna, and Rudnicka.

A group of Jewish Partisans.

From left: Nisn Rojtbord
Mordechei Szames

Judith Solonojc

TWO LIVES ON MY CONSCIENCE...

I HAD become friendly with a refugee from deep Poland—Yehuda Kuszinsky—who was now in the Vilna ghetto. I worked with him for a while in the same German labor unit. I knew that he was an experienced soldier and had smelled gun smoke on the German-Polish front. I therefore considered him good material for the U.P.O. and had some talks with him about setting up a resistance to the Nazis and so on. As a result of our conversations he gradually got to know about the existence of the U.P.O.

Before you knew it, I heard one day that Kuszinsky and several other Jews had been arrested for dealing with non-Jews outside the ghetto at his place of work. This was a common practice of the ghetto for it was the only source of earning some money or getting some food to supplement the starvation diet.

Suddenly I felt guilty that I had already spoken a few words to Kuszinsky about the U.P.O. I thought to myself: who knows, perhaps while sitting in jail awaiting his turn to be shot, he might cave in under the pressure and say something. Then the blame would fall on me, and I naturally wanted to be free of such a suspicion.

I therefore decided that the best thing would be to rescue him from jail and thus avoid the ordeal. I went to the command staff and said that a certain Yehuda Kuszinsky was an ex-soldier and knew what combat was as he had served in the Polish army. I thought that he was good material for the U.P.O., and so on and on. I argued so well that the command believed it was essential to save this man. Of course, I did not tell them what was bothering me inside.

Only one who has been in a ghetto, and especially the Vilna ghetto, knows what it means to sit in the Lukiszki jail and to be extricated from those walls. There were only a few cases in which the ghetto leaders tried desperately to save someone, who was considered in their opinion valuable for the

ghetto Jews. Large sums of money were required and even then
it was 99 per cent uncertain that they would succeed. But that
one per cent chance was worth trying and in a handful of isolated cases there was success, before the victim was sent off to
be killed at Ponary.

Yehuda Kuszinsky was a refugee. Nobody here knew him
well and none was ready to put up a large or small sum of
money for his rescue. Not only that—a rooster would not have
crowed if he had been killed, for he had no family in the ghetto
and there was nobody who would even *attempt* to do anything
for him.

In these circumstances, I continued to hammer away that
he must be saved, as he would be an asset to the U.P.O. At that
time there were strained relations between the U.P.O. staff and
Gens, and when the staff approached Gens about Kuszinsky,
they found him in a cooperative mood, wishing to show the
U.P.O. that he reckoned with their wishes, and he promised to
try. After eliciting such a promise, a miracle was also necessary
—that after Gens had talked to the Gestapo, they would comply
with his request. It turned out that the Gestapo knew that I was
very much interested in Yehuda Kuszinsky, the Polish refugee,
and they released him . . .

Yehuda did not actually know how it happened. He saw it
as a great miracle and personal luck, and thanked Glazman and
the other U.P.O. commanders for doing such a thing for him.
However, when he expressed his thanks for this miracle, among
a circle of friends, Yehudith Solonojc spoke up: "You should
thank one man—Isaac Kowalski. He turned the world upside
down for your liberation and you should thank only him that
you are among us today."

Kuszinsky opened his eyes with wonder and only now did
it dawn on him who had rescued this stranger in the Vilna
ghetto from a sure death.

*   *   *

The so-called pink pass "action" was going on in the

ghetto. Those who did not identify themselves with a yellow pass, or as a family member with a pink pass, were caught by Nazi agents and dragged off to death.

A young man standing in the middle of the street noticed that the agents had entered the ghetto and were not many steps away from him on Rudnicki Street. In desperation, he ran into the Judenrat which was on the same street and dashed into Glazman's office, deathly afraid, and pleaded for help. Quickly Glazman took a pink pass from his desk and said, "Your name is Isaac Kowalski. Remember the name."

The young man left the office at once and at the exit met the Lithuanian kidnappers, identifying himself to them with that pink life-saving pass he had just received.

* * *

After the "action" I found out about this incident. All U.P.O. members who did not have yellow passes, were provided with pink passes by the command staff, which had connections with the ghetto administration. Such a pass had been prepared for me, but I had already fixed myself up with one from another source, so I did not come to get it the previous night. That is why my pass was available . . .

The young man, whose name I no longer recollect, found me in the ghetto and thanked me for the lucky coincidence.

Along my rambles through various European countries after the war, I met him again, on the eve of his departure for America, and I found out that he was among the most successful merchants in post-war Germany. If he is as lucky and successful as he was in the Vilna ghetto and in Munich, he must be quite a wealthy man, and hopefully a happy one, somewhere in America.

The "Herrenfolk" are freezing . . .

Partisans are transporting food to the base.

Partisans are bringing
wounded
to the base.

FROZEN APPLES

Hundreds of Jews were employed as slave-laborers on the railroads. My sister Luba also worked there in various capacities.

Almost daily, in the winter months, transports filled with German wounded arrived in Vilna. Those slightly wounded recovered there; the badly wounded died there. This was the normal scene of war throughout Nazi Europe.

But the transports of frost-bitten soldiers presented another picture. My sister used to describe to me the pitiful appearance of the "master race" who could not stand up to the Russian frost. She related that they looked like "frozen apples." The comparison appealed to me and I repeated it to my ghetto friends and we decided to use "apples" as a password. It was soon spread around that if one said, "A large transport of frozen apples came today," it meant a large transport of frozen German soldiers or chopped cabbage—severely wounded Germans.

That is how the word was adopted in the jargon of our ghetto life.

Besides the Germans, the Italian troops also suffered from the bitter frost. They were more to be pitied, for they were less conditioned to withstand Russian winters. In addition to Mussolini's soldiers, there were the so-called "volunteers" of the Spanish Brigade. The last-named had their own military hospital in Vilna, and some Jews were assigned there as slave laborers. Some Jews even learned to speak a little Spanish and they were propositioned to go to Spain with their charges. They would be given military uniforms and would be covered by the Spanish soldiers. This was an honest offer, but the Jews were afraid to accept it.

In general, the Spanish soldiers were friendly and they felt no special antipathy toward Jews. They complained about their sad state in that they were taken as so-called volunteers. The truth of the matter was that entire military units were forcibly taken and transported to the cold and bloody front.

THE NEWSPAPER WILL NOT APPEAR

IN honor of New Year's 1943, the Polish-German newspaper *Goniec Codzienny* prepared a special edition. All except the first and last pages were ready for the press. I looked at the galley sheets hanging on the hook in order to get, as usual, the latest news and articles in advance.

I was disheartened to see that there would be two "pogrom" articles in the issue. They had taken one article from *Der Stuermer* and had written a new one themselves, accompanied by all kinds of dirty caricatures of Jews.

As I was reading these articles, they were finishing a major repair job on the electric cables in the shop. The presses, which had stood still all morning because of the power shutdown, began to turn at full speed. The air was full of their whirring noises.

I went to my corner where I worked, and after thinking the whole thing over, decided: the newspaper must not appear! The Poles must not have the pleasure of seeing this compote that would be served at their holiday.

Had it not been for the fact that the presses had been stalled all morning on account of the electrical breakdown, I would probably not have engaged in such an adventure without having the agreement of the U.P.O. Under the circumstances, however, I had to go through with it on my own responsibility.

From decision to execution there is a big distance. How could I manage the job?

In the yard near the printing plant, the Germans had begun to build a wooden movie house. This was to impress upon the people that the Germans intended to stay quite a while, especially since the movie house was to be open to the civilian population. Tens of Jews worked on the construction. The building work stopped a half hour before our printing plant did. Electric cables lying in the area which had been dug up were also feeding part of our plant. I decided to sneak into the partly finished movie house and cut the cables.

I went out of the printing plant as usual with all the others. I said goodbye, going on the sidewalk while they went along the pavement. When we got to the central Mickiewicz Street, I turned around and headed for the yard and the cinema. Slithering in so that the watchman would not notice me, I did my work according to plan . . .

The form which was all set with its eight pages was waiting. The director was in the shop, going about nervously in the typesetting section. A trifle! Again the newspaper could not come out. This smelled of danger. Soon the technical director of the plant came and then the second technical director. After a long search the editor was also found.

Breathlessly the editor flew into the room. After learning the situation, he telephoned to the electric power station. He explained the seriousness of the matter and demanded that an engineer and electricians come at once to set presses in motion again. He warned that if his request was not promptly fulfilled there would be severe consequences.

An engineer and four workers promptly came to the rescue. None of them had any supper that evening. After hunting for the defect for two hours, the engineer called the station to send over some special equipment. After two more hours of search, he concluded that the failure was in the cables of the regional electric station located in the cinema yard and it would take a long time to do the repairs.

The directors of the press had to announce that the newspaper could not appear with all its pages as five hours of work had already been lost. Had this occurred on a weekday, they could have mobilized men for the smaller presses, but since the workers had gone home to celebrate the New Year and were at their holiday feasts or asleep, this was out of the question.

All agreed that it was late . . . the watchman shut the gates.

Early in the morning I stood at the ghetto gate and looked out, to see if the newshawks were running about as they did every day, shouting, *Goniec Codzienny.*

I watched for two hours but saw no one. I dispatched Molka Chazan, one of our ghetto police, to go to a second street and see if any papers were being sold. He met a young non-Jew with an empty bag in which he usually carried papers.

"Sell me a paper."

"The papers did not come out today."

The comrades of our command staff commended me and were highly pleased, even though the job had been done without their direct approval.

The whole incident went along peacefully for me.

Later it was explained that the cables had been accidentally torn while the excavation was going on for the cinema. One of the Christian workers must have been responsible for it. So they believed.

After New Years, thousands of Poles read outdated news together with the two anti-Semitic articles. However, I could do nothing about this.

From left: Sonia Buksztelski, Fania Warszawczyk

THE FIRST CONTACTS WITH THE FOREST

THE forest—used to be a concept among Jewish youth of a place where you can hide from the rays of the sun on hot summer days, take cover under the shade of trees and pick mushrooms or berries. The forest—in winter time, for some people, was the place to practice winter sports. But for the ghetto, the forest had quite a different significance.

First of all, it was not the forest to which the Jews went in pre-war days. Then it was found hard by the periphery of the city. Lovely pine trees grew there and the soil was dry and pleasant. But in Hitlerian times, the forest meant running away to wooded areas which resembled j u n g l e s , abounding in wild animals, swamps, moss, tangled trees, etc. Such forests were ideal spots for wild animals but they were far from being an ideal place for people. On the other hand, they were of great strategic value.

Of course, you cannot rest in the forest but you can carry on a struggle against the Nazi war-machine. In such a place you can take revenge for the spilt blood of Jews and non-Jews.

Therefore, there was an urge among large sectors of youth to go into the depths of the forest. That was not so simple. Those who risked it were exposed to great dangers.

First, you had to have arms, which were not available to you. Then it was very dangerous to make your way across Vilna to the nearest Rudnicki wilderness—a distance of 40 kilometers. You could be captured on the way by two-footed human beasts and be spared the terrors of the forest. If you reached the forest, you would have been met by other great dangers, like veteran bandits who spent years there or by Lithuanian and Polish fascist-partisans who murdered unarmed Jews in the same way the Nazis did in the towns and cities.

On May 30, 1942, the special "Central Staff of the Partisan Movement" was created by the Soviet military chief. In

August, 1942, Marshal Clementi Voroshilov was placed at the head of the movement.

The work of the Central Staff of the Partisan Movement, which was to harass the rear flank of the enemy, actually commenced in the beginning of 1943. Later it was extended to our own Vilna region.

There were other partisan units up till then, but they were not as centralized as when Voroshilov took over the leadership.

Zvi Rozanovicz, a friend of the U.P.O. brought the news in February 1943 that a parachute group descended upon Biala-Waka, eight kilometers away from Vilna. The U.P.O. staff decided to delegate Itzik Wittenberg to go to Biala-Waka and make contact with them. Wittenberg conferred with them and learned that this was a group which would recognize the U.P.O. as an integral part of the Central Partisan Movement in Moscow. Our mission was to engage in intelligence activities in all German units where Jews were employed as slave-laborers. We were to relay information to the parachute group. They in turn, would unite with the U.P.O. and form a diversion group to back up the fighting in the ghetto and in the city.

Before we were able to organize ourselves properly, they were betrayed by certain peasants and almost all of them fell in battle with the exception of the commander Margis.

After this failure, the U.P.O. staff decided to send Sonia Madejsker and Cesia Rosenberg to Moscow in order to establish contact with the Central Partisan Movement. They were provided with documents and all other information by our secret printing press and they set out on this extraordinary and dangerous mission. They were arrested in Polock, because they lacked special supplementary documents. This was a front zone, and we in the ghetto of Vilna did not know that they needed these special documents which would give them the right to be in such a zone. As they were being led to jail, they ran away and took another road leading to their goal. They were captured again near Vieliki Luki, 12 kilometers from the

Sonia Madejsker as Katarzyna Romanowska

Cesia Rosenberg

front. Not knowing that they were captured once before, the arresting officer led them back to Polock for execution. At the last moment, there was a stay of execution, and it was decided to bring them back to Vilna, from which their documents originated. This was done to establish their identity more firmly. They kept on asserting their claim that they were two speculators and that they lost their way by accident.

When they arrived at the Vilna station with their guards, they took advantage of their superior knowledge of the ins and outs of the station which they knew as well as their ten fingers, and they escaped again. They arrived safely in the ghetto. The municipal police were led on a useless chase to find the whereabouts of their charges. Since their documents showed them to be Polish, it did not occur to anybody that the two "speculators" were Jewish girls. Now they were back in the Vilna ghetto. Nothing came of their mission.

*   *   *

After this the U.P.O. decided via the commandant Wittenberg, to make a workable contact with the Municipal Progressive Resistance Movement. A certain Vitas was at the head of this movement. He was the former chief of the Vilna city council at the time when the Soviets were in Vilna. A combined partisan general staff came into being for mutual benefit activity in Lithuanian territory. Vitas was the chief. Itzik Wittenberg was chosen as the representative of U.P.O.

Our group requested that the municipal partisan division provide secret hiding places for U.P.O. fighters when they would have to leave the ghetto so that they could sustain

Griko and Bugnas
preparing to blow-up a railroad.

themselves in the city until it was safe enough to proceed to the forest. A promise was made to that effect.

First the joint staff decided to start an intensive propaganda campaign. A plan was formulated whereby I was to be transferred from the ghetto to live with Jan Pszewalski, my most important assistant in the secret city printing press. The staff instructed me to make all necessary preparations so as to be ready in a few days to leave the ghetto permanently, for better or for worse.

I took stock of the situation and thought of what it meant to operate a secret printing press in the city. The slightest misstep and I end my life in the dungeons of the Gestapo under extreme torture. I therefore decided, that in addition to being armed I would always carry cyanide with me. That was promised to be supplied to me. No matter what, I made up my mind that they would never take me alive.

The next day when I was supposed to leave permanently, the ghetto was surrounded by the evil hordes of the Gestapo and I was hemmed in. This was the beginning of the final liquidation of the Vilna ghetto.

* * *

In the spring of 1943, word reached us that in the Narocz woods, about 180 kilometers away from Vilna a partisan group was functioning headed by a certain Markow, a teacher from Minsk. A second group functioned under the leadership of Yurgis, also a teacher from Kovno.

Through our city Lithuanian co-worker, Vitas, we established contact with the two leaders. The general staff received a letter written by Markow in which he invited the youth into the Narocz woods to join his brigade.

This was the first and best contact with the partisan movement which was in our vicinity and in the beginning of its activity.

The problem as to what action to take arose before the

partisan general staff of the ghetto. The idea of the U.P.O. was to engage in armed resistance in the ghetto—the scene of Nazi crimes. The Nazis would have to pay with their lives. Whoever would survive after the Hitler campaigns, would then have to withdraw to battle positions in the forests.

*   *   *

Much earlier, many attempts were made by unorganized groups to leave the ghetto and take to the forest, and for the most part they were successful.

Mitzka Bastomski worked with a few hundred Jews in Torf and Biala-Waka. Before the war Bastomski was a woodsman, and therefore, he knew the region and the peasant inhabitants thereof very well. In talking to the two peasants, Nicolajczyk and Romka who were Tatars living in the village called Sorok Tatarof (Ten Tatars) which was behind Biala-Waka on the periphery of the Rudnicki wilderness, he learned that scores of armed partisans were to be found within its confines.

Chayim Solc, a second Jew, with the nickname, "Chayim The Fat One," was a simple man from the town of Olkeniki. Previously he had rescued himself from a pogrom there. Chayim found one of his friends in the forest by the name of Germilowski. He was a peasant of about 70 years who led a band of partisans, whom he had recruited from soldiers in hiding who refused to give themselves up when the Soviet military forces left the area. Chayim Solc made the contact for us with this group of partisans.

The two villagers used to provide wood for the Warszawczyk bakery in the ghetto. The three brothers, Lole, Hirsh and Yechiel Warszawczyk were members of the fighting unit of Yechiel Scheinbaum and when Mitzka Bastomski came with the peasants of the forest with the wood to the ghetto, he told the Warszawczyks about the partisan unit. The brothers immediately reported it to their leadership and thus we made valuable contacts in the forest.

During the one year of the Soviet regime in our area, Germilowski, whose nickname was "Batya" (Father), was in the Soviet militia, and when the military forces left, he ran away to the woods, and lived there—uniform and all. These "A.W.O.L." combatants were the nucleus of the first partisan group in our area.

When the "Thousand Years German Reich" took over, "Batya" revealed himself in his Soviet uniform and his weapon. He warned the peasants who knew him well, that they should not collaborate with Germans, on pain of paying dearly for such collaboration.

One day, as we returned from a partisan mission, when we were already in the forests, we met up with "Batya" and his group. We sat down to rest and started a conversation. It was a surprise to me to hear how well versed he was in politics, and though he was a backwoodsman all his life he knew about Ze'ev Jabotinsky. Though he had no praise for Jabotinsky, he did say that if he were alive, the Jews would not be in the Vilna ghetto, but in the forest . . .

On the night of April 20, 1943, a group which was formerly led by Scheinbaum, till they incorporated in the U.P.O., left the ghetto. The first group was led by my good friend, Engineer Boria Friedman and the aforementioned Bastomski, who was the guide. Together they consisted of 28 men. Among them were Jews who knew how to handle weapons well.

Later we were notified in the ghetto that the first group in the Rudnicki wilderness under the leadership of Boria Friedman arrived in the forest at a most unfavorable time. Just then German punitive expeditions were sent to comb the woods, and the partisans had to break up their ranks and hide in peasant huts where they remained until the storm had passed. One of these peasants was a fascist. He informed the Land Army partisans about our group who hid in his hut and a fight took place. There were casualties on both sides. Relief Land Army units arrived which wiped out the survivors of our group. Thus they died as heroes—not at the hands of the Hitlerites, but by the anti-Semitic independent "Niepodleglosc" Polish partisans.

When we later became a big power in the woods, we punished the treacherous Polish landowner by shooting him point blank and burning his hut with all the contents thereof.

* * *

After making contact with the parachutists it was for us, confined to the ghetto and having paid with thousands and thousands of lives at the hands of the Nazis, an event of importance comparable now to the launching by the Russians or Americans of the first man in space. It made a terrific impression on the very few who heard about it. Generally, the ghetto inhabitants had no idea of what was going on. Only the staff and a select few in the U.P.O. knew about it.

It came as quite a surprise, therefore, when the parachutist Margis, the only survivor of the first group in the area, turned up at the German press with my closest co-worker, Jan Pszewalski. It was quite an experience to meet with him, especially since, as slave laborers, that morning like every other morning, promised death.

Months later, when I was already a partisan in the forest, they brought Margis under heavy guard to the staff headquarters in the woods. I happened to be at the base when he arrived and he immediately recognized me and came over with a warm greeting. I was the only one at the base who had met him before and who knew him, with the exception, of course, of the parachutist commanders. They knew him from the days in Moscow when they all attended parachutist school and were later dropped with other detachments in our area to serve as the nucleus of the commanders who later developed the widespread movement.

Joseph Glazman

JOSEPH GLAZMAN

BEFORE the war, Joseph Glazman lived in Kovno, Lithuania. He was a highly intelligent and energetic man. When the war broke out, Glazman was in Vilna.

When the Germans began to drive the Jews into the ghetto, Glazman was sent as a forced laborer with other Jews to the village of Resza in the vicinity of Vilna to dig turf.

One day, by the end of September, 1941, he came to the ghetto. Jacob Gens was overjoyed to see him; he had known him well in previous years, and appointed him assistant chief of the ghetto police, since Glazman was an excellent organizer. Joseph Glazman was extremely well-liked as a high ghetto official.

After a year, "well-wishers" began to whisper to Gens: "Look at the good name Glazman has in the ghetto, while your reputation is growing worse and worse. Glazman is considered a cultural and civic leader, and you are thought of as a man whose hands are dripping with Jewish blood." These people also told Gens that his "strategy" of surrendering *some* Jews to the Germans in order to save *many* others was not appreciated by the ghetto residents.

Gens was deeply disturbed. He had felt that his policy was the only one that was correct and statesmanlike under the circumstances. Besides, he had great respect for the concept of "history." He did not want to enter history in an unfavorable light. He therefore decided to rid himself of his rival, Glazman, so that the ghetto inmates would not see before them a living example of good, as opposed to bad administration.

Gens dismissed Glazman as assistant police chief and appointed him manager of the housing department. This subsequently turned out to be of great benefit to the U.P.O. Glazman used his new position to transfer some residents to other places and thus create strategic points in the ghetto where U.P.O. fighters were concentrated.

For the first time in the history of the Vilna ghetto, the Gestapo pressed the ghetto police into a joint action in exterminating 400 Jews in the nearby small city of Oszmiana. The ghetto police were given special blue uniforms (formerly they had worn only blue military caps) and took part in the extermination, winning an even worse reputation than they already had.

Gens and Dessler called in Glazman and suggested that, as housing manager, he should move to Swenciany, near Oszmiana, and put the housing situation there in order.

Glazman, however, understood their plan to discredit him and guessed that a similar action was being planned for Swenciany. He flatly refused to take any direct or indirect part in their dirty game.

At that point, Gens ordered him to go to Swenciany. Glazman's reply was again contemptuous and categorical refusal.

Soon after that Gens called a meeting of the entire ghetto police, at which he attacked the "rotten intellectuals" who hampered the work of the police. It did not take long before Glazman was arrested.

Itzik Wittenberg, the commandant of the U.P.O., and Chiene Borowski, one of our "ambassadresses," went to see Gens to discuss the matter. They demanded and obtained Glazman's release. Later, Glazman and certain other close comrades were arrested again several times by Jacob Gens and Salek Dessler.

Through its agents, the Gestapo learned of the existence of a secret movement in the ghetto and decided to liquidate the Vilna ghetto at the first opportunity in the spring of 1943. To this end, the Gestapo decided that the first step was to exterminate all the young Jews in the Vilna province, who were already preparing to withdraw into the forests as guerrillas and would have proven a serious obstacle to our extermination. The Gestapo was also afraid that, should there be resistance in the ghetto, the Polish population might also stage an uprising, which would bring serious consequences to the occupation authorities.

The Gestapo therefore ordered the ghetto police to break the back of the resistance movement inside the ghetto, and took all the rest upon itself. There was an implied promise that this action would be rewarded by sparing the lives of the police for the time being.

On a certain day in July 1943, Raphael Aster, the leader of the criminal police in the ghetto, came to Joseph Glazman's room and declared, in the name of the ghetto commandant and chief of police, that he must leave the ghetto and return to the village of Resza, from which he had come some time earlier. Glazman refused to leave the ghetto. Aster reported to Dessler that Glazman had refused to obey. Dessler ordered Glazman removed from the ghetto.

Five policemen armed with rubber truncheons and iron gloves came to Glazman and took him away by force. They threw him into a cart and put him in chains. Then they began to drive him toward the gates of the ghetto, systematically showering blows upon him. The ghetto residents were shocked and outraged, and within minutes the U.P.O. was mobilized and given orders to free Glazman at any cost.

The U.P.O. fighters came running with saws and cut the chains that bound Glazman to the cart. All this time Glazman kept repeating to our men: "Don't shoot! Don't shoot!" In the fight, the police were overpowered and driven off, and Glazman was taken back to his room at No. 6 Rudnicki Streeet, in the building which also housed the Judenrat.

Taking part in the freeing of Joseph Glazman were the comrades Janek Sztul, Szmulke Kaplinski, Hirsh Gordon, Raszke Markowicz, and others.

The streets were full of people. The ghetto population rejoiced in the victory over the ghetto police.

Soon, however, the Jews began to ask themselves: "Was that the end of the matter?" "Wouldn't the Gestapo learn what had taken place? After all, the ghetto police had been compromised, and the Gestapo was behind it."

Gens had left the ghetto at the time in order to avoid the charge that he had ordered the police to beat the prisoner. Five minutes after Glazman had been freed Gens entered the gates of the ghetto and received a report from his police on what had happened. He flew into a rage, pulled out his revolver and began to fire into the air, shouting orders to the people to disperse, which they soon obeyed.

Gens called in representatives of the U.P.O. and tried to convince them that Glazman must leave the ghetto and go to Resza as ordered. Otherwise, he said, the entire ghetto police would be compromised and lose its authority, and hence would be unable to carry out its duties and keep order in the ghetto. Furthermore, he said that he and Dessler would soon have to leave the ghetto, and all power would then be assumed by the S. S.

His arguments had their effect. The leadership of the U.P.O. was persuaded that persistence at this point would place the ghetto in danger *prematurely*. Glazman, accordingly, left the ghetto of his own free will in the same cart, accompanied by U.P.O. members, and went to Resza, which was then a labor camp. Exiled along with him was the sergeant of the ghetto police, Janek Faust, who had taken a hand in liberating Glazman instead of siding with the ghetto police.

Some time later, Glazman was smuggled back into the ghetto with the aid of D. Rogalin and other U.P.O. members. Janek Faust was also brought back to the ghetto.

Thus, Glazman was able to remain in the ghetto until its final days, and to continue his activities as a member of the U.P.O. leadership.

Itzik Wittenberg

ITZIK WITTENBERG

THE secretary of the city's partisan organization, Witas, and the committee member Kozlowski, an engineer from the town of New Swienciany, both non-Jews, were arrested by the Gestapo.

Kozlowski was mercilessly beaten and forced under torture to reveal organizational secrets. He told the Gestapo that the leader of the resistance movement in the ghetto was Itzik Wittenberg. He also revealed the existence of the clandestine printing shop in the ghetto, which served the entire underground both inside and outside the ghetto. (Fortunately, Kozlowski did not know my name.)

On the following day the Gestapo officer Kittel came to the ghetto and demanded that the Judenrat surrender Itzik Wittenberg. He gave the ghetto leadership two hours to arrest and turn him over to the Gestapo. After the expiration of the two hours, Kittel was informed that Wittenberg had died and was therefore no longer in the ghetto.

Kittel left and returned on the next day to arrest the policeman Itzhak Averbuch, who was our contact with the Lithuanian underground in the city.

We were in dismay, fearing that he might break down under torture and reveal his contacts in the city. But the Gestapo had already learned from Kozlowski the identity of our Lithuanian comrades. The Gestapo men made a deal with Averbuch, promising to release him if he revealed his contacts. He accepted the deal. After several hours in the Gestapo cellars, he was sent back to the ghetto. When he returned, everyone understood that there was something suspicious, but no one knew just what had happened. In the morning, when I met Averbuch in the street, his eyes were the eyes of a dead man.

The Gestapo wanted to impress us with the fact that they could arrest a man, but could also release him. In this way they hoped to lull the vigilance of the resistance leaders.

Naturally, their calculation was quite foolish, for it was the prime motto of the resistance movement that the Germans were not to be trusted. The only thing we believed was their oft-repeated intention to exterminate all the Jews in areas under their control.

*　　*　　*

On Friday, July 16, 1943, a woman courier came running to me with the code words, "Lisa is calling!" This meant full mobilization, and she ordered me at once to a certain specified point. Although it was still quite dark, the entire ghetto was on its feet. The ghetto police ran from yard to yard, shouting: "All men must gather at once in the yard of the Judenrat, the ghetto is in danger!"

In the middle of the night, Jacob Gens and Salek Dessler had summoned several members of the U.P.O. command to the Judenrat: Itzik Wittenberg, Aba Kowner, Abrasha Chwojnik and Chiena Borowski. In the middle of the discussions, Salek Dessler left the group and went outside the ghetto; soon he returned with several Lithuanian policemen. They bound Wittenberg and began to drag him toward the gates. The U.P.O. was already mobilized, suspecting a possible betrayal. Our comrades attacked the police, gave them a thorough beating, and rescued Wittenberg. Since the police, aware that they were faced with the underground, refrained from shooting, the affair was confined only to blows.

After that it was Gens himself who called together all the men in the ghetto and addressed the huge crowd from his balcony:

"In a raid on the city, the Gestapo captured the Polish man Kozlowski. During the interrogation, he confessed that he was in contact with a certain Wittenberg in the ghetto and revealed the existence of a secret printing shop inside the ghetto walls which published anti-Nazi materials and prepared false documents. The Gestapo is therefore demanding the surrender of Wittenberg *alive* within two hours. If he is not surrendered, the German tanks and planes will demolish the ghetto with bombs."

"What shall we do?" Gens asked the crowd. "Shall we surrender Wittenberg and so save the remnants of the Vilna ghetto, or shall we sacrifice the ghetto for one man?"

"Give up Wittenberg and save the ghetto!" came voices from the crowd.

Gens continued:

"Wittenberg is hiding. Go out, then, and find him!"

The pre-war underworld, which had been organized by Dessler into an auxiliary to the ghetto police, set out with sticks and iron rods to look for Itzik Wittenberg. They attacked a house on Niemiecka Street No. 31, which was one of our armed points. (One side of this street belonged to the ghetto.) A well-known agent provocateur, Shapiro, who was a member of the ghetto police, fired the first shot in the direction of the U.P.O. group. A hail of stones flew at the windows of the rooms where the fighters were assembled. Our people fired a volley of warning shots. Everything was thrown into panic. Everyone ran to get out of the line of fire.

The ghetto residents felt that those were the last hours. The ghetto was doomed.

*   *   *

We had waited for three bloody years to hear the news from the front that was reaching us now. The Germans were sustaining terrible blows on the Russian front and were in retreat. Italy was crushed. We felt that now, more than ever, we must hold out. It was a matter of only a few more months, and we might still be saved.

Many people asked in despair: should we all perish now for just a single man? Should the twenty thousand Jews still surviving out of the original eighty thousand be sacrificed for one man?

The prevailing mood in the ghetto was: Wittenberg must be surrendered.

* * *

As I stood at my post with my group, I observed what was happening. How long I had hoped for the day when Nazi corpses would litter the streets, just as Jewish corpses had littered them for years! The day when the Germans would be brought down by my hands and the hands of my partisan comrades! I had dreamed that I and the others would be the vanguard of an uprising, followed by the Jewish masses who had learned from the past years that they no longer had anything to lose, that they could only win, morally and physically. And now suddenly we found almost the entire ghetto against us. There was even danger of civil war inside the ghetto! Who could have foreseen such an irony of fate?

The partisan command faced a terrible dilemma. The choice was between postponing the liquidation of the ghetto by surrendering the commander of the U.P.O. and thus winning time, or engaging the Germans in immediate fighting at a time when the partisan movement was in a most unfavorable position.

After careful analysis, the command decided to surrrender the commander.

One of our branches was given orders to find Wittenberg, who was hiding and out of contact with the headquarters. But he could not be found. Time was running out, and the German ultimatum hung like the sword of Damocles over the remaining ghetto residents.

Ghetto police ran through all the courtyards, shouting: "The ghetto will soon be reduced to ruins! We shall all die! Help find Wittenberg! He is hiding somewhere dressed as a woman! Save the ghetto!"

* * *

At last, headquarters made contact with Wittenberg. Sonia Madejsker, Wittenberg's close friend, and Nisl Resnik, came to Wittenberg at 15 Straszuna Street where he was hiding and brought him the tragic news of the decision of the U.P.O. command. Wittenberg did not accept this decision. He escaped again, and everyone lost sight of him once more. Kryzhanowski, another old party comrade of Wittenberg's who was now a courier of the Judenrat, sought him everywhere, hoping to persuade him to sacrifice himself and thus save the ghetto from immediate destruction. He failed to discover his whereabouts, but a group of other old acquaintances, including Anatol Frid, Dr. Milkanowitski, Trapida, and Mina Swirski, found him. If he surrendered, they assured him, he would be brought back alive from the Gestapo. Gens and Dessler guaranteed this.

Shortly after their visit, the ghetto police captured Wittenberg, dressed in woman's clothes. He began to shoot over the heads of the police and succeeded in breaking away and running into the house at No. 21 Niemiecka Street.

The partisan command met in continuous session to discuss this tragic problem. It decided to send another, larger delegation to Wittenberg to explain to him the true state of affairs, as the command saw it. This time Wittenberg was visited by Sonia Madejsker, Aba Kowner and Joseph Glazman. Wittenberg could not have the slightest doubt of their friendship and honesty. They informed him once more of the *unanimous* decision of all the commanding staff that he must surrender himself to the Gestapo. They told him that, after long and detailed talks with Jacob Gens and Salek Dessler, the two ghetto governors assured them that they would do everything possible to save him after the Gestapo arrested him; they had promised to try to bribe the Gestapo heads, even if it took all the gold owned by the Judenrat.

Itzik Wittenberg did not consent to this. He said that the ghetto was in any case on the verge of the final liquidation. The Gestapo was trying to destroy the leaders of the resistance, and would immediately turn to the ghetto itself. The others replied that they agreed with him entirely in his assessment of the situation, but that the ghetto as a whole unfortunately did not agree. The ghetto population felt that, unless he surrendered, everyone faced immediate destruction; on the other hand, his surrender, the people believed, would gain time, so that the ghetto could perhaps be saved by the advancing Soviet armies which were marching forward in a great offensive.

Furthermore, the command explained that the entire organization was now out in the open, and there was danger that it might have to fight its own brothers in the ghetto instead of the Germans.

After listening to the pessimistic assessment of the situation by his best and most devoted comrades, Wittenberg decided to submit to the wish of the U.P.O. headquarters. He would commit suicide, and so yield to the demand of the ghetto masses who were grasping at a straw.

The command reported Wittenberg's decision to Gens and Dessler, but they would not hear of it. The Gestapo had told them unequivocally that they wanted Wittenberg *alive*. Surrender of Wittenberg dead would leave the ghetto in the same danger.

There were more discussions between representatives of the command and Itzik Wittenberg. At last, seeing that there was no other way out, he declared himself ready to surrender, on condition that he was provided with a dose of Prussic acid. He was given the poison and hid it in his ear. Then he ordered the ghetto police to be called. They would take him out of the ghetto, and so it would appear that they had caught him and were delivering him to the Gestapo.

I stood on the corner of Rudnicki Street when the police, with revolvers in their hands, led him past. When I saw that he noticed me, I stood at attention and he smiled at me. He walked proudly with his head high toward the exit gates. He did not have the slightest doubt that he was going to his

The court-yard at 6 Rudnicka Street where the Judenrat was located and also Joseph Glazman lived there, as many other ghetto officials like Gens and Dessler.

martyrdom. A Gestapo car was waiting at the gate. He entered the car.

The next morning, Jewish laborers who worked in the Gestapo building found him lying dead in the yard. When the labor brigade returned to the ghetto in the evening, they brought the tragic news.

The members of the U.P.O. felt broken and ashamed. But such was the reality of our situation.

Witas didn't reveal any secrets and was also killed by the Gestapo around the same time, July 1943.

Note: The Itzik Wittenberg story is now known all over the world. In Vilna a street bears his name. In many countries of the world plays have been performed in the theatres, based on this episode.

ITZIK WITTENBERG

English: Esther Zweig | *Yiddish*: S. Kaczerginski

I

Our foe lies there crouching,
Like a beast of the jungle,
My pistol is ready in hand,
Watch out—the Gestapo!
They're leading a captive
At night—our Commander-
in-Chief!

II

A flash tears the ghetto,
The night is electric,
"Look out!"warns a tower, a wall;
Rescue our comrades,
They're with our Commander-
in-Chief!

III

The night is foreboding,
There's death lurking 'round us,
The ghetto's in fever and dread;
The ghetto is restless,
And Gestapo threatens
Our Commander-in-Chief!

IV

Then Itzik spoke to us,
His words were like lightning—
"Don't take any risks for my sake,
Your lives are too precious
To give away lightly."
And proudly he goes to his death!

V

The foe again crouches
Like beasts of the jungle,
My pistol is ready in hand,
My gun is my guardian,
My rescuing angel,
It's now my Commander-in-Chief.

I

S'ligt ergetz fartai-et
Der faint vee a chaye,
Der Mauzer er vacht in main
    hant,
Nur plutzim—Gestapo,
Es feert a geshmidten
Durch finsternish dem
    Commandant!

II

Di nacht hot mit blitzn
Dos ghetto tzerissn,
"Gefar!"—shrait a toier,
    a vant;
Chavayrim getrai-e,
Fun kaytn bafraien,
Farshvindn mit dem
    Commandant!

III

Dee nacht iz farfloign,
Der toit far dee oign,
Dos ghetto, es feebert in
    brand;
In umruh dos ghetto,
Es droht dee Gestapo:
"Toit,—oder dem
    Commandant!"

IV

Gezogt hot dan Itzik—
Un durch a blitz iz—
"Ich vill not eer zollt tzuleeb
    mir
Darfn dos lebn
Dem soine opgebn . . ."
Tzum toit gayt shtoltz der
    Commandir!

V

Ligt vider fartai-et
Der feint vee a cha-ye,
Vachst vider, main Mauzer,
    in hant;
Itzt bizstu mir taier,
Zai du main bafraier,
Zai du itzter main
    Commandant!

198

ITZIK WITTENBERG

A resemblance of Itzik Wittenberg as he is being led out of the Ghetto.
(Published in *Sovietish Heimland* in Moscow February 1968).

THE U. P. O. COMMAND ISSUED A PROCLAMATION THAT WAS POSTED ON THE GHETTO STREETS

"Jews! Defend yourselves with weapons.

"The German and Lithuanian hangmen have reached the Ghetto gates. They have come to massacre us! Soon they will lead us, group by group, through the gate.

"This is how hundreds were led astray on Yom Kippur! This is how they were fooled on the 'pass' night, the white, the yellow the pink colored.

"Thus were fooled our brothers and sisters, our mothers and fathers, our children.

"Thus were tens of thousands led to death! But we shall not go!

"We shall not bare our throats like sheep being slaughtered!

"Jews! Defend yourselves with arms!

"Do not believe the false promises of the murderers. Do not believe the words of traitors. Whoever leaves the Ghetto gate has one path—to Ponary.

"And Ponary is Death!

"Jews! We have nothing to lose, because death will come anyway. And who can still think that he will remain alive while the murderer exterminates us systematically?

"The hand of the hangman will reach each and every one. Neither experience nor cowardice will save your life!

"Do not hide in secret places and the malinas. Your destiny will be to fall like rats at the hands of the murderers.

"Only armed defense can save our life and honor.

"Brothers! Better to fall in the Ghetto battle than to be led like sheep to Ponary! Know, that in the Ghetto walls there is an organized Jewish force that will rise up in arms.

"Lend a hand to the revolt!

"Jewish masses! Go out on the streets! Whoever lacks weapons, let him take an ax, and if there is no ax, grab some iron, or a pole or a stick!

Ilya Scheinbaum

On August 1, 1943, the following announcement apppeared in the official bulletin of the Jewish ghetto administration *Geto Yediot* No. 50 (Ghetto News):

According to the order of the German Security Police and S. S., a number of Jews, and among them brigadiers, were arrested.

We want to remind the ghetto of the words and warnings of the Ghetto Representative, that as of the latest order received from the German Authorities, all Jews are collectively responsible.

It is your duty to yourself and to the ghetto to inform on any activity which might endanger the existence of the ghetto.

"For our forefathers.

"For our children who have been murdered!

"In repayment for Ponary.

"Hit the murderers!

"In every street, every yard, every room. In the Ghetto and out of it. Hit the dogs!

"Jews! We have nothing to lose! We shall save our lives only if we destroy our murderers.

"Long live freedom! Long live the armed revolt! Death to the murderers!

Command of the United Partisan Organization—U.P.O.

1 September 1943, Vilna Ghetto."

12 STRASZUNA STREET

THE ghetto was already in its last agony. On the morning of September 1, 1943, it was surrounded by Gestapo units and Esthonian S.S. men. It was an iron ring that nobody could cross, and no one could either enter or leave the ghetto any more. The final liquidation was on the way.

The ghetto residents ran, panic-stricken, to any place that offered some hope of shelter. Any place seemed safer than the streets.

The Gestapo chief Neugebauer demanded that the Judenrat turn over the last ten thousand Jews—to be sent to work in Esthonia. Here, he claimed, they were superfluous, while Esthonia was short of labor power.

The entire partisan movement was ready. It had been fully mobilized since the Glazman and Wittenberg incidents. Every partisan was already at his assigned defense post. The partisan headquarters had abandoned the idea of resistance in the ghetto itself and decided to retreat to the woods and wage the fight from there.

Our defense posts were on Straszuna Street, in houses No. 6, 8 and 12. Instructions from headquarters were: if the Germans attacked partisan units, we were, as a last resort, to fight on the spot as well.

The Gestapo began to round up Jews and collect them at the gates of the ghetto.

The post to which I was assigned with twelve or thirteen other fighters was No. 12 Straszuna Street. The Gestapo blew up No. 15 in an attempt to frighten the hiding Jews into coming out and reporting for deportation; otherwise, their action implied, they were faced with immediate death.

Looking out of the side windows at the wreck of the demolished building, we saw wounded men running in all direction. Our orders, issued by our commander Ilya Scheinbaum, were to fire at the Gestapo demolition men in the street as they stood admiring the results of their work. Ilya Scheinbaum, a former officer in the pre-war Polish army, threw a grenade into the group of Nazis outside. It was a direct hit. Those who were able to escape ran, but not for long.

We saw them take dynamite sticks and run to our side of the building. We fired at them, but soon lost them from sight, for they took up positions at the walls of the building, where they could not be seen. For a while it was quiet. Then we heard commands to mine and blow up the entire house. We tried to find positions from which we would be able to fire at them and prevent their action. Ilya Scheinbaum leaned slightly out of a window to see where the Gestapo men were. At that moment there was a shot from below. I felt a violent thrust and saw Ilya falling. I knelt down to him, but could see no injuries. He lay stretched out tautly in his officer's boots, with his ski cap on his head. There was no blood, no sign that he had been struck by a bullet. I thought he might have fainted. I felt his pulse, his body, but I saw he was dead. His wife Pesia was already kneeling by his side too, and she cried: "Ilya is dead!"

We could not allow ourselves to lose any more time. Ruszka Korczak gave orders to jump from the back windows, to the cement yard. Ruszka twisted her ankle in falling. I was the last to jump, but at that moment I recalled that in the confusion the bag of ammunition was left with the dead Ilya. Although every second might be the last, I ran back to the window where Ilya's body lay and managed to snatch the gun and the ammunition from under him. Then I jumped. I barely had time to recover from the shock of falling when I heard the tremendous explosion that turned the entire building into a smoking heap of rubble.

With the exception of Ilya Scheinbaum, the entire group succeeded in retreating to the position at No. 8 Straszuna Street, where a larger group of our fighters was posted, under the leadership of Aba Kowner.

Many residents of the building and many other fighters

like Chaim Napeleon, Gurwicz and others from a different unit were buried under the ruins.

The Gestapo learned that every second building was a partisan stronghold and quickly withdrew from the street.

We realized the mistake of trying to defend ourselves through the window, which did not allow enough people to concentrate fire at the same time, and we moved our bomb-throwers to neighboring roofs, providing a wider sphere of action. The Nazis, however, were heroes only until they realized that Jewish bombs and bullets could also be deadly. They got cold feet. As soon as they discovered that Straszuna "Strasse" was a place from which a man might not come out alive, they stayed away from it.

In the course of this "action," the Nazis rounded up some six thousand Jews, who were sent to Estonia for slave labor.

The ghetto calmed down for a while. We dug the dead and the wounded out of the ruins. Among the dead was Ilya Scheinbaum, whose body was not crushed because it lay under a pile of beams that formed a sort of tent which prevented the bricks from falling on him. When we examined him, we found that the bullet had hit him in the throat, and his collar made it impossible to see the wound at the first moment when we kneeled over him.

Ruszka Korczak

Aba Kowner in front of
the casket with Ilya Scheinbaum

Pesia Scheinbaum-Bernstein

Here rests the *Chalutz* Yechiel Scheinbaum,
born in Odessa in 1914. Fallen
in defense of the Ghetto Vilna.
XI.I.1945.

206

From left: Isaac Kowalski, Abraham Suckewer
(The ruins of Straszuna 12)

The partisan movement held a funeral that was the only one of its kind, for the men still remaining in the ghetto took part in it. After the war, when we returned from the woods where we had fought, we raised a gravestone for Ilya Scheinbaum in the Jewish cemetery where he was buried.

Such was the chapter of No. 12 Straszuna Street in the history of the martyrdom of the Vilna ghetto—the single known collective armed resistance in the ghetto proper.

However, almost the entire vanguard of the partisan army succeeded in breaking through the encirclement, making its way across the city and getting safely to the Narocz and Rudnicki woods, where our partisan comrades fought Hitlerism in the heroic ways described in the following chapters.

U. P. O. Command

URGENT COMMAND
TO ALL INSTRUCTORS AND COMMANDERS

In connection with the intensive exercises now being conducted, I ask of all instructors and commanders:

1) Reduce to the minimum the dismantling of weapons.

2) Refrain from bolt action if the weapon is not oiled.

3) Do not lower the bore (To lower the bore only when a bullet is inside)

4) See to it that the magazine is inserted properly, according to rules. (Otherwise, the magazine will expand and spoil.)

5) Lately, after exercises, many weapons are returned in bad condition. In every case of a defect, do not try to use force—send the weapon back for repairs.

Instructors and Commanders—Spare our weapons.

A defective weapon—disarms a fighter.

Points 1, 2, 3, 4 are to be made known to all fighters.

—Uri

Vilna Ghetto, 4 July 1943

Berl Druzgenik

Berl Szereszyniewski

WORKING IDENTITY CARD

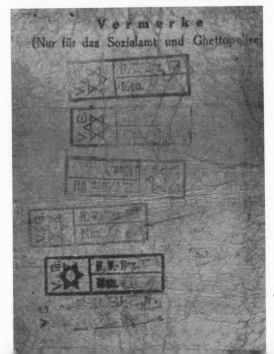

THE TRAGIC FIRST BATTLE

O N July 24, 1943, the first organized group of U.P.O. fighters, headed by Joseph Glazman, left the ghetto at dawn and set out on a dangerous journey across 180 kilometers to the so-called Narocz forest. The forest was already the refuge and operating base of the incipient Byelorussian partisan movement under the command of Brigadier Markow and of the Lithuanian partisans under the leadership of Brigadier Yurgis. These partisan movements were soon to develop into large organizations with many units stationed far and wide.

Thirty kilometers from Vilna, the Jewish partisan group was intercepted by a German ambush as it was crossing the Mickun bridge. An ambush is never the best of situations to be caught in. The enemy sees you, but you cannot see the enemy. Glazman's group was compelled to face it without any previous battle experience.

In the violent skirmish that developed, several Germans were killed. But we also lost eight U.P.O. men. The survivors included Joseph Glazman, Chayim Lazar, Berl Szereszyniewski, Berke Druzgenik and others.

The dead were Molke Chazan, the Gordon brothers, Izke Mackiewicz, Rosa Szereszyniewski, Chayim Spokojny, Zundel Burakiski and his wife Rachel.

The Germans searched the bodies and found their ghetto documents. Accordingly, the Gestapo arrested their families. The thirty-two arrested persons were immediately shot.

Such was the tragic end of the first U.P.O. march away from the ghetto. Naturally, it did not prevent other fighters from following in the footsteps of the first partisan group. On the contrary, it hardened their resolve and taught them several lessons. Subsequently groups of partisans did not carry any documents. All they had was revolvers, grenades and ammunition to fight the enemy.

YOUTH SONG

English: Esther Zweig

(This song is dedicated to the Child and Youth Club of the Vilna Ghetto. It was sung by the youth choir at all functions of the club.)

I

Our song may be full of sadness,
But our step is firm and gay,
Though the foe is at the border,
With our song we'll win the fray.

Chorus.

Youth will always stay with
Anyone who thinks young,
Years may pass by you and me,
For together with the old folks
We are children
Of an era brave and free.

II

Some may wander on strange
pathways,
Some may do and dare alone,
From the ghetto youth sends
greetings
And a hearty welcome home.

III

We remember those who hurt us,
We remember friends as well,
And we bind our past to present,
By the stories that we tell.

IV

We shall pull ourselves together,
Steel ourselves to keep our file.
If a builder and a smith lead,
We shall follow them in style.

Yiddish: S. Kaczerginski

Music: Basye Rubin

I

Unser leed iz full mit troier,
Drayst iz unzer munter gang,
Chotch der soine vacht baim
toier,—
Shturemt yugent mit gezang.

Chorus

Yung iz yeder, yeder, yeder
Ver es vil nor,
Yorn hobn kain badait,
Alte kenen, kenen, kenen
Oich zain kinder,
Fun a naier, fraier tzait.

II

Ver es voglt um oif vegn,
Ver mit draistkait shtelt
zain fus,
Brengt di yugnt zay antkegn
Funem ghetto a gerus.

III

Mir gedenken alle sonem,
Mir dermonen alle fraint,
Aybik velln mir farbindn
Undzer nechtn mitn haint.

IV

Klaibn mir tzunoif die gleeder,
Wieder shteln mir ojf die ray,
S'gayt a boier, s'gayt a
shmeeder,
Lomir alle gayn mit zay!

YOUTH SONG

OUR song may be full of Sad-ness But OUR step is firm and gay, Though the foe is at the bor-der, With our song we'll win the fray. Youth will al-ways stay with a-ny one who Thinks Young. Years may Pass by you and me, For to-ge-ther with the old folks we are Chil-dren, of an e-ra brave and free.

The Story of the Jewish United Partisan Organization in Vilna

THEY HELPED JEWS

Dr. Kutergene

Janowa Bartosewicz

Sofia Binkiene and her daughter

Maria Fedecki with her daughter

213

THEY HELPED JEWS

Jadzia Dudziec

Anna Shimajtis

Masha Iwaszkiewicz

Marila Wolski

214

Szmerke Kaczerginski and
Victoria Grzmilewski

SHINING FIGURES

IN every war, law and order are trampled upon by the boots of the aggressor. So, at the outbreak of World War II, all the exalted ideals of mankind were trampled under foot by advancing Nazi forces. This was true throughout the war. All the slimy degradations of the nations under the heel of Hitlerism swam like oil to the surface.

The "intellectual bigwigs" in Berlin devised various tricks and low propaganda in order to attract the masses to their devilish schemes. People with weak characters and with all sorts of mental aberrations participated in Nazi "activities" by murdering Jews—young and old.

One did it for a pound of sugar, or for another product which was at a premium due to the exigencies of war. Another did it to satisfy his sick sadistic tendencies. A third did it in the hope that by placating the Germans, he would not be touched. In the end all these excuses for action were proven false.

They promised the Lithuanians that if they cooperated in establishing the "law and order" of the Third Reich, they would get autonomy. The same thing was promised to the Ukrainians and other nationalities. But first they were required to risk their lives on fighting fronts for the greater glory of the Third Reich. When fortune's wheel began to turn backwards, then the Lithuanians and the other nations in turn, began to realize that their dreams of independence were only an illusion. In the meantime, the youth of all these nations were being wiped out. An insurrection arose among the former collaborators and their armed youth gradually turned upon the Germans in the hinterlands—and also against the Jews. There was still peril and danger in rebellion against the Germans. It was much easier to turn their guns upon the Jews.

Therefore in such an oppressive atmosphere of treason against the concept of man it was refreshing to note that there were people among the Lithuanians, Poles and other nationalities, who showed courage and human sympathy to their fellow citizens. It is worth while mentioning the following as shining examples:

A group of Lithuanian university-workers had collected a small sum of money for the Vilna ghetto. Professor *Birszysko Michal* (Literat) used to give 2,000 to 6,000 Rubles every month and hide Jewish children.

A group of socialist sympathizers gave 20 per cent of their earnings for material help for the ghetto. The initiator of the idea was a Lithuanian called *Yurgaitis*.

Professor *Zwironas* (Fizic), a social-democrat, used to show an active interest in the Jewish problem. He also sent in Prussic acid to his friend in the ghetto (Dr. Mowszowicz).

Professor *Zezman* who taught logics and also Professor *Karsowin*, the historian, and Professor *Birziszko Victor* had hidden some Jews, and helped Jews change their clothes. *Wilajszys* used to help Dr. Cemach Feldsztajn: Professor *Victor Felczar* rebuked a Polish doctor because he refused to give back Jewish belongings. Professors *Januszkiewicz* and *Michaida* helped their friends who were Jewish doctors.

Rutkauskas, a Lithuanian worker, saved a Jewish girl from the Riga ghetto. When Rutkauskas' daughter, Margarita. went to work in Germany, he made out for the girl Zenia Ran papers under the name of his daughter. Later these papers entitled her to an important position in Minsk. She used to come to Vilna in a German uniform. She transferred German materials for the Soviets. After the liquidation of the ghetto, she hid Jews from the Vilna ghetto. Among others she hid Smilig, a lawyer, a good friend of my brother Aaron, Branszweig, and the wife of Frucht. Refugee Jews came for food. *Rutkauskas* sent one hundred and fifty Jews to Germany to work with counterfeit Aryan papers, before the liquidation of the Vilna ghetto, because he wanted to save them from disaster. *Dr. Jazas Sztakauskas*, director of the government archives. together with a Lithuanian teacher *Zemaijtis* and the Polish nun *Milkulska*. hid

12 Jews: Dr. Alexander Libo with wife and daughter, Grigori Jaszunski and wife, Engineer Jacob Jafe with wife and daughter, Miss Ester Jafe, Mrs. Bak and her son, the young artist Zalman.

Professor *Aka*, Professor *Czizowski*, Professor *Petrusewicz*, lawyer *Josef Czlecki* helped hide some Jewish acquaintances. *Merila Abramowicz-Wolska* made counterfeit papers for Jews. At 16 Pohulanka Street she hid tens of Jewish people and helped them with food and money. *Mrs. Wiktoria Grzmiliewska* hid scores of Jews in every apartment and showed friendliness to them. It is in place here to mention *Mrs. Maria Fedeka*, who saved a lot of Jews from death, by helping them to run from the ghetto. The above women carried out their mission from pure human motives.

A great many Aryan domestics showed human feelings for their employers, by helping them with food and in some cases, even hid them. It is also in place to tell about cases where Aryan governesses hid Jewish children, whom they helped to raise. Some help for Jews came from Catholic priests. *Markowicz*, a Pole, and *Lipniunas* had spoken to their people to give back Jewish property. Lipniunas was arrested. Father *Krupowicius*, who showed sympathy to the Jews was sent away to a German concentration camp, Tilzit. Father *Waltkaus* hid the Trupianski child in a Catholic orphanage, and helped save other Jewish children.

Theosophists, members of a mysterious cult, helped hide Jews. There were occasions when priests met Jewish workers on the street and encouraged them by telling them that they would soon be free.

Our friend, the old Masha, told me one day, when she met me on my way to the ghetto from work, that her Pastor from the "Wszystkich Swietych" church which was located only a few feet from the ghetto gates, advised her during confession that she should help us with everything possible.

The Jews in the ghetto knew about his human attitude to

217

our suffering people and dug a tunnel from the ghetto to the church. A few escaped on the day of the liquidation of the ghetto through the church to the city and then to the woods.

Eta Lipenholc tells about *Leokadia Piechowska* and others.

"We were nine people in our family: Mr. Isaac Glazman and son Aaron, Jacob and Dora Glazman and daughter Cyla, Mina and Zelman Kurgan, my mother, Mrs. Rachel Joffe and I, Eta Joffe (Lipenholc). We all came from the ghetto and the H.K.P.

"Then there were the families that came from Kailis, Mrs. Szeskin with two daughters, Lolek and Riva Krawczynski, Mr. and Mrs. Dimensztein with their little girl and two sisters-in-law, Mr. and Mrs. Schneider with their two daughters, Mrs. Gitelson and her daughter Mira.

"We were 24 people saved at this place called Tuskulany farm.

"She was the one that found a place for us to stay and took us there. Every week she visited us and many times risked her own life. She wanted no money and accepted nothing, just wishing to save us.

"The Polish people who kept us for a whole year until the liberation, were *Mrs. Stankiewicz* and *Mr. Gieda.*"

Dr. Anthony Panski, the Social Democrat, helped the writer Herman Kruk financially. Kruk kept a ghetto diary and after the war the manuscript was found buried in the Vilna ghetto although the writer himself was exterminated in Estonia. His diary in Yiddish was published in New York in 1961 by YIVO.

Almost daily I used to meet with my close friend Boria Szneider at his sister Batya's apartment, who lived at Rudnicka 6. This was a cooperative dwelling shared with other partisans. In order to camouflage the nature of the place, some outsiders were also allowed to live there. One of them was Taube Rolnik and her daughter Mascha. I also saw them daily. The mother was broken, a sick woman. No wonder, since she had already lost two small children in the ghetto. Her daughter was about 14 or 15 and worked in the ghetto office, because Gens knew the family, whose father had been a prominent lawyer. The girl survived the liquidation of the ghetto and, half dead, was rescued in the village of Streletin near the Stuthof concentration camp in Germany, where she had been dragged.

Shortly after the liberation, she came to my office at the Polygraphic Trust, with a large order for a Lithuanian office where she worked. She was thus one of the first customers. Mascha told me then the glad news that her father had saved himself by fleeing to Russia and that as an army officer he had stormed Vilna with the regular Lithuanian brigade; she was now living with him again.

Years passed and the young girl blossomed into a gifted writer, graduating from the Moscow University. Among other works, Mascha published a diary, *I Must Tell*, about her experiences in the ghetto and various camps in Germany. She is known as the Anne Frank of the eastern countries. Her book appeared in Lithuanian, Russian and Yiddish in 1965.

In her diary she wrote in her youthful naivete, "I never knew that in the ghetto there was an illegal organization, unknown even to their families. But they were there. Their New Year calls made a great impression. Really printed (perhaps even printed in the ghetto itself). They call for resistance, not to allow themselves to be led like sheep to slaughter. They write, that in Ponary there already lie the bodies of our mothers, brothers, sisters. Enough victims! We must not allow it!

"The mood is elevated. People re-read the words of the declaration."

Although I met many partisans almost every day at the home of Boria's sister, that young girl knew nothing at all about our activities.

Immediately after the German occupation and before the Rolniks came into the ghetto, they were systematically helped by

Mascha's French school teacher, *Henricas Jonajtis*, who frequently gave them the last bit of food he had.

In 1967, there appeared in Israel a book, *Stronger than Iron*, by the pharmacist Mendl Balberiszki, who had lived in Australia after the war. From his memoirs and my personal knowledge of him, one gathers that he was a communal leader of some stature, unlike the teen-age Mascha Rolnik. Even he discovered the U.P.O's existence quite late, in the Wittenberg period, in the middle of July, 1943, when the organization was fully deconspirated.

In his book Balberiszki describes a neighbor, *Kozlowska*, who returned golden valuables even after the Balberiszkis had been in the ghetto for quite some time and thus helped them to overcome hunger and need.

Victoria Nazmilewski, Maria Fedecki, Dr. Kuturgene, Sophia Binkiene, Maria Wolski, at one time or other, helped the partisan-poet Szmerke Kaczerginski and other Jews.

In a concentration camp in Magdeburg, Germany, there was a factory where all sorts of ammunition was produced. Thousands of prisoners were working there, mostly Poles, Russians, and Jews.

My wife Masha was among 20 girls chosen, at the end of 1944, for work in the kitchen of the officers canteen. The chief was a 6-foot German girl, *Gertz*, who was very helpful to the Jewish girls and gave them sandwiches to take back to the barracks after a day's work in the kitchen.

It happened on one occasion that a sentry by the kitchen searched one of the girls, but luckily she didn't have anything on her. The girls reported this to Miss Gertz the following day, and she said that she would take care of the matter. The next day (and many other times), she stayed by the side of the entrance to make sure that nobody would get caught.

The co-worker Chafcia Igelska was very sick and Gertz managed to get medicaments for her. Thanks to her the girl recovered, and later on survived.

Entrance to Choir Shul

Herman Kruk

Magister M. Balberiszki

221

Gertz was in tears, many times, when she heard of the conditions and inhuman treatment of prisoners, behind the fences of the camp.

Jadzia Dudziec was a practicing Catholic. She was in contact with the Scheinbaum-group and supplied them with small arms. She perished August 13, 1944.

Irena Adamowicz was also a devoted Catholic. She was a very active scout-leader and was very friendly with some Chalutz-leaders. Irena volunteered to be a courier for the Hechalutz and travelled many times to various ghettos in Poland and Lithuania. Irena is one of the few to engage in such dangerous work and survive.

A two and a half-year old child from the well known Vilna family Kulbis, was brought into the ghetto by their good friend *Marian Bilinski,* an executive of an insurance company. Bilinski was arrested a few times and was compelled to give up the child to the ghetto authorities. Kulbis' divorced wife in the ghetto took the child because her divorced husband and his second wife, the parents of the child, were no longer alive. She wanted to tie up the destiny of the child with her own.

One of the forced laborers in the German-Lithuanian Pharmaceutical Division was a well known Jewish pharmacist of Vilna, Miron Abelowicz, who died at the end of April, 1943.

The director of the Pharmaceutical Division, a representative of the labor force and a very famous Polish pharmacist, *Iwaszkewicz,* came to the funeral in the ghetto in honor of the deceased. All three were Christians.

Under the ghetto rules and regulations this was a most unusual thing to do, because Christians were strictly forbidden to enter the ghetto without a special, official permission from the Gestapo. This restriction of entry was especially applied to attending the funeral of a Jew. At the eulogy, the three Christian mourners cried bitterly.

The wife of the deceased and other members of the family who were alive at the time, could accompany the coffin only up to the ghetto gate, because it was forbidden for them to leave the ghetto. Outside the ghetto gate, many Christian colleagues of the deceased waited, and they accompanied the coffin to the Zarecza cemetery.

A certain *Naroshis*, was a friend of the bloody Nazis, Hingst and Franz Murer. Naroshis was the head of the Housing Division of the city of Vilna.

When the two German Nazis proposed that the choir-synagogue (with its distinguished choir so beloved by my mother) be converted into a circus, Naroshis did all he could to dissuade them. His argument was that a much bigger building was needed for a circus and he proposed the empty great halls. Hingst and Murer accepted his proposals and the synagogue was spared. It is still being used for services. Naroshis told this story to his Jewish friends in the days that the ghetto still existed.

A Jewish peasant named Joel Levine, who lived in a suburb of Vilna, was murdered by the Germans and buried in an out-of-the-way place.

When his Christian neighbors got the news, they went to the village sheriff and applied for a permit to bring the murdered Jew to the Vilna ghetto. They brought the corpse to the Vilna ghetto wrapped in white linen in lieu of a shroud, and they asked the Jewish community to bury their dead neighbor according to Jewish tradition. They were even ready to pay for the plot in the Jewish cemetery. They were thanked and were assured that everything would be taken care of and that they would not have to pay anything for the burial service. The three peasants who brought the body to the ghetto also accompanied the funeral procession when the dead man was brought to his eternal rest in the Jewish cemetery, outside the ghetto.

Doctor Kutergene helped Gesia Glezer (Albina), a partisan woman from the Rudnicki forest, with a hideout in Kovno.

Miriam Ganiszczyker, a teacher in pre-war Vilna, was arrested in the street by a Lithuanian policeman who recognized her as a Jewish girl, after the ghetto was already liquidated.

She saw she was doomed, and did not even try to ask for mercy. When they were close to the entrance of the First Police Precinct of Zawalna Street, the policeman told her to run, and she did. She ran and ran, until she landed in New York, where she is now living.

In the last days before Vilna was liberated Esther Geler, wounded by a bullet, Robotnik and Feiga Itkin, the last survivors of the H.K.P., managed to escape. They came to a Polish woman in the Antokol section of Siostry Milosierdzi Street, where *Mrs. Guriono* let them sleep in the basement and gave them food, until the liberation of the city.

The Germans massacred the remaining H.K.P. Jews on July 4. Vilna was liberated on July 13, 1944.

These are only a few of the stories about decent people which came to my attention. Unfortunately, I must admit that a much greater number of people became demoralized under the Nazi regime and they betrayed their Jewish fellow-citizens.

However, let the shining deeds of the few be given full credit. In this manner, I honor those noble people who helped the Jews in the hours of their greatest need.

It is also worth while commending those nationals who,

Masha Rolnik as a child

although they did not proffer any direct help, yet they made believe they did not see the Jew, disguised as an Aryan, when they met him in the street; they did not run as informers to the authorities, as many of their debased co-citizens had done. Now their conscience can be clear, that they were not partners to the spilling of innocent Jewish blood.

Even though this is only a fragment of the list of people with whom I came in direct or indirect contact in my years as an underground ghetto partisan, I must mention that in this connection, I intend to devote myself in the near future to a more detailed account, where I intend to cast light upon a large number of shining figures. For it behooves the world to know, that in brown-shirted Europe there lived not only human beasts, but also human beings—ordinary human beings.

THE GHETTO PROCLAMATION OF 6 JULY 1943

By command of the Security Police and the S. D. no Jew is allowed to possess more than 30 Reichsmarks for each member of the family.

Possession of valuables, such as gold, silver and precious stones is absolutely forbidden to the Jews.

All residents of the Ghetto must hand over, by 7 July 1943, 21 hours, all money in their possession above the limits set forth above, as well as all valuables.

The Jews are also commanded to turn in all their valuable possessions that were hidden by them in the city or that were left with Aryans. In case the valuables are found through informers, a reward will be paid to the informants.

I ask all residents of the Ghetto to comply with this order, as all who hide any valuables will be punished by death.

Money, valuables and information about their hiding places have to be given to the police station, to the manager of economic affairs, Wacker.

Head of the Ghetto

Ricowicz—two Jewish Partisan brothers.

From left: Witka Kempner, Ruszka Korczak, Zelda Treger

MOTHER OF THE BENEDICTINE CLOISTER

To the noble persons of our account, we can for sure add the Mother Superior of the Benedictine Cloister in Vilna.

The Mother herself was a college graduate and outspoken anti-Nazi. A former socialist, she had some friends in the left-wing Zionist youth organization, Hashomer Hazair. Among her friends were also the leading members of this youth organization Aba Kowner, Arie Wilner and others.

I heard in our circle about the Mother of the Benedictine Cloister. I heard that she even wanted to reside in the ghetto, and live with us as a camouflaged Jew.

The underground command told her that her place was in the cloister and not in the ghetto, because she could in one day there be more useful to us than she could be a year in the ghetto.

The Mother understood this well, but wanted to express solidarity with her Jewish friends.

The Mother was the one who brought over the first four handgrenades and gave them to her friends of the U.P.O. Many times she brought over small arms of all kinds.

One day I met her with a group of friends in a conspirative house in the ghetto. I saw before me a young, beautiful nun in a black cloak talking as if she were one of us.

As one in the special detachment my duty was, among other tasks, to protect the security for the U.P.O. I had complained to my chief Joseph Glazman, as previously in Schmidt's case, that in my eyes it was ridiculous for her to come into the walls of the ghetto in this garb and put herself on display before thousands of eyes.

The story is that the Lithuanian sentries at the gates took her to be a Nun-Nazi, because her papers showed this to be true. The risk was too big to play around with such a worthful life. After my intervention, the nun was clearly told that it was forbidden to come any more. Thus she never came to the ghetto walls again.

From that time on, our "Aryan" girls were in constant contact with the nun. She was of considerable help to the U.P.O.— she survived.

A PROCLAMATION

"CITIZENS OF ALL THE CONQUERED TERRITORIES!

"The blood of the enemy is flowing on all fronts.

"The fire of the Red Army has gripped the reinforcements of the enemy.

"Death and destruction encircle the trapped German troops. The German divisions on the battlefield are tired, without strength, without combat capacity.

"Hitler committed his forces to battle in the belief that in 14 days they would conquer Moscow. The days became weeks. The weeks—months. And when summer passed, he commanded to wait until autumn, and when all his efforts to split the defensive forces of the Red Army failed in the fall, the timetable was postponed until winter.

"But the winter was a catastrophe for the Germans. Millions of German soldiers are milling around on the battlefields. Vast amounts of war equipment were smashed by the relentless pounding of the Red Army.

"With the arrival of spring, the opposing forces face each other. Twenty million Soviet troops fully armed. Nine million on line. Eleven million as reserves. The Red Army, whose might has grown because of new and powerful military equipment, is preparing a great offensive, that will inflict death upon the enemy and finish him off once and for all.

"Citizens of all the conquered territories!

"The enemy, in his fear of rebellion, wants to wipe you out first. He is shooting your best sons, taking them to Germany by the hundreds and the thousands. In Warsaw, Kalisch, Vilna, Lwow, the Hitler terror has already seized the masses.

"Do not let yourself be led like sheep to slaughter! If the enemy is forced to break the resistance of each, one by one, he will be prevented from accomplishing his end.

"Thousands among you fall as passive victims. But freedom is bought only by active sacrifice.

"Join the Partisans!

"Destroy the highways, transports, factories!

"Death to the occupier!

"To us is victory!

Organization of Fighters against the German Invader."

SOVIET BOMBARDMENTS OF VILNA

(From the Archive note about Vilna)

"**W**HO kept us alive, sustained us, and brought us to this time . . ."

Jews who met each other in the street today had cheerful faces in general. Conflicting reports were passed around. It develops that last night, besides Vilna, they bombed Kovno, Molodeczno, Wilejka, etc.

In Vilna: Everybody waited anxiously for press reports. But the newspapers did not print a word. A few people began to circulate around spreading news, and it became clear.

A bomb fell on a train and landed on the third rail. A few cars were damaged. Ten people were killed.

On 51 and 53 Zawalna Street not far from the Halle, opposite the railroad tracks, a bomb fell and killed 2 Lithuanians.

On Niemiecka Street, near Jatkowa Street, traffic was halted. On 17 Niemiecka Street a bomb fell. A second bomb landed on the only Lithuanian Church on Dominikanska Street, which lies close to the walls of the ghetto. Here a Lithuanian priest was killed and Bishop Reines was severely wounded.

The Ignatowska army barracks suffered badly. Rumor has it that four convoys of dead Lithuanian soldiers were carried out of there.

The Poles are cheerful. The Lithuanians suffered 90 per cent casualties; the rest of the population only 10 per cent. In reality the impression was that the bombs chased after the Lithuanians in particular. The Lithuanians are downcast. They contend that this was a special toast to their declaration of independence . . .

In the suburbs of Vilna, the Soviets threw down leaflets calling the population to keep up their resistance and bear up. On Parubanek airfield they found a multitude of leaflets directed to the German soldiers that they should not believe in Hitler and that they should throw away their weapons.

"Out with Hitler,
Down with the War,
Let yourselves be taken
  prisoner,
Let your motto be:
'Hail Moscow. Down with
  Hitler.' "

Fort mit Hitler.
Nieder mit dem Krieg.
Gibt Euch gefangen. Die
  Parole ist:
"Leb wohl Moskau. Nieder
  mit Hitler."

"Weisst du wofur du kampst? —Diejenigen von Euch, die in den Reihen der Okupanten bleiben, werden vernichtet werden." (Those of you who will remain in the ranks of the occupiers will be destroyed.)

* * *

This proclamation was issued, with illustrations, under a caption which read:

"What is going on in Germany?"

The issue bears the number 77 and is dated February, 1942.

Famous Straszun library that was bombed out.

THE EDITOR ARCISZEWSKI

IN the printing shop, which put out the Polish-German news-paper *Goniec Codzienny*, I had to perform a variety of tasks required in producing a newspaper.

In the course of my work, I had daily contact with the paper's editor Arciszewski. Actually I had no special business to bring me into contact with him. Nor did his work have much to do with mine. Nevertheless, he would come over to me from time to time and ask me to set a headline or perform some similar task. In fact he even thanked me on occasion.

A Pole entrusted with an editor's job under the Nazi occupation was sure to be a trusted Nazi himself, otherwise he would not be permitted to hold such a responsible position.

The newspaper was thoroughly German, but appeared in Polish and was, of course, hostile to the Polish underground.

One day I heard some of my Polish co-workers tell each other in strictest confidence that the editor had told them of a warning he received from underground sources. He was warned not to publish anything against the resistance and the Poles who were active in it, at the risk of his head. The editor had once boasted to a certain Pole that he had no fear of the underground, since he was at all times protected and guarded by the Gestapo.

One Sunday, however, several shots were fired at him as he was coming out of church, and he fell down dead.

The Polish workers in the print shop were very alarmed, and I was even more so. One never knew. It was a standard German trick to blame the Jews whenever a traitor was shot. Since I was the only Jew working on the newspaper, I could easily become the scapegoat. especially because the assassins succeeded in escaping and the all-powerful Gestapo did not manage to catch them.

Fortunately, my fears did not become reality. As for fear, I had long been accustomed to living with it.

THEY FOUGHT BACK!

(From the Chronicles)

Tevia Belak, who had escaped the slaughter in the town of Braslaw, in the Vilna district, was residing in another town, Swieciany. When the remnants of the town's youth were transported to Vilna, he used to help his friends in the Vilna ghetto to join the partisans. On one of these "excursions" in August, 1943, when he was going without a Jewish "patch," he was detained by the Lithuanian police. He tried to shoot his way free, but ran out of bullets and was captured alive.

Belak's friends in the ghetto became nervous out of fear that he might blurt out, under duress, the names of his contacts. Belak was tortured to death, but he did not give away his comrades.

Shortly after this event, when the Gestapo hangman, Martin Weiss, came to the ghetto and talked with Gens, he said, "I never saw such a fellow before. He died like a hero."

Feivel Benski, a youth in his early twenties, was hidden by his Polish friend, Jurgelanec. When Jurgelanec informed him that the Jews of Kalwariska Street were being driven out, Benski dashed out of the house to see the people on the move, and spotted his own parents among them. Without hesitation, he opened fire and killed a number of Gestapo men and their Lithuanian aides. He broke loose, and fire was poured on Feivel by the Germans. Feivel jumped into the nearby Wilja river and crossed to the other bank. There, a machinegun got him, and his riddled body was left lying in the open for several days, so that the people could see it. Then the body disappeared.

Eliahu Baron, an engineer by profession, was a wholesale thief, specializing in weapons. He supplied our people with guns. He also stocked the Polish underground with vast quantities of weapons.

He was shipped from the Vilna ghetto to Estonia, but he escaped and returned to Vilna. Some time later, he and two

Polish colleagues in the smuggling action, were caught. He was cruelly tortured and half-dead he was sent to Ponary. Midway he attacked his guard and leaped from the moving auto. He was shot and killed.

Stanislaw Braunszweig was a Warsaw lawyer. In the Vilna ghetto he headed the information office. He ran away from the ghetto and posing as an Aryan, with appropriate documents, he became the moving spirit of the general Polish underground. He helped the Jews in Kailis and H.K.P. a great deal. In the spring of 1944 he was arrested in his dwelling at 18 Pohulanka Street. The Polish underground exerted every effort to rescue him, as eventually he might have been pressed into disclosing secrets to the Germans. He knew many secrets. But despite the inquisitorial tortures, such as tearing out his finger nails and poking out his eyes, he took his secrets to the grave.

Taibe Winiski was from the Narocz group. In the Rudnicki wilderness she joined one of our partisan groups on a mission. Because of the negligence of their Russian commander and betrayal by a peasant, who was an informer for the Germans, the group was discovered and ambushed by a large German unit. In the fighting many fell on each side, and Taibe was taken alive. When they wanted to tie her up she pulled the ring of a grenade and blew up her captors and herself.

The neglectful commander was tried by the partisan field court and executed.

Yitzhak Jabrow, before the war, lived only two courtyards away from me and was one of the first partisans in the Narocz forest. General Markow sent him to Vilna to act as a guide for the U.P.O. members who had to go to Narocz. Jabrow came just on the eve of the liquidation of the ghetto and was stuck there, unable to fulfill his mission. He therefore decided to break out of the surrounded ghetto in spite of everything that Sonia Madejsker and I said. We advised him that it was better to remain with us where we would all make a joint effort to escape. Jabrow did not listen to us and was detained at the ghetto gate by the

Lithuanian-German guards. Kittel, the Nazi officer, found arms and grenades on him. Jabrow was tortured in the Gestapo cellars.

* * *

In February, 1942, a large transport of Jews was brought from Belgium, Holland and other West-European countries to an extermination camp in the 9th Fort*near Kovno.The forcibly transported Jews put up a stiff resistance and many of their exterminators were destroyed at their heroic hands. Some of them succeeded in running away, and some even got as far as Vilna.

* * *

In a hideout on Szpitalna Street No. 13, the bodies of Moshe Hauz, his wife and child were found. Moshe Hauz came to Vilna with a stream of refugees from Poland. His aim was to go to Palestine together with a certain Mr. Goldstein. When Moshe Hauz refused to go to an unknown relocation center outside the ghetto he and his family were shot on the spot.

The next day this obituary was posted on the ghetto walls:

"On Sunday, Hauz and Goldstein died on Szpitalna Street No. 13. Honor to their memory." This obituary was also posted:

> # HONOR TO THE MARTYRS
> # HAUZ AND GOLDSTEIN
> # HONOR TO THE FALLEN!

June 12, 1943.— A partisan, named Chayim Levin, was arrested by the guard at the ghetto gate. He had come on a mission from the partisans in the forest to act as a guide to a group of city Jews, who came from Swienciany, Oszmiana and other nearby cities.

When Levin was put in the jail near the ghetto gate, he confided to the local Jewish police commissar Mayer Levas, that he would do well to free him because he had come on a partisan mission. When Levas refused to free him, Levin shot the policeman, Moshe Gingold, who was assigned to guard him and who tried to prevent his escape.

In the meantime, the ghetto police chief Gens rushed over

---

*The 9th Fort was the equivalent of Ponary near Vilna.

234

to the scene, and he ordered the prisoner to surrender. When Levin refused to do so, Gens opened fire and shot him.

The Jewish police received official commendation from their German commanding officers for shooting down a partisan.

In this instance, there was another ceremonial funeral for the victim, the policeman, Moshe Gingold.

After this, the so-called "provincials" were kept under special surveillance. They were the remnants of the small communities around Vilna which were exterminated. These remnants were driven into the Vilna ghetto.

Since their point of origin was in the neighboring small towns, they were familiar with the surrounding forests. There was a tendency among them to go to their own regional forest from which they were previously driven out. The Germans did not want loose Jews to be found on the outskirts of greater forests.

In general, these groups were not organized and they did not belong to the U.P.O. But they tried to keep together in accordance with their place of origin.

After the liquidation of the Vilna ghetto, a special German unit of the H.K.P. was created at 37 Subocz Street. All those who had worked in various units of the H.K.P. in other parts of the city were gathered here.

When Vilna was bombarded by Soviet planes, and the attacking partisan forces were on the edge of the city, the Germans liquidated the remaining Jews in the H.K.P. As this final action began, the Jews resisted fiercely, and many Nazis were killed by the Jewish partisans Motke Nemser, Yankel Zalbi and David Eigenfeld. The last named was slain in the battle.

There were many more cases beside those enumerated here, in which Jews, single Jews unaffiliated with the U.P.O., got hold of weapons and set out to fight the Nazis directly. This does not include the untold cases of *passive* resistance which required, frequently, just as much courage and sacrifice.

One more Ghetto document.

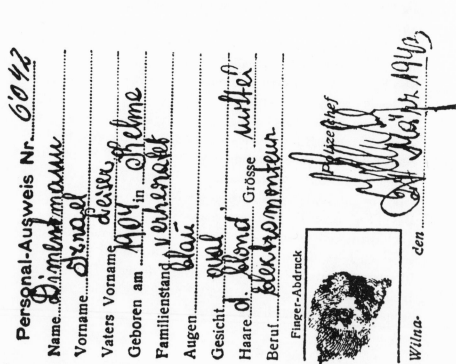

Personal-Ausweis

GÜLTIG nur ZUSAMMEN
mit dem ARBEITS-AUSWEIS

M

Personal-Ausweis Nr. 6042

Name. Dimenstmann

Vorname Israel

Vaters Vorname Leiser of Selma

Geboren am 1904 in Selma

Familienstand verheiratet

Augen blau

Gesicht oval

Haare d. blond Grösse mutter

Beruf Elektromonteur

Finger-Abdruck

Wilna- den

FROM THE GHETTO CHRONICLE

In one of its broadcasts, the secret radio station "Swit" announced that the Bishop of Kovno, Reines, in the Sunday sermon in the Basilica, denounced the Lithuanian participation in the atrocities perpetrated against Jews in Swienciany and Oszmiana.

*   *   *

July 4, 1942—Among the Vilna ghetto police force, there was a certain Nathan Schlossberg, 34 years old, a pre-war lawyer. He often had to make official visits between the ghetto and Sorok-Tatar, some 18 kilometers from Vilna, where a few hundred Jews were working as slave labor. He had supervision over them.

Schlossberg had a bad reputation among the Jewish workers of Sorok-Tatar.

The first Soviet partisans began to appear around that section and they established contacts with the camp Jews. At one of the meetings, some workers complained about Schlossberg. The partisans took heed of the complaints, and when Schlossberg was on his way back to Vilna, they shot and wounded him. He was brought to the Vilna hospital where he died.

The leadership of the Jewish police was incensed, because outside partisan powers were brought in, who were doubly odious in the eyes of the German occupation force.

An honor police guard stood at the head of Schlossberg's coffin for an entire day. In every street of the ghetto there were posters announcing his death and the police wore black armbands of mourning.

They transformed the funeral march into a grotesque martyr's procession. For the first time in the annals of the Vilna ghetto, the German District Commissioner, in accordance with a special directive, empowered a group of Jewish policemen to escort the hearse to the Jewish cemetery on Zarecza.

*   *   *

On July 25, 1942, Neigebauer, a Gestapo officer, and his escort, drove to the ghetto hospital at breakneck speed. Shortly thereafter, the Jewish police chief, Jacob Gens, also arrived.

Neigebauer introduced himself as the head of a division assigned to extinguish all lights at night. He informed Gens that light signals were being flashed from the hospital to Soviet airplanes.

Gens denied this categorically. The commanding officer got very angry at Gens and said that if there was any more back talk from him he would be shot on the spot.

In the dialogue, Gens repeated his denial that signals were given from the hospital to Soviet airplane pilots, who thereupon bombed Vilna.

The commander did not shoot Gens, but he left the ghetto with the warning that if any more signals were sent to the enemy, he would personally shoot down every Jew in the ghetto with a machine-gun.

The ghetto got away with an extra portion of fright and with that the incident was closed.

* * *

"Residents of the ghetto who may have fur pieces elsewhere —fur vests or other fur apparel—are under strict orders to report to the police by March 1, 1942, 9 P.M., the exact whereabouts of such furs."

The above announcement appeared on the ghetto walls. Later on, the Christian population were also ordered to "donate" a part of their furs and woolens. At first it was a "voluntary" collection from the Christian sector of the population; later on, warm apparel was conscripted.

* * *

In the Torf Camp Bezdan near Vilna, there was a Jewish-Lithuanian doctor named Yudel Grulianski.

The Lithuanian guard wanted to rescue the doctor before the liquidation of the camp, but the Lithuanian commander Mankiewiczus prevented such action.

Later on, the Jewish partisans caught Mankiewiczus and killed him.

* * *

Nonjoji Lietuva, No. 207, November 11, 1942.

LET US DONATE GLOVES AND STOCKINGS

"At this time, quite a few of our youth work with the transport service. Outside of the borders of Lithuania, there are also battalions for self-defense.

"The Lithuanian community should take it upon itself to see to it that the men working in the transport service, as well as those in military service, should not suffer from frozen hands and feet. With that in mind, all people sympathetic to our cause are asked to donate gloves and stockings.

"Anybody with an extra pair of gloves, don't be lazy and bring them down to the Mutual Aid depot, on Wielka No. 12. Donations are accepted from the eighth to the 14th hour.

"If grandmothers have a moustache . . ."

Everything would be in order if not for the last cryptic sentence.

The next day there was an explanation or a "correction of error" which ran something like this:

"In the previous issue we had a statement reading, 'Let us donate gloves and stockings.' Because of the carelessness of a proofreader, a sentence was put in which had no connection with the subject in hand. We apologize to the reader for this unsavory error."

In reality it was a sabotage done by a printer to make it look funny, that Germans were appealing for warm clothes.

The Warsaw Ghetto in flames.

THE WARSAW GHETTO UPRISING

BY THE PRESIDENT OF THE UNITED STATES OF AMERICA
A PROCLAMATION

Of the more than 400,000 Jews whom the Nazis had previously walled into the Warsaw Ghetto, only about 70,000
remained in April of 1943. With deadly efficiency, most
of the other inhabitants had been transported by the Nazis
to concentration camps and had there been exterminated.
The surviving Jews, suffering from malnutrition and disease,
with pitifully few weapons and virtually no hope of assist-
ance from any source, determined to sell their lives as
dearly as possible. They engaged the Nazis in battle.

The result was known by the Jews to be foredoomed.
Yet, though they lacked both military resources and a
military tradition, they were able to conduct their struggle
against the overwhelming forces of the Nazi occupiers for
more than three weeks, thereby providing a chapter in the
annals of human heroism, an inspiration to the peace-loving
people of the world and a warning to would-be oppressors
which will long be remembered.

NOW, THEREFORE, I, JOHN F. KENNEDY, President of the
United States of America, in consonance with the joint
resolution of Congress approved August 28, 1962 (76 Stat.
407), do hereby invite the people of the United States to

observe the twentieth anniversary of the Warsaw Ghetto uprising, April 21, 1963, with appropriate ceremonies and
activities.

IN WITNESS WHEREOF, I have hereunto set my hand and
caused the Seal of the United States of America to be
ixed.

ONE at the City of Washington this *fourth*   day
of *MARCH*   in the
year of our Lord nine-
teen hundred and sixty-
three, and of the
Independence of the
United States of America
the one hundred and
eighty-seventh.

By the President

John F. Kennedy

Dean Rusk

Secretary of State

U. P. O. PROCLAMATION TO THE JEWS OF ALL THE GHETTOS

Parts of the Proclamation sent by the U.P.O. Command "To All the Jews under the Nazi Occupation" have been lost. In the missing section, the proclamation laid bare for the first time (April 1942), the awful truth about the fate of Eastern Jewry in the ghettos of Vilna, Kovno, Vilejka, Minsk, and went on to say:

"The fate of the Jews under the yoke of the Hitler conquest is the fate of general annihilation *despite* the economic factor.

"Brothers! Tear off your illusions—we shall not be saved by economic necessity. Desist from false hope: that the 40,000 in the Bialystok ghetto and a half million in Warsaw will not be destroyed by the Germans on account of economic interests. The annihilation of the Jews is a central program that has no foundation in any local institutions.

"The Germans in Grodno, Bialystok, Warsaw—in order to avoid going to the front—are prepared to delay the end of "their" ghettos for a time. The process of annihilation is a systematic one that will sooner or later affect all. The political program takes precedence over any economic factor. Wherever there is a Jewish community under the rule of Hitler—there will rise a Ponary!

"Jews organize yourselves! Take hold of weapons!

"Jews—to the defense!

"The Command of the United Partisan Organization in the Vilna Ghetto (U.P.O.)"

Mordechai Anielewicz

"Now it is quite clear to us that what happened has by far surpassed all our expectations . . . The last wish of my life has come true. Jewish self-defense has become reality. Jewish resistance and vengeance have been transformed into acts."

> *Last letter written before his death by Mordechai Anielewicz, commander of the Jewish Fighting Forces of the Warsaw Ghetto Uprising.*

(This document is to be found in the Jewish Museum in Vilna)

HIMMLER'S COMMAND FOR THE DESTRUCTION OF THE WARSAW GHETTO

Number 2494   S E C R E T :

Reichsfuhrer S. S. Nos. 38, 33, 38 Police Headquarters, February 16, 1943

To the Supreme Commander S. S. and Police, East

Obergruppen fuhrer S.S. Dreieger, Cracow.

For purposes of security I order the destruction of the Warsaw Ghetto after the Concentration Camp has been transfered to another place; the various materials and parts of buildings which can be put to further use should be preserved.

The destruction of the Ghetto and the transfer of the Concentration Camp are a necessity; we will never be able to placate Warsaw and put an end to the delinquency as long as the Ghetto exists.

I ask that a complete plan for the destruction of the Ghetto be forwarded to me. In any case the dwelling places of the 50,000 inferior people which are not suitable for Germans, anyway, must disappear from the face of the earth. The area of Warsaw, that dangerous permanent center of seething and rebellion, must be reduced.

On the ruins of the Warsaw Ghetto. On August 4, 1959, Vice President Nixon and his wife, Pat, made a pilgrimage to this most solemn shrine to the memory of the six million Jews who were victims of the Nazi holocaust. Mr. Nixon said from that spot that: ". . . the sufferings of the Jews of Poland and other European countries served as a reminder, at a time when the world hoped for peace, that men of good will must battle against those forces that spread prejudice and hatred."

Jewish children
fighter s

Burning Ghetto fighter
jumps from building.

Gen. Jurgen Stroop leads the Major Operation inside the Warsaw Ghetto

TO THE DEFENDERS OF THE WARSAW GHETTO, TO THE JEWS WHO REMAIN ALIVE!

The population of Warsaw has been conducting an armed struggle against the German invaders for the last three days. This is our struggle, too. A year has passed since we raised the flag of the famous revolt in the Ghettos and labor camps, since we began the battle for our lives and honor, and we again join the entire Polish nation in the fight for freedom. Hundreds of Jewish youths and members of the Jewish Fighting Organization stand shoulder to shoulder with their Polish comrades at the barricades. We send our greetings to the fighters.

Together with the rest of the Polish nation we are, today, struggling for freedom. All of the members of the Jewish Fighting Organization who have survived and all Jewish youths capable of fighting are hereby called on to continue the struggle. No one should stay behind. Join the ranks of the rebels. Through war we shall achieve victory, and a free, sovereign, strong and just Poland!

The Jewish Fighting Organization
Signed: Antek, Commander
(Yitzhak Cukerman)

Warsaw, August 3rd, 1944

German soldiers shoot down the Jewish and Polish flags hoisted in challenge by Warsaw Ghetto Fighters

THE WARSAW GHETTO UPRISING AND ITS ROOTS

"**W**E'LL be seeing you again!" Thus we bade farewell to the two emissaries, Yehuda Pinchevski and Israel Kempner, as they left the Vilna ghetto.

Pinchevski raised the collar of his leather jacket and the two of them left the ghetto gate. Instinctively, I thought: who knows whether we would really meet again? Before them stretched a train ride of twelve or thirteen hours, but the way to Warsaw was full of danger and there were a thousand doubts whether they could penetrate the thorough military check points. I knew that they had been provided by us with good counterfeit papers, but you could never tell what would happen.

While I was in this mood, they left, and they got to Warsaw safely, bringing the first call for resistance to the ghetto there.

Although Vilna had been occupied by the German troops about two years after Warsaw had fallen, Vilna was the first large city where the annihilation of the Jews on a large scale began. As a result of this bitter experience, the United Partisan Organization (U.P.O.) wanted to rush the facts to every community where there was a large number of Jews, in order to warn them in advance about the true intentions and immediate plans of the Germans.

When our messengers arrived and met with the underground leaders and informed them that the Nazis had murdered 50,000 of 70,000 Vilna Jews in several months, they would hardly believe it.

The Warsaw ghetto, with its half million Jews, had been in existence for about a year, but they had not known of such a record of annihilation. In the Warsaw ghetto, each day hundreds of Jews died of hunger and epidemics as well as by out-

Note: This fragment about the Warsaw Ghetto, written by Isaac Kowalski, was printed in *The Jewish Herald* in Johannesburg, South Africa, April 13, 1966.

right murder, but not of mass murder on such a scale or proportion. So it was shocked to hear such a report from Vilna. However, it did arouse them and put them on the alert, which was extremely important in those days.

The former Vice-Commander of the Warsaw ghetto uprising Yitzhak (Antek) Cukerman, writes in his memoirs:

> The police and the Judenrat were against all communal movements, and battled all forms of open resistance. After the evening of April 18th, Chernikov gathered the heads of the Jewish underground and argued that the underground activities were dangerous to the Jews. He implored that they be stopped—that we should refrain from congregating; from establishing educational activities. The police and Judenrat suppressed any form of Jewish communal activity—and shortly afterwards, were traitors in the 'Jewish Affair.'
>
> They, though, were not the only deterrent powers in the Ghetto. There were high-minded, idealistic people, who objected to a Jewish revolt from other points of view. Some based their disapproval on general historical grounds and political considerations, while others still were against a Jewish war and Jewish violence, because of their religious faith.
>
> The chief advocate of containment—if we are to mention anyone—was Ozech. He did not preach, 'Let us not fight', but only 'Let us fight when the Poles fight—in the meantime, no!' He upheld that the coarseness and the despotism of the occupancy were not reserved for Jews only, but were meted out to the population, in its entirety. Our war was defensible—according to him—insofar as collaboration with the non-Jewish underground was possible, and if the non-Jewish underground forces were ready to open a united front together with us. As long, however, as they did not find it necessary to conform to Jewish needs, the legitimate conclusion was that we must adapt ourselves to the make-believe needs of the non-Jewish underground.
>
> In combined sessions we heard Ozech argue: "We, a portion of the fighting world,—are but one group among an entire underground. Why are you so shocked at the Jewish slaughter in Vilna? Are you altogether oblivious to the many thousands of Poles who are killed—day in, and day out—on Poland's streets and are interred in Auschwitz? We all wage one war—one war for all the oppressed. And when the time comes, the Polish worker and the Jewish worker will rise together and press their common purpose!"

As we see from this quotation, there was a difference of opinion about the practicality of beginning a revolt against the Germans without the help of the Polish population. The arguments of the two Vilna emissaries won out, however, and the idea was accepted that the Jews could no longer wait.

The Germans had a large special staff of skilled "technicians" who day in and day out, were scheming how to fool the Jews best, so that they would not know what was going on until the last moment, when their end had come. So, for example, they induced the Dutch Jews in Auschwitz to write letters to their relatives in Holland and to the then existing publication, "Joodse Weekblad," which appeared as late as September 1943, to print their letters from which one could conclude that the Jews were engaged in work at Auschwitz. In reality, immediately after the letters were written, the writers were killed. Time after time they pulled similar tricks so cleverly that they fooled and destroyed large numbers of Jews.

When the U.P.O. in Vilna caught a secret radio communication of the Polish underground radio "SWIT,"* which said "Hello, Hello, the Warsaw ghetto has begun to resist," I became excited and saw in my imagination the two emissaries whom the U.P.O. had sent off not so long ago and knew that they had a large share in this uprising, for which they had agitated. Later we found out that Israel Kempner died a hero's death in the revolt, and Yehuda Pinchevski succeeded in escaping to the forests around Lublin where he, too, died in the unequal battle against the Hitlerites.

When the radio, in a later broadcast, told the world of the heroic, bloody struggle in which hundreds of Nazis were killed within the walls of the Warsaw ghetto, we gleaned from the communiques that aside from the sympathy of the radio station,

*) "SWIT" was located in Great Britain and used as a relay, was thought to be broadcasting from Poland. It was not until 1944 that the Germans discovered the location of the station. Also we in the ghetto, as all the nations in occupied Europe didn't know that the station was not located some place in Poland.

the Jews had no real help from the Polish underground. Therefore, we in Vilna ghetto were surprised how the Jewish fighters
succeeded in halting the powerful tanks, airplanes and other
heavy weapons that the Germans brought into the fray in an
effort to crush the revolt. Yet, the Jews held out for 27 days,
until most had died and the survivors ran out of ammunition.
They retreated into the sewers of the city, to escape and take up
the battle later during the general uprising in Warsaw, when
many more Jews fell. Only a handful came out alive after both
uprisings.

Jacob Kaplan

Asia Bik

Jewish people are hanged.

THE EXECUTIONS

EVEN before my group had left the doomed ghetto for the forest of the Rudnicki wilderness, several units of the U.P.O. fighters had already gone in the direction of the Narocz forests which were situated about 180 kilometers from the city.

One such group, which was sent by the command in Narocz a few days earlier to escort U.P.O. fighters out of the Vilna ghetto, was headed by Nisl Resnik, a staff member. Accompanying the group was Rudnitzki, who served as a guide. Rudnitzki, a veteran partisan, always made it a point to brief the others on the various dangers threatening the group along the way. He knew from experience that crossing railroad tracks or bridges involved the greatest risk.

When the group reached the end of Subocz Street, they realized that one of their members—Moshe Shapiro—was missing. Only later did they learn what happened. After losing his way in the darkness, Shapiro proceeded on his own to cross the tracks behind Subocz Street. He was spotted by sentries who opened fire and killed him.

Another group, headed by Abrasha Chwojnik, a staff member who had been a lawyer before the Nazi occupation, also met a tragic end. As they reached the treacherous Subocz Street, the group, which also included Asia Bik, Jacob Kaplan, Grisha Lewin, ran into a large military police patrol on a routine check up of all persons in the area.

When asked for their identity papers, the partisans immediately answered with a hail of bullets and the ensuing exchange of fire shattered the stillness of the night. Kaplan, a staff member, was killed in the shooting melee. Their resistance crumpled and they were captured when police reinforcements arrived and the hopelessly outnumbered partisans ran out of ammunition.

Later, we found out that among the killed Germans was none other than the head of the Anti-Partisan-Division, Gross.

At Rosa Street, meanwhile, the remaining Jews from the

ghetto were rounded up by the Gestapo and herded into a large open field near the railroad behind Subocz Street. Troops, heavily armed with machine guns, surrounded the area.

Although they had been informed that they were to be shipped out to labor camps in Estonia, each one of them feared that it was just another trick and that they would be sent to their death.

As they were pondering their fate, the Gestapo commander abruptly ordered them to stand up and announced over the loudspeaker that they would have to witness the execution of three "criminals" who had armed themselves and tried to flee to the forest. He warned that any others who tried to escape would meet the same fate.

The Gestapo men then dragged out the three partisans captured in their ill-fated struggle on Subocz Street and they were brought to the gallows and hung, while several thousand Jews—many of them weeping silently—looked on.

All three of the partisans went to their death courageously. When it was her turn on the gallows, Asia Bik nodded her head toward the spectators as if to assure them that, while lives must be sacrificed, the United Partisan Organization would survive to avenge the dead.

A group of Kovno fighters eulogizing their fallen comrades after the war.

MAIMONIDES IS QUOTED . . .

Only a few rabbis remained in the ghetto because the majority of them had been killed before the Jews were driven into the enclosures or soon after they entered the two existing ghettos.

Simultaneously, the rabbis composed prayers in which they implored the Almighty for pity on behalf of their suffering people.

After the action of the yellow certificates, the rabbis remaining in the ghetto (Gutman, Mendl Zalmanowicz, Pilovski, Yitzhak Kroniks) met with the ghetto commander Jacob Gens, and told him that according to Jewish law it was forbidden to deliver to the authorities any Jew, *just because he was a Jew.*

A GOOD JEST—"A Good Year to All Jews"—the sign posted by the Jewish sentries at the gate of the Vilna ghetto on Rosh Hashana, 1943. Four Jewish policemen stand at the gate

Gens replied, however, that by delivering a few Jews he was saving the majority, and under the circumstances this was the only way he could act. To this, the rabbis quoted Maimonides, that if the idolators threaten to annihilate all Jews if one of them is not delivered up to be murdered—let all make the sacrifice rather than betray a single soul of Israel . . .

Note. Maimonides, Moses ben Maimon (1135-1204), refered to as Rambam), philosopher, Talmudist, physician and codifier of Jewish Law. He was born in Spain.

The selection by the gates during the "Yellow Certificate"-action.

But Gens continued to apply his own laws and collaborated with the bloody Germans. At a later date he, too, paid for his Jewishness with his life. When the Gestapo murderer, Martin Weiss, warned Gens to run off as he was on the list of those to be shot, Gens told his companions that he would not do so. He reported to the Gestapo when he was called. on September 13. 1943, so that the remaining Jews would not have to pay the penalty for his escape. He had a good chance to get away. but he went to the Gestapo headquarters where he had been such a frequent visitor as the ghetto representative, and was shot. Salek Dessler was then appointed by the Germans as the head of the ghetto.

So strange are the ways of God's world. The murderer Weiss, who had thousands of lives on his conscience. tried to tip off "his" Jew—Jacob Gens—about the immediate danger: but Gens believing that with his running away he would bring a new catastrophe for the remnants of the ghetto Jews. went to his doom.

THE TRAGEDY OF THE SECOND BATTALION

A TRAGEDY befell to the Second Battalion of the U. P. O. Five o'clock in the morning, on September 1, 1943, the ghetto was suddenly surrounded by heavily-armed Estonian S.S. troops.

Notices were quickly pasted on the signposts of the streets reading, "Lisa Calls!"—the signal for mobilization. In minutes members of the U.P.O. manned their posts.

The Second Battalion assembled on Szpitalna Street No. 6, and they waited for one of our special units which was supposed to bring over weapons from one of our arsenals. This was scheduled to take place within an hour.

In the meantime, an act of treachery was committed by Gens' brother, Salomon, and the hated slave-labor brigadier Hyman. They led in a strong unit of S.S. troops through a side entrance along the rear—an area which bordered our Szpitalna Street station. One part of the street extended outside of the ghetto. The U.P.O. unit, which numbered about 100 members, was ambushed and commanded to line up at the ghetto gates in order to be transported to Estonia with other ghetto Jews.

Our fighters saw that they were cut off from the possibility of receiving any weapons in time, and the Lieutenant Commander Zwi Cepelewicz ordered the units to set themselves free by force.

With bare fists they threw themselves upon their captors and 25 of our fighters succeeded in getting away to other positions on Straszuna Street No. 6. But 75 of our members were captured and dragged away (together with thousands of other Jews) to Estonia.

Among those who were dragged away, was my best friend Boria Szneider; the poet-partisan, Hirsh Glik, who wrote the *Partisan Hymn*, Moshe Szymeliski, who instructed our members in the way to use firearms, Jona Wirszup the group-commander, as well as many other members.

When the group arrived in Estonia, Szneider and Glik joined a few others in a daring escape to nearby forests. But they perished a short time thereafter because none of our partisan·units had as yet taken over that region, and they could not fend for themselves there. Only few of our U.P.O. members survived.

An anonymous poet wrote in Auschwitz: "There is no more hope in the white skull,/Among the barbed wire, under the ruins,/And our dust is scattered in the dust/Out of the broken jars . . ./Our army will go forth skullbone and jawbone,/And bone to bone, a merciless line,/We, the hunted, who hunt, will cry to you:/The murdered demand justice at your hands!"

Mayer Blit

Moshe Szymeliski

THE BEGINNING OF THE END

WHEN the last Jews had gathered at the gates of the ghetto to be transported to unknown destinations, I was with a group of partisans in a small room directly over the gates of the main entrance of the ghetto. The room was the home of two girl partisans.

I do not know how it happened, but I was then the only man in the room with nine or ten of our women. I wondered at the whim of fate which led me to be the only man in the company of these women fighters in this defense post. I did not know which of us was the commander of the unit. However, the girls instinctively turned to me as the leader.

In reality, this group was a scouting unit. It was to observe what went on at the gates and in the nearby areas. The windows were boarded over, for they looked out on a street that was outside the ghetto. But we could see everything through the cracks between the boards. One half of the unit watched by the windows, the other half rested. The room was silent. No one spoke. Each one was absorbed in his own thoughts. Every few minutes the observers reported what they saw. Every few minutes large groups of Jews with sacks on their shoulders left the ghetto, allegedly to march to the railway station, from which they would be taken by train to Estonia for forced labor.

I had been informed through one of our contacts that across the street from us, on the opposite side, there was another fighting group, under the command of Szmulke Kaplinski. who had a large machine gun at his disposal.

When we judged the time to be right, we were to open fire as we were nearest the gate. The Germans. we calculated, would turn to us, and then the machine gun would open a barrage against them.

Again, during those hours in the room, waiting for the coming battle, I tried to sum up the various facts of my still young life, and again I wondered at the fate that brought me into this situation with ten women and laid upon me the fearful responsibility of throwing the first grenade. The ghetto was being liquidated, and according to all indications this time people were not lured out with false promises, but were really about to be sent to Estonia. They might be going to heavy labor; but all the same they were not going to immediate death. Yet this was the moment when we had to offer resistance. True, it was a hopeless resistance, but it was the realization of our dream of dying in the ghetto itself, and of taking along a number of our murderers into the ghetto grave.

The group of girls consisted of Feige'le Milsztein, Zelde Treger, Dina Grinwald and others. They were our leading intelligence scouts and liaisons throughout the years of our life in the ghetto. They had shown incredible courage and devotion, and now our last hour was approaching. Those were the last minutes of our lives. Each of us was taking an accounting of his life and knew that this was the end.

We spoke quietly and, in a sense, offered our final confession when the watchers at the window reported that a large military column was marching toward the ghetto gates. I quickly ran to the window and saw a column of some two hundred soldiers coming from Zawalna Street toward Rudnicki Street. They were some fifty feet from the gates of the ghetto. I ordered everybody to cock their guns and stand ready. I held a grenade in readiness, prepared to throw it as soon as the soldiers entered the gate. These were my instructions, and I counted their steps. The boards on the windows had already been loosened to allow for their quick removal. I watched the ghetto guard making ready to open the gates to the column, but suddenly the officer gave orders to the troops to turn right; the men marched off toward Konska Street instead of entering the ghetto. This column, it turned out, had nothing to do with the proceedings in the ghetto and was marching somewhere else on its own business.

The ghetto police shut the gates again and looked at one

another in wonder. We in the room above the gate also looked at one another, with faint smiles on our lips.

I said nothing, but left my post at the window and lay down on the sofa for a rest. Who wants to be the first to be responsible for opening the revolt for which we had been preparing for three long years with so much effort and so many sacrifices? How lucky that I did not lose my head at the critical moment and waited. If I had thrown the grenade when they were at the gate I would have started the revolt at the wrong time. There were too few Jews left in the ghetto, while we had always planned to have thousands of Jews join us in an effective and large-scale resistance action.

It was thus that the Vilna ghetto never staged a revolt that might have become famous as a heroic episode in which all the Jewish fighters had fallen in the unequal fight against Hitlerism.

*   *   *

Below, in the street, the last residents were being led out of the ghetto. A woman liaison officer came to us with orders to leave our posts, for the entire partisan movement was withdrawing into the forest, where we would be in a more favorable position to square accounts with the Third Reich.

Partisans
are hanged.

Ghetto entrance. To the left a warning sign: "Attention Jewish Quarter. Danger of Epidemics. Entry to Non-Jews Forbidden!" Some Ghetto police at the entrance. (x) the window of the room (battle point)

Chawa Glezer-Kozlowski   Danke Lubocki

LETTER TO THE PARTISAN COMMAND

To Comrades Markow and Yurgis
Combrig.

I hereby transfer to you the additional unit of the Jewish fighting partisans organization of the Ghetto (U.P.O.)—to the troop being formed under the name of "Nekama."

Unit Commander: Ziss.   Deputy: Raff.

Composition: 32.

Equipment: Own, acquired from the Germans.

Character: Know warfare, ardent Partisans.

—We are in the last stages of armed defense.

With combat greetings, Uri, Commander

Grisha Gurwicz

Szmulke Kaplinski

THE SEWER

IT was my fate to leave the ghetto with the last group. By that time the Germans had tightly sealed off the area so that it was no longer possible to leave through what had been taken for granted as "normal" channels accompanied by a Jewish police escort under the guise of going into the city on a labor detail or on some similarly legitimate mission. By the time we left, the only way open to us was through the sewer.

Among those in my group were the last commander of the U.P.O., Aba Kowner, and Szmulke Kaplinski, the weapons instructor. Kaplinski was our guide in the sewer, a route with which he was quite familiar since he was one of the few who used it to smuggle arms at a time when the ghetto was in full use.

When we entered the hole opening at 7 Rudnicka Street and heard the sound of the flow of the smelly water, I thought that this could easily turn out to be our grave.

We had to wade in sewage, either stooped over for long periods of time or, on occasion, to crawl on our knees for several hours at a stretch while we passed under the entire city. From time to time, Kaplinski had to look out of a manhole cover in the middle of a street to find out where we were.

For technical reasons, we were unable to leave the sewer where we planned and had to leave through an alternative exit which was practically in the back yard of the Central Police Station on Jasinska Street. This point was chosen mainly because it was the least likely place that the police would expect to find a Jew. It was a street that even Poles were afraid to use.

One by one, we crawled out of the sewer and sneaked into a nearby store. We had the key to the shop, which was empty, its Jewish owner and his merchandise no longer to be found. Slowly the store filled up with U.P.O. members. Nearby, another group of partisans assembled in another empty store. All this was taking place in the very shadow of the main police headquarters. When I realized where we were, I could not help but think what an odd combination of circumstances.

After we were in the store about an hour, Witka Kempner came in. One of the more heroic figures among the partisans, she was then serving in a liaison function which she carried out by posing as an Aryan, a role she carried off well with the aid of her blonde hair and with her excellent Polish accent.

Witka told us we were to make our way, one by one, to Kailis Camp on Wiwulska Street. The camp was allowed to remain in existence because its Jews produced fur coats for the freezing German troops on the front. She said we would regroup in the camp and then proceed to the forest. She told us exactly where we were and warned us not to shoot if we saw a Lithuanian policeman in front of the shop because he was one of us.

Everything went according to plan. It was already dark outside and no one was around except for our own partisans, a number of other "shikses" who showed us the way and our Lithuanian policeman who was there to protect us if anything went wrong.

Our group was luckier than those who left a day earlier and were ordered to go to the Narocz forests. All the groups arrived at the designated rendezvous points. One of them hid out in the attic of the Central Police Station where they remained for four days. They could not move for fear that they would be heard in the floor below which was swarming with Lithuanian police.

Our "shikses," however, came every night and brought them food until they got word that the way to the forest was clear and no large military units were about. It took a few days until our scouts were satisfied that it was safe. One of the scouts was my good friend Jan Pszewalski.

In Kailis, the several hundred Jews who lived there reacted to our presence with mixed feelings. Some feared that if word reached the Gestapo of our presence, they would suffer for it. Others envied us that we might soon have an opportunity to be saved.

I was notified by one of the liaison girls that the U.P.O. commander, Aba Kowner, who was hidden in a different part of the city, had appointed me acting commander of the group in Kailis and that I was to lead them immediately into the forest. Knowing what had happened on the previous day to the group headed by Chwojnik and the public hangings of the three partisans, I realized the full significance of the responsibility that had fallen on my shoulders for the lives of the entire group.

From Wiwulska Street, where the Kailis was, to the periphery of the city, was a long walk. We would have to pass all sorts of streets, in many of which there were no Jews to be found even before the war. And we had to know where to go. To complicate matters, there were a number of persons in my group who were complete strangers to the city and who made it a point to stick close to me in spite of the fact that they were instructed to spread out and to proceed in groups no larger than two. This would give us ample room to maneuver in the event of any exchange of fire.

Soon after leaving Kailis, I was surprised to see Niomka Lubocki carrying a rifle on his shoulder and smiling at me from the distance. He later told me that he had previously tried to carry the rifle under his coat but found out that this interfered with his walking and, anyway, it was apparent that he was hiding something. It occurred to him, therefore, that, if he carried the rifle openly on his shoulder, no one would suspect that he had no right to the arms. They would probably assume that he was a Lithuanian Nazi plainclothesman and that he had a perfect right to carry the rifle. He was right. Passersby even treated him with proper respect and greeted him courteously.

While crossing Radunski bridge, I noticed that one passerby kept staring at our bulging forms—we did carry our arms under our coats. I stopped and let him approach my companion, Chava Glezer and myself. When I asked him what he was staring at, he said that he was always scared in such dark and lonely places. I ordered him to go in the opposite direction to ours and he complied immediately. He did not know, of course, that we were Jews headed for a new world. He knew instinctively that he had to do what he was told.

I brought the entire group numbering a score of partisans to a rendezvous point outside the city where all those who made their way out through the sewer met. There, in a cave, we all took out arms and assembled our automatic machine guns— we were ready to take on in open battle anyone who would try to prevent us from reaching the forest. We covered a considerable distance, however, like regular partisans and we did not meet any obstacles even when crossing the various rail lines and bridges.

One of the partisans, Shlomo Kowarski, had seriously injured himself in the sewer where, because he was tall, he had to crawl the entire way on his knees. His knees were scraped and badly infected in the filth and he was unable to move either leg. From time to time, we would call out all the names to make sure no one was missing. So it was that on one roll call we discovered that Kowarski and his wife Rachel were left behind. Nataniel Lewin volunteered to go back and he found them. Together with Rachel, Lewin managed to drag Kowarski as one would drag a corpse, creeping along the ground. Shlomo later recovered completely in the forest and he was able to take part in regular partisan activities.

Jewish Partisans

Children-hideout in H.K.P.-concentration-camp at Subocz Street
(H.K.P.'s last location after liquidation of the Ghetto.)

Esther and David Ehrlich

Part IV

Forests

NAROCZ FOREST

THE hangings did not deter our partisans from getting to their goal—the Narocz forest.

A few groups arrived sooner and a Jewish battalion called "Revenge" was created, consisting of about 500 people. The commander was a certain Bomke, a pre-war Soviet Jew who wandered into the Vilna ghetto where he was a policeman for a time. Then he was among the first to join a group of provincials in the forest. Joseph Glazman was staff officer and Chaim Lazar, a unit commander. Under the leadership of Bomke, Glazman and Lazar, the partisans were ready to face the fire of the fighting front. They waited only for the orders from Brigadier Fiodor Gregorowicz Markow, who commanded six battalions called " *Voroshilov.*" Now, "Revenge" was supposed to be included as the seventh battalion in his brigade.

On a certain day at 3 P.M., an inspection was planned in a large, empty spot in the forest. Markow rode in with his corps of officers. Bomke stood at attention and reported to him in military fashion. Later on Markow whispered an order to Bomke. All those with arms were to arrange themselves at the right, women at the left, shoemakers and tailors at the front, and others were to remain in their places. Bomke gave the order.

There was some nervous tension. Nobody understood what was happening. Those with weapons and the women carried out the order immediately. But the others did not hurry and they delayed in going to their assigned places.

Markow was astounded to see that his order was not carried out punctually and he asked irritably, "Where are the shoemakers and the tailors?" A few stepped forward and Markow asked why the others had not carried out the order of their commander.

One answered: "We came here to fight and take revenge on the Nazis, and not to be shoemakers and tailors." To that Markow replied that fighting and taking revenge can also be accomplished when they made boots and warm clothes for the partisans.

A certain Lea Margolis voiced her opinion that the women wanted to fight side by side with the men. Markow answered that he did not need so many women and that there were not enough weapons to go around.

Then Markow called over a few fighters who had weapons, and he asked them to hand them over to others who in his opinion looked more combative. Furthermore, Markow reported that the partisans Suckewer and Kaczerginski were being transferred to a newly created work group. Morris Grajneman was appointed commander of the household force, and four armed partisans were assigned the job of providing the entire group with food.

In this manner, non-combative units were brought into being, until more weapons could be obtained. Then they would be changed into combat units.

One day, after a week's absence, an order came from Staff-Officer Wolodka Szaulewicz, that at an appointed hour, all the new partisans should report to the bunker house where the recently organized Jewish Staff was to be found. The Jewish partisans were very quick to notice that a heavily armed partisan group stood on guard at the entrance.

One after another they went into the bunker and soon came

out of it, without loitering a moment to talk to the others in line who were waiting to enter. They were told one by one that they were to penetrate further into the forest.

Everyone understood that something was going on, but nobody knew exactly what it was. It was only when they entered the bunker that they saw a table laden with all kinds of watches, money and other valuables. Szaulewicz greeted each man with the directive that he had to contribute something to the defense fund of the Soviet Union—anything of value he had brought along. Each had to sign a paper that he had given his valuables voluntarily.

All this would have been acceptable, if Szaulewicz had not led a group of strong-armed men the next day and surrounded the unarmed Jewish partisans, forcing them at gunpoint to take off their good boots, leather jackets, and hand them over to his men. When the Jewish partisans began to grumble and complain to Markow, they were met with a cold shoulder. The Jews considered this episode as an act of anti-Semitism.

About this time Markow was visited by Major General Klimow who flew in from Moscow. In 1940-41, Klimow was secretary of the Wilejka region, not far from Vilna and he had a rank comparable to an American governor. He had come now to inspect the ranks of the Partisan Movement in White Russia. He called in the new Jewish partisans in order to get acquainted with them. In the course of his tour of inspection he remarked: "How come that so many of you lack weapons?" He continued with: "And if you had no weapons why did you come into the forest?"

The partisan Kaczerginski wanted to explain to the general that it was not easy to get weapons in the ghettos. To which the answer was that it was only easy to take a stroll . . .

We of the Vilna ghetto were aware of the fact that the first condition of being accepted into any partisan unit was the possession of at least a revolver and bullets. We did everything in our power to get hold of enough weapons for everybody even when the U.P.O. was in the ghetto. Then it was already an integral part of the partisan movement and we were considered a collective unit. Because of this we were not under any obligation to provide such weapons to our fighters as individuals in the forest.

All this depressed the Jews in the forest to a great extent. The birds in the forest sang quite a different tune from that which had been imagined. But the impetus to resist, to enter into direct combat with the hated Nazis was uppermost. They waited stoically for a more propitious time which would be more favorable for the Jewish partisans who did not have any weapons.

There were thousands of Jewish partisans in various mixed battalions, where the problem did not exist. Together with other nationality groups, the Jewish partisans carried on a tireless campaign against German installations. They tore apart hundreds of military echelons which were on their way to the front, burned countless bridges, sawed down telephone poles, etc. The only problem was the few hundred unarmed Jews of the so-called household group. The same problem existed in other parts of White Russia, Ukraine and Poland.

About the same time, two brigade commanders arrived from the other side of the front. One had the pseudonym Kazimir (his real name was Tadeusz Szumauskas) and he remained in the White Russian city which was already a partisan town. The other had the pseudonym Yurgis (his real name was Henoch Ziman), and he came to Narocz in order to recruit new partisans for his Lithuanian brigade. He needed manpower at the time in order to bring them into the heart of the Rudnicki forest.

Yurgis had to give up his plan to recruit Lithuanians for his brigade, because they did not come into the forest. They fared very well in those days under the German rule. There were only some Lithuanians who had retreated with the Soviet military forces at the start of the war, and like Yurgis they were parachuted into Lithuania and White Russia. They became partisans and partisan commanders in Narocz. From their ranks came the "Lithuanian Brigade." When Yurgis saw that he did not have enough genuine Lithuanians, his staff decided to attract Lithuanian citizens. In this category were all those from Vilna, since Lithuania was incorporated in 1940 into the U.S.S.R.

Yurgis' staff officer then chose 20 partisans, almost all of them former members of U.P.O.—like Joseph Glazman, Liowa Ziskowicz, Michal Kowner, Miriam Bernstein, Moshe Brause, Chaim Lazar and others. The rest of the partisans were very envious of this group which was accepted into the Yurgis Brigade. That meant they would have a real chance to fight the enemy. This group of 20 consisted of the best of our U.P.O.-fighters of the ghetto.

Narocz forest produced a great amount of heroes. To mention just one of our co-workers, the partisan Isaac Blat who was post-mortem awarded the highest title as Hero of the Soviet Union for his tremendous courage in fighting the enemy.

Szmerke Kaczerginski

Abraham Suckewer

THE PARTISAN JEW

YEED, DU PARTIZANER

English: Esther Zweig   *Text*: S. Kaczerginski

From the ghetto's prison walls,
To the forests' wonders,
On my hands there are no chains,
But a gun that thunders.
When on duty, my dear gun,
Kisses neck and shoulder,
With my friend to give me heart,
I grow bold and bolder.

Fun di ghettos' t'feese-vent,—
In die velder fraie,
Anshtat kaytn oif di hent,
Ch'halt a biks a naiye—
Oif die oifgabes, main fraint
Kusht mir haldz un aksl,
Mitn biks chbin not fun haint
Fest tzunoif gevaksn.

II

Though we number very few,
We find strength in union,
And we blow up bridges, tanks,
High and low, we storm them.
The Fascist is pale with fear,
Cannot get his bearing,
Facing Jewish partisans,
Men with grit and daring.

II

Vaynik zenen mir in tzol,
Draiste, vie millionen,
Raissen mir oif barg un tol,
Brikn, echalonen.
Der fascist fartzitert vert,
Vayst not vu fun vanen—
Shturmen vi fun unter erd,
Yeedn Partizaner.

III

We have written down "REVENGE"
With blood and death's rattle,
For the dawn of a new day,
We unite in battle.
No, we shall not be compared,
To the last "MOHICANS,"
After night, the dawn will rise,
For Jewish partisan men.

III

S'vort "NIKOME" hot a zin,
Ven mit blut farshraibst eem,
Far den haylikn bagin,
Feern mir die shtraitn.
Nayn, mir velln kaynmol zain
Letzte MOHIKANER,
S'brengt der nacht—dee zunenshain,
der yeed—der PARTIZANER!

(Written in a partisan camp named after Voroshilov, in the White Russian forests around Narocz.

THE PARTISAN JEW

Moderato

From the ghet-to's pri-son walls

To the for—ests' won-ders,

on my hands There are no chains,

But a gun that thun-ders.

When on du-ty my dear gun,

Kis - ses neck and shoul - der

With my friend to give me heart-

I grow bold and bold -er.

Poet-Partisan From Vilna Ghetto Says Nazis Slew 77,000 of 80,000

Lithuanian Jews Fought Back in Their Agony —Gorky and Tolstoy Letters Seized From Germans and Taken to Moscow

By Wireless to THE NEW YORK TIMES.

MOSCOW, April 14—The desperate, heroic struggle of the Jews of the Vilna ghetto against the Germans, who reduced their numbers from 80,000 to 3,000, was described today by the poet Abraham Sutskever, a Partisan in a Lithuanian detachment which he had joined with a few hundred other Jews who crawled from the ghetto via sewers.

The poet brought to Moscow a letter written by the late Maxim Gorky. He also saved a diary of one of Peter the Great's servants, letters written by Leo Tolstoy and Sholem Aleichem and many other valuable relics.

He had smuggled these from Vilna's famous Jewish Museum and from Russian collections transferred to Vilna by the German organization for pillaging Soviet museums. For a time Mr. Sutskever was employed by this organization as an expert and this gave him an opportunity to keep certain treasures from being sent to Berlin.

Not Thinking of Verses

The poet spared no details of Vilna's travail. In June, 1942, a German train carrying arms was blown up near Vilna. The mines had been laid by captives from the Vilna ghetto; the doomed were still struggling.

The Germans did not kill all the Vilna Jews at once. That would have created "disorganization" and sacrificing the sadistic pleasure of prolonging the Jews' agony. They organized two ghettos. The doomed were destroyed over a two-year period. Two months ago 3,000 remained alive.

Before the war there was a Berlin movie actor named Kittel. Occasionally he played minor villains in Ufa films, but his work was considered mediocre. When the war began he found a new vocation; he became an executioner. He had four assistants picked up from the fringe of the Berlin film world. It was they who killed thousands of Riga's citizens. Then Kittel went to Vilna, where he was commissioned to liquidate the ghetto.

Once the Germans said they were going to open five new theatres in the ghetto. The people concluded that there was to be a change of policy, that they were going to be allowed to live. But the day after the first theatre was opened 5,000 were killed.

One day Kittel said to Mr. Sut-skever, "Here are some presents for you." The poet recognized his mother's clothes. She had been shot the day before.

The Germans burned Vilna's Jews alive. They buried them alive. They put out their eyes and twisted their arms.

What took place in this world of death, where women gave birth to children who they knew were already under sentence of death, where doctors treated patients knowing death awaited the sick, the convalescent and the doctor alike?

A partisan detachment was formed in the ghetto in January, 1942. It was headed by a 41-year-old Vilna shoemaker named Vittenburg. The Germans announced that if Vittenburg did not give himself up all the Jews would.be killed immediately. The leaders met for the last time in a cellar and drank together. Then Vittenburg went to the Germans. The next morning his mutilated body was found at the ghetto gate.

But guerrilla activity increased in strength. A rebel from Vila, the

German Arsenal Razed

A German arsenal was blown up at Burkickiai and two Jews from the ghetto perished. Kittel thought it was an accident, but it was warfare.

A 16-year-old boy broke into a freight car and stole some hand grenades. He was caught and grilled. "Why did you steal the grenades?" Kittel asked him. "I wanted to throw them at you. You killed my father and mother," the boy replied.

Once when a party was being led out to be shot the victims flung themselves on the German soldiers and throttled seven with their bare hands.

Three hundred partisans in the ghetto obtained arms and the Germans blew up a house in retaliation. In the confusion 300 Jews broke from the ghetto and joined the Lithuanian partisans, Mr. Sutskever among them.

Partisan Sutskever had a tommy gun in his hands, poetry in his mind and Gorky's letter on his heart. And now the pages of the letter covered with writing in faded ink are in Moscow. Gorky wrote of Russia's future, of man's strength. A rebel from Vilna, the ghetto poet and soldier saved this letter as a banner of humanity and culture.

Article published April 14, 1944 in *The New York Times*

THE BIG RAID

THE battle scarred unit of the U.P.O. which arrived at Narocz scarcely managed to heal the sore feet they had suffered from the dangerous 180 kilometer march from Vilna to Narocz. They had scarcely managed to put up their temporary huts constructed from intertwined branches—when the reconnaisance brought the news from headquarters that a large detachment of enemy soldiers had taken possession of the railroad station at Kobilnik. The news was confirmed by other partisan units. It was clear that a large-scale raid was in the offing. Many raids had taken place in the forests of Narocz before and the veteran partisans knew the feel of them. But for the Vilna newcomers a raid or blockade in the forests was a new experience.

The commander of the task force, Boris Greineman, contacted headquarters and was told that the situation was grave. Intelligence units estimated that 30 to 40 thousand German soldiers and their collaborators were getting ready for a large scale raid or maybe a blockade of their region.

Greineman was told that his unit was assigned the special mission to evacuate their base and transfer the seriously wounded of all surrounding camp units to "America."

What was this "America"? It was a tremendous island surrounded on three sides by tall grass, trees, countless thick bushes and swampy footpaths. On the fourth side there was the magnificent blue water of Lake Narocz. In pre-war times tourists came to sail in gondolas there. Since it was considered a far-away and secure place, it was called "America."

The regular, well-armed partisans evacuated the forest shortly before the aggressors gathered their forces to comb the forest. The masses of Jews who did not belong to any combat unit suffered casualties. They were open to attack. Seventy were killed in action.

The partisans divided themselves up into small groups. They hid among the tall swamp grasses and bushes. This time the Germans also forced their way through the lake region and combed the island in small groups. They kept on shooting to the right and to the left. They did not catch sight of a single partisan and they were probably glad of it. Otherwise it might have proven fatal to individual soldiers. They were also unaware that a great number of unarmed people were there who only had a few weapons at hand.

The entire raid was favorable for the "Americans." The one exception was Lieutenant Lisicki who was brought with the badly wounded. Lisicki peeked through the tall grass and saw a detachment of six German soldiers coming in his direction. Fearing that he would fall into their hands alive, he fired a bullet through his own neck. The Germans thought it was one of their own number who fired the shot and they passed the mortally wounded Lisicki without taking notice of him. After a few days of intense suffering, Lisicki died.

Yurgis and his brigade weathered the bitter battles and arrived at the Rudnicki wilderness where he had to organize his own base of operations.

My nearest and dearest friends fell in the bitter campaigns led by Yurgis: Joseph Glazman, Liowa Ziskowicz, Moshe Brause, Miriam Bernstein, Michal Kowner and many others.

Within a few days the partisan units began to return to their bases in the forests. These bases had been burned to the ground. This act of savagery later produced fresh contingents of partisans who were appalled by the barbarism practiced upon the innocent peasant population.

After the raid the ranks of the partisan movement were greatly strengthened to the extent that the Germans lost the courage to spring a new raid on the forest. On the contrary, in the surrounding garrisons the German military forces dug into their bunkers and feared any movement of the partisans as they came out into the open.

When Yurgis transfered from the Narocz to the Rudnicki forest, the field commander, Kazimir, replaced him in Narocz. He had come from the neighgboring Kazan forest. When homeless Jews got wind of the Narocz base, they tried to make contact. Jews who belonged to other combat groups wanted to join him also, because he had a good reputation and he had enough weapons. In addition, the Lithuanian high command in Moscow gave him supplementary weapons. But at that time, Kazimir did not accept new recruits.

In the meantime, the Jews who did not belong to any combat group were between the devil and the deep blue sea. They subsisted on that which the regular partisans could spare from their own provisions. Others established primitive shoemaking or tailoring stands, etc. and served the regular partisans who paid them in products.

After all the units returned from the Narocz forest. Brigadier commander Markow empowered the Jewish commander Boris Greineman, to have his task forces designate a base, 10 kilometers from headquarters and establish there work benches for tailors, shoemakers and leatherworkers. A bakery was to be set up to service all the partisans in the surrounding areas.

The Jewish partisans of the task force were highly satisfied with these new productive duties assigned to them.

In this corner of the wilderness they began to set up new dwellings and work benches with the thought that they would withstand all the elements not only during the autumn, but also during the winter of 1944.

That really happened. The task force provided everything necessary for the partisans in combat. These in turn were able to keep body and soul together and share their provisions with the Jewish masses who did not belong to any combat group.

This went on until the partisans really became a mighty force and had enough weapons. Then, all the men and women capable of bearing arms, were enrolled in various regular partisan units and they fought side by side with partisans of all other nationalities.

Later on, the partisans Suckewer and Kaczerginski were given permission to write the chronological history of the partisan activities in the Narocz forest.

The Jewish writers of the Soviet Union requested that the poet Abraham Suckewer and his wife, Freidel, be brought to Moscow. They were soon brought by airplane. Suckewer was the first delegate of the U.P.O. from the other side of the front.

Suckewer lucidly described the vital work of the partisans and he faithfully recorded the events of the Vilna ghetto and the U.P.O.

German SS in pursuit of partisans

Pol Bagranski

Dr. Leon Bernstein

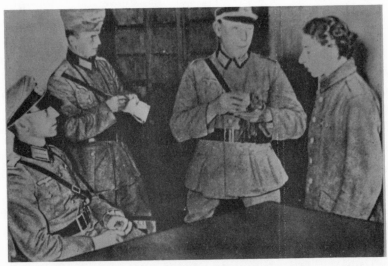

Beila Gelblath—a girl partisan dressed in Polish military uniform was caught by Gestapo. She is interrogated before her doom.

MY WORK AT THE BRIGADE STAFF

AFTER spending a few days with my Vilna friends in one detachment, I was summoned by the brigade commander Yurgis. He was the chief of the Lithuanian brigade. The Russian section had its own commander.

Yurgis told me that I had been transferred to him and that my assignment was to run a printing plant in the forest. The plant did not exist yet and had to be created. He told me that aside from himself and the brigade commissar, Gabris, I would take orders from no one. From now on I would work for the high command.

I was shown by the officer in charge the space on which I was to sleep, in the headquarters bunker, and I was to have the same menu as the headquarters staff. I freed myself of these two privileges and had my own way.

"Yurgis" was a pseudonym. His real name was Henech Ziman, and he was a Jew. He did not reveal this in the forest and passed for a real Lithuanian. Apparently, he thought that this would be best. Before the war, he had been a teacher of the Lithuanian language in the Sholom Aleichem Gymnasium at Kovno. In the years 1940-41, he was editor-in-chief of the communist daily in Kovno, *Tiessa* (Truth). He retreated with the Red Army, and in the middle of 1943 he was parachuted from a Soviet plane into White Russia. In the first days of November 1943, he came to the forests of Lithuania with a unit of paratroopers, which included some former U.P.O. fighters.

The transfer to the new place meant a great improvement in my living conditions. We were still "green" in the forests. Hunger and cold were ever present. A shortage of weapons and unfamiliarity with the outdoor way of life afflicted the Jewish partisans at first. It was as though they had come half way around the globe.

At the post, there were partisans who had lived in the forests for a long time. Here there were enough arms for everyone and more than enough food. Sure enough, I began to still the hunger of my Vilna friends, bringing them small quantities of food. Needless to say, I was not supposed to do this for each base was a kingdom unto itself. In due time, the Jewish units became experts at foraging for themselves and the non-Jews began to envy them. It was not only in the actions to get food that the Jews showed heroism and courage. They excelled in the diversionary military activities, too.

The Jewish partisans in the woods were greatly excited when American condensed milk was dropped to them by Soviet pilots using American stub-winged planes. The instructions on how to use the contents were printed in many languages and also in Hebrew! Another highlight of our ghetto and forest life was the comforting news that came to our shattered people from that part of Jewry which still lived somewhere in freedom.

After we had taken root in the forest, we brought part of our printing plant which had been left behind in the city. We began to issue anew our weekly, *Za Wolnosc* (For Freedom) in Polish and *Kova* (Battle) in Lithuanian, as well as many proclamations in various languages, including German.

I then recommended to headquarters, which was composed of parachutists who had been dropped from Soviet planes, that in honor of the Allied invasion of France, we should put out a proclamation in German. They agreed to this and ordered me to take care of it. For this purpose I summoned two partisans, Dr. Leon Bernstein and Paul Bagrianski to the headquarters, where I kept the press. They knew German perfectly and could help write the text. They came from the units a few kilometers away.

The document was excellent. It contained a safe passage form, which guaranteed to any deserters a cordial reception by the partisans. The results were fairly good. Many former Soviet soldiers in German uniform now deserted and came over to the partisans. Even when Vilna was recaptured and masses of German troops were taken prisoner, many of them had this proclamation on them, and used it as evidence that they were deliberately holding back instead of fighting. Incidentally, this was true. They also claimed that they simply could not find a way to reach the partisans to surrender. This was probably also partly true.

Later on, as the front moved toward the Lithuanian border, a small press was dropped from a Soviet plane to us. It was a miniature flat press, and looked good, but I could not use it because of its poor construction. I therefore used only the press that we had brought along.

At first, Yurgis was editor of the forest newspaper. Then he gave the job to the radio-transmitter, a former teacher, Vitas. Later, when Margis (his real name was Markowicz), came over to the forest, he became editor of the publication.

One thing was clear: our work was not in vain. We could tell by the German reaction to our proclamations. Throughout the entire Rudnicki forest district, the Germans put up warnings not to listen to the announcements of the bandits (that is what they called the partisans) because, in addition to it being all lies, the commissar is a Jew and the head of the printing plant is a Jew. The Germans offered a reward of 100,000 Reichsmarks for either of these two heads. The Germans knew very well what we were doing, as they had their spies who posed as partisans and run away, whenever they had a chance, to report to their bosses, the Germans. More than one was caught and paid for it with his life.

The work did not cease for a minute. Our proclamations used to cover kilometer after kilometer. The best man in this operation was the group commander Yitzhak Schwarc, who belonged to one of the Jewish partisan units.

*   *   *

Once, as I was setting in type a story about a battle that had erupted in the Rudnicki forest, Sonia Madejsker burst in on me. We embraced and she told me that she had just come from Vilna; after some conferences with the top brigade commanders, she would go back to the city. Incidentally, the story I was setting concerned my good friend the Jewish partisan Motel Gopstein, who had been with a group on a patrtisan mission to blow up an enemy train. Seeing he was critically wounded and that he was in a trap, he shot himself in the head rather than be taken prisoner.

In May 1944, a bitter fight broke out when the Gestapo came to the house at Zarecza 3, a partisan stronghold. Sonia's underground co-worker, a Lithuanian named Julian Jankaus as, was killed as he tried to shoot his way free through the window. Sonia herself was badly wounded and she died therea in the Lukiszki prison hospital.

Montage of our clandestine publications in Polish, Lithuanian and German

THE PARACHUTE DROPS

ONE day our staff got word by radio that arms and munitions would be dropped by parachute at a pre-arranged time. The drop landed some distance from the target area and, since our forces were spread out over a large area, we could not maintain proper control over the region. When the arms and ammunition landed near the more densely populated peasant villages, the peasants plundered the sacks. We learned later that the peasants mistook the rectangular shaped yellow sticks of dynamite for soap and took much of it home.

The partisans managed to recover only a small part of the arms and the "soap." This angered Moscow and, for a long time afterward, no further shipments were dropped in our area mainly because they felt that we were too weak to prevent the material from falling into the hands of the Germans or of the peasants.

The staff was in a very unpleasant situation. They felt that they had lost much of their prestige. Later on, they began to secure munitions themselves to fill their needs. This was apparently the aim of Moscow—defeat the Nazis and take their weapons—and that is what we had to do.

When the Soviet forces broke through the German lines around Smolensk, Orsha and other places, Russian planes began to appear more often. They dropped weapons, ammunition, medical supplies and even doctors.

In time we became a major force in the woods and we had enough manpower to occupy the entire area to protect the sacks that were dropped and make sure that they were recovered only by partisans. The peasants in the region were warned under penalty of death not to venture to the edge of the partisan zone unless they wanted to join the partisans. If any of them even took the pieces of "soap" again they were in for trouble.

Often I would be in the group who knew in advance about the scheduled airplane arrivals because I would be assigned to the unit which had to carry wood to a large clearing to prepare it for the parachute drop later in the evening. After dark we would make a large bonfire to guide the pilots. The sacks would be dropped when the brigadier signaled with a colored flare. In other areas in White Russia, the planes would actually land since the partisans were in complete control of the region. After unloading the cargo, the planes would take the wounded to the other side of the lines.

Our task was to gather the large heavy sacks, load them on wagons and bring them to the base where they would be distributed to the various units who would come to pick them up according to schedule.

During one such operation in the pitch dark I found one sack that had been torn in the fall. When I looked at the contents I was surprised to see that the entire sack was full of German money (presumably counterfeit). When I saw that I could not budge the sack, I took one bundle of money and showed it to Brigadier Yurgis. He told me with a smile that he was looking for that particular sack. He sent me back with some men, who divided the sack into four parts and carried it off like a corpse.

The front was coming continuously closer and it was urgent that we distribute the money in order to add to the confusion. Only then did I understand the saying: "*U nas wsio yestz.*" (We have everything . . .).

* * *

Another time, a doctor nearly fell on my head—a Russian surgeon. We were all standing around the place where a parachute jump was scheduled. Just where I was standing, this doctor parachuted down.

After we exchanged passwords to establish our identity, he put away the revolver he had aimed at me. He placed it in his holster. Then he took out a bottle of vodka and offered me some of it.

I led him some 200 meters along the road to the center

where five fires were burning, which were the signals to the airplanes. He went in to report to the commander.

During our short walk he told me that before he parachuted into the Rudnicki forest, his plane flew over Bialystok (which is half-way between Vilna and Warsaw). They carried out a successful bombing mission.

The doctor told me that he could not remain with us. His mission was to carry out a partisan raid along the old Polish-German border. The next morning he left with a group of diversionary specialists.

*   *   *

On another occasion, in the middle of a fiery circle, which marked the landing place for parachutists, a slender, blonde woman came down. Wearing military boots and carrying ammunition, she landed right on her feet and looked as if she had dropped from a few stairs.

After she looked around, she ran over to some nearby lady partisans and began to kiss them. She recognized them as her former classmates in the Polish-Jewish Epstein Gymnasium in Vilna and she conversed with them in Polish and in Yiddish.

There were two Russians standing near me and they asked me what was the idea of the lady partisans speaking Yiddish among themselves. I explained to them that they studied together and knew each other well.

A short time later, an officer approached and said half in earnest, that it was customary to report to one's superior officers first, and then she was free to follow her fancy.

*   *   *

Gesie Glezer (Albina) was a woman in the middle forties. She was one of the leading communists in pre-war Lithuania, with a jail sentence behind her. She retreated with the Soviet army and later parachuted into our region. She was assigned to "party duty" in Lithuania.

Until the time for action would come, she was stationed

on our base and did not attend to her own assignment, for some reasons unknown to me.

I just knew one thing: that she did not agree with Yurgis and Gabris.

I had the impression that a feeling of nationalism awoke in her. and she saw things differently now, than at the time she parachuted down in the forest. That is why she criticized the commanders in their private conversations.

For a period of time she worked with the underground in Vilna. At one of the contacts she had to make at the entrance of a city park in Zakret, she was surrounded by the Gestapo. Realizing that her number was up, she opened fire on the Gestapo, wounding a few of them. Since she saw no chance of escape, she shot herself.

*   *   *

The majority of the parachutists were with me on my base, since they belonged to the High Command of the forest. As the occasion demanded, they were sent to take command over other local partisan groups. Thus it came about that the parachutists Didialis (h:s real name was Isser Schmidt), the telegraphist Leon Sendorov.icz, and many others were with us for a time.

The arrival of people from the "other world" was always a pleasant experience for us. All were part of our partisan ranks.

A Nazi strongman is herded to the rear of the front.

Father Daniel
(Shmuel Rufeisen)

Ruth Ben-David
(Madeleine Perrie)

SHMUEL RUFEISEN (OSWALD)

THE town of Mir in the Vilna District achieved fame throughout the Jewish world mainly for the Mir Yeshiva located there. It turned out many great rabbis, not one of whom still occupies a pulpit anywhere in the world. However, a yeshiva of the same name exists today in New York.

The German troops occupied the town of Mir a few days after they took Vilna in June 1941. The Jews were immediately driven out into a ghetto occupying a number of small side streets in the town.

One cold evening in November of that year, a sharp pounding on the floor was heard by the inhabitants of one of the houses of the ghetto. When the door was opened, a fully armed police officer, in a black uniform with a Red swastika, walked in and demanded that all members of the household show their identification cards. He examined each one and returned it. When he came to the card of Ber Reznik, however, the officer turned to him and said: "I see that the photograph shows you smirking. No matter, you won't be smirking very long. Come with me." The officer led the frightened young man out of the house.

When they were some distance from the ghetto, the officer took the young man aside and said: "I'm Shmuel Rufeisen from Vilna." Reznik nearly fainted when he heard this. He got up the nerve to look at the officer squarely in the face and recognized his old friend from the Vilna days.

Rufeisen then told him how he had made his way to Mir in the German uniform. While going along a road he had found an identification card of a German Pole named Yuzef Oswald. Since he came from western Galicia, he knew German fluently as well as Polish and it was not difficult, therefore, to assume the identity of the German Pole.

On arriving in Mir, he reported to the authorities as a German who was wandering around looking for his parents who were supposed to be in that area at the outbreak of the war. He told the authorities that he was unable to find his parents and was ready to work in Mir.

He immediately got a job as a watchman in the local school. However, when they learned that he was fluent in German and Polish, they appointed him as an interpreter for the police.

Oswald, as he then called himself, became very friendly with the police chief who appointed him as his aide.

As soon as he was named to his new post, he began to seek out ways and means of helping the local Jews, but he needed one of them whom he could trust to confide in and share his secret. That was why he spent time carefully examining the identification papers—to find someone whom he had known. Otherwise his story would never be believed. He said that he was glad that he found Reznik.

The two of them immediately began to make plans to help the Jews in the Mir ghetto. The next day they met again but this time Reznik brought his friend, Salomon Chackes. Only these two knew who the police officer Oswald really was.

In order to operate more effectively, Reznik and Chackes decided to confide in the head of the Judenrat, a man named Shulman. They told him that they got to know a Pole who was posing as a German Pole; that he occupied an important post in Mir and that he was ready to help the Jews.

Shulman did not believe their story. A few days later, however, Reznik and Chackes again came to Shulman and reported to him that their contact had informed them that in a few days the Jews were going to be removed from the ghetto and crowded into the Mirski farm on the outskirts of the town and that the Jews would be allowed to take only a small part of their belongings.

This sounded incredible to Shulman but he decided to pass on the information to the Jews, telling them that it was "advisable" to bring some of their belongings to the designated place, since it was possible that they would be forced to move there later. The Jews knew the meaning of the word "advisable" and they brought part of their belongings to the deserted Mirski farm in advance.

When they were ordered by the authorities a few days later to move, most of them already had brought part of their things to the new place and were able to move with their remaining possessions. The incident, naturally, raised the prestige of both Reznik and Chackes among the members of the Judenrat. The entire operation went along smoothly because, in the meantime, Oswald was promoted to the post of commandant of the Mir police and he was in charge of moving the Jews out of the ghetto.

In the surrounding towns, the Nazis began wiping out the Jewish population and it was soon clear that the Jews of Mir would suffer the same fate. The young people began to rebel and made up their minds that it would not happen without a struggle.

Oswald encouraged them in their resistance and even helped them out with weapons and ammunition which he took from the police arsenal. He also helped them organize. A staff was soon assembled which was headed by Oswald, Reznik and Chackes who spent nights teaching the youth how to handle arms. The Judenrat knew nothing about this.

The Germans, meanwhile, received reliable information that partisans were operating in the area of Mir. Oswald planned that the youth would form small groups and leave the ghetto to join the partisans. Before the plans could be carried out, an order was received in Mir that the town's Jews should be massacred on August 13, 1942.

There was no time to lose. Oswald called together his aides and told them that four days before the planned massacre, on August 9, he would take the entire local police force into the woods on the pretext of fighting partisans. At that time, the entire Jewish underground would leave the ghetto with their arms and head for the woods in another direction from where he would be with the police. Some 300 young persons, all armed, left the ghetto and reached the woods safely since the town was completely without police.

After Oswald returned with the police from his search for partisans in the woods, the chief commandant Hein told him that about 300 Jews fled from the ghetto to join the partisans in the woods. Hein was quite put out but he sought to suppress the entire incident because it reflected on him. Nevertheless, he ordered an investigation.

Someone informed Hein that none other than his own right-hand man, Oswald, was behind the escape of the Jews. At first he took it as a joke, but he later decided to look into it and called Oswald in, and told him that someone had accused him of being behind the arming of the Jews and making possible their escape to the woods. He told him he knew that he had a good heart and wanted to help people but how could he possibly give them arms if he knew that they would eventually be used against Hein and Oswald himself? "Why did you do such a thing?" he demanded.

"Because I am a Jew," was Oswald's immediate reply. "I did what I had to do and I am not afraid to die for it."

Hein was stunned by the confession. When he recovered his senses he ordered Oswald placed under arrest. For Hein this was a horrible tragedy—his own right-hand man a Jew, and a Jew who is ready to die for his people.

Oswald's former subordinates were shocked at the disclosure. The prisoner was able to take advantage of the fact that his guards had "forgotten" that he was their prisoner and not their commander. He was able to sneak out of the police station and head straight for the woods.

On the way to the woods he sought refuge in a monastery where he was welcomed. They dressed him as a woman and he was able to stay there for three months. He then left the monastery to actively join in the fight against the Nazis. When he reached the woods, however, he was picked up by the partisans who recognized him only as the police commandant of Mir. They arrested him, tried him and sentenced him to death. When the Jewish partisans heard about it, they rushed to the partisan leadership and told them all that Oswald had done and who he really was and he was immediately released. He then resumed his fight against the Nazis.

I first heard this unbelievable story from a number of partisans when I was in the woods some 150 kilometers from Mir. Oswald and his fellow partisans also operated in the Narocz forests where we had a number of U.P.O. fighters who left the Vilna ghetto with the first group under Joseph Glazman.

Later, when Vilna was liberated, I had the opportunity to meet Oswald, a young blonde fellow, and I regarded him as a hero.

The war left him, however, broken in heart and spirit. Seeking an answer to all the suffering that he had experienced, he converted to Christianity. He came to this decision as a result of his lengthy stay in the monastery where he studied the New Testament.

What also apparently played a role in his decision to convert to Catholicism was the factual or rumored report that a Jewish wagon driver by the name of Stanislavski who had worked as forced laborer in the police station, was believed to be the one who gave him away to Hein. Stanislavski, according to the rumor, betrayed Oswald in an effort to save himself from a death sentence. Stanislavski was executed anyway and I could never find out if he was really the one who betrayed Oswald.

After the war, Oswald studied for a number of years in a seminary in Cracow and was ordained a priest at which time he took the name, Father Daniel. First he served in the priesthood in a number of towns in Poland and later went to Rome. Finally, with the blessing of the Pope, he emigrated to Israel where he joined a Carmelite monastery.

He attracted considerable attention in Israel when he demanded the right not only to settle there, but to become a citizen under the Law of the Return which gives that right to every Jew. The Israeli authorities, however, decided that he did not have the automatic right of citizenship since he was no longer a Jew. The courts later reversed the decision and gave him the right of automatic citizenship, since he was born a Jew.

*　　*　　*

In contrast to the story of Shmuel Rufeisen, the Jew who came out of the war with the decision to convert to Catholicism and become a priest, was the case of a French Christian woman, Madeleine Perrie who converted to Judaism as a result of her wartime experiences.

She lived a quiet life in a French town where she attended the local gymnasium and later the university where she majored in history and geography. She was married to a devout Catholic man and they had a child.

When the war broke out and France was occupied by the Germans, she became a fearless partisan in the French Maquis where she volunteered for many dangerous missions. It was in the Maquis that she got to know Jews. She was able to observe at close hand the bestiality of the Nazis and the heroism of the Jewish partisans. When the war ended she began studying and she converted to Judaism in 1951. She adopted the name Ruth Ben-David.

Like Oswald, Ruth Ben-David was the cause of a major controversy when she emigrated to Israel. Israelis were stunned to read in the papers that she was engaged to none other than Rabbi Amram Blau, the leader of the ultra-orthodox Naturei Karta and that they were soon to be married. Many of his followers felt that the 70-year-old rabbi should not marry a woman who was 30 years younger and that there were more suitable ladies he could marry. He won out, however, and he was supported by many who felt that her devotion to Judaism and her courageous deeds in wartime made her a suitable match for the rabbi. Not only the Israeli press, but newspapers throughout the world reported on this controversy. Articles appeared in the New York Times, the London Times, Le Figaro of Paris and other papers. Rabbi Blau was forced to leave Jerusalem after his marriage and live in another town.

When Ruth was asked why she took such a step, to leave her family and wealth to marry the poor old rabbi, her face would light up and she would say that for the first time in her life she now found contentment. She was overjoyed that she found the one, true faith and she was thankful that God had mercy on her and in spite of all obstacles she was able to become the wife of such a pious man as Rabbi Amram Blau.

Both Oswald and Ruth were fighters against Nazism. Both were war heroes. But they came to opposite conclusions in their choice of faith.

Destruction of eight 150,000-volt high-tension pylons on the Paris-Hendaye line on Hitler's birthday, 20 April 1944, in anticipation of D day.

Destroyed railroad tracks in Nazi Europe.

„1 " *Август* 194 4 г.

№ *3/0/2*

СПРАВКА

Дана настоящая *Чайковскому Ив. Ант*

в том, что он действительно состоял в партизан-
ском отряде *П Четвый* бригады „*Железняк*"

с „*4* " *Июля* 1943 г. по „*1* " *Август* 194 4 г.

в должности *рядовой*

Просьба местным органам власти оказать

товар. *Чайковскому* содействие в

устройстве жажительсто и работу.

Начальник Отдела Кадров
Белорусского Штаба Партизанского
Движения

Certificate that Eban Cikowski was a partisan in White Russia.

PONARY

Niema dzisiaj na świecie ludzi, dla których straszliwe mordy masowe niewinnej ludności cywilnej dokonywane przez katów faszystowskich we wszystkich krajach okupowanych, stanowiłyby jakąkolwiek rewelację. Dużo materiałów zebrano o zbrodniach, popełnionych przez faszystowskich zbirów. Dla każdego stało się jasnym, że wojna, którą prowadzi Czerwona Armia i państwa Sprzymierzone z Niemcami jest walką między prawdą a kłamstwem, między wolnością a niewolą, między duchem tworzenia a duchem, który pustoszy i niszczy. Bezbrzeżne morze łez i krwi, niezliczone bratnie mogiły w bestialski sposób zamęczonych starców kobiet i dzieci, brutalny sadystyczny gwałt na każdym kroku — to są obrazy które ilustrują krwawy ustrój barbarzyńców.

Niezliczone są miejsca zbrodni i mordów znajdujące się wszędzie, gdzie tylko panował lub jeszcze panuje krwawy reżim hitlerowski. Piękna, znajdująca się obok Wilna letniskowa miejscowość Ponary stała się jednym z wielu miejsc straszliwych mordów masowych, dokonanych przez gestapowskich przestępców. Dziesiątki tysięcy niewinnych ofiar z pośród różnych narodowości znalazły swoje miejsce w ciemnych ponarskich mogiłach

Może się wydawać, że koszmar lasów ponarskich jest epickim krwawem o dramatu historycznego. Zimny, wyrachowany sadyzm niemiecki nie ma jednak granic. Dwunożne zwierzęta faszystowskie nie dają spokoju swoim ofiarom nawet w mogile. Grobowy spokój w bestialski sposób zostaje naruszony przez nowoczesnych Hunnów. Zawdzięczając bohaterskiej ucieczce zatrudnionych w Ponarach ludzi, którzy pracowali przy spalaniu trupów, mamy możność opublikowania dokładnych wiadomości, dotyczących ponarskich zbrodni. Przeprowadziliśmy, między innymi, rozmowy z następującymi ludźmi, którzy uciekli z Ponar:

1. Gol Sz.; ostatni adres wileński — ul. Bosaczkowa 3—15.
2. Potanin Konstanty — jeniec wojenny z Kazania.
3. Zinin Piotr – jeniec wojenny Krasnaja Podgora, Mordawska ASSR.
4. Owsiejczyk L. z Oszmiany.
5. Moskowski Z. jeniec wojenny z Moskwy.
6. Bielic J. z Wilna – ostatni adres, ul. Algirdo (d. Piłsudskiego) 55—9.

Z opowiadań powyższych osób, możemy zestawić następujący obraz ich przeżyć:

Władzy hitlerowscy, widząc swe rychłe i ostateczne załamanie się, postanowili prze

opuszczane tereno... ...stkie ślad... ...owych zbrodni. ...owód rze... ...ny ich krwawego panowania. W tym celu gestapo wileńskie, przy pomocy sprowadzonych gwałtem ludzi, jeszcze w końcu 1943 r. rozpoczęło palenie trupów, znajdujących się w grobach ponarskich. Przy tych pracach byli zatrudnieni więźniowie gestapa jak również sprowadzeni jeńcy wojenni. Gestapowcy w straszliwy sposób znęcali się nad tymi ludźmi. Chorych, pod płaszczykiem odsyłania do szpitala, rozstrzeliwali. Na nogi nakładano im kajdany, a mieszkać musieli w specjalnie dla nich wyrytych podziemnych lochach. Praca tych ludzi odbywała się w następujący sposób: Po wykopaniu trupów (Niemcy zabraniają używać wyrażenia trup, a zamieniają słowem "figura") zdejmowano z nich wszystkie cenne rzeczy, które jeszcze zostały jak to złote zęby, obrączki i t.d. Trupy przenoszono na miejsce specjalnie rezłożonych ognisk, rozmiaru 8 m. szerokości, 18 m. długości. Trupy układało się rzędami. W każdym rzędzie znajdowało się od 200 do 250 trupów. W ten sposób powstawała wysoka wieża, składająca się nieraz więcej z 3500 trupów. Stos podpalało się benzolem i włożonymi rakietami świetlnymi. Spalenie tego ogniska trwało od 4 do 7

dni, zależnie od wiatru. Popiół, po spaleniu trupów, mieszano z piaskiem, i wsypywane do wolnych już od trupów jam.

Pierwszy grób, znajdujący się w odległości 150 m. od szosy grodzieńskiej zawierał 9 tysięcy trupów. Trupy były ułożone warstwami i zalane cementem. W bli... gile znajdowały się, trupy jeńców wojennych, Żydów i około 500 księży w ubraniu.

U przewidzianej ilości trupów można było skonstantować że w kark. Układanie trupów, jak również miejsce strzału, niezupełnie masowania porównanie zbrodnię katyńską, zawierające analogiczne cechy charakterystyczne.

Oto jeszcze jeden dowód do magościnnej kampanii morderców hitlerowskich zmierzającej do faktyczego obrócenia krwawej tragedii katyńskiej.

W drugim grobie znajdowało się około 8 tysięcy trupów wyłącznie mężczyzn. Wśród nich pewna część jeńców wojennych w ubraniu.

W trzecim grobie znajdowało się 10400 trupów mężczyzn, kobiet i dzieci. Strzał — przeważnie w kark. Prawie u wszystkich dzieci jak również u części dorosłych nie stwierdzono żadnego strzału. Widocznie zostali zasypani żywcem.

Czwarty grób, największy –

PONARY

TEN kilometers from Vilna there was a place called Ponary. Before the outbreak of the war, young people used to come to this spot to spend the summer days in the beautiful surroundings. This region was blooming with a great variety of vegetation. Winter time, it was perfect for skiing and sledding down the numerous large and small hills.

During the one year Soviet forces were in Vilna, they dug large holes in which they planned to install gasoline tanks. The holes were twenty meters in diameter and six meters deep.

However, when the black flag with the skull, the emblem of the Gestapo, appeared in our city of Vilna, Ponary was designated as an extermination center for the region.

During the first year and a half of German occupation, twenty thousand persons were killed there. They were of various nationalities. Besides the Jews and local residents, victims were brought from White Russia and other places.

In the next year and a half, 80,000 more were killed at Ponary. The greatest percentage was Jewish, but there were also thousands of Poles, Russians, Lithuanians, gypsies, and others.

When the Soviet army cracked the front and pushed forward rapidly, a special officer came from Berlin with directives to wipe out the evidence at Ponary. This was the new Berlin "line." Such special emissaries were sent to countless Ponarys.

* * *

Early in 1944 a group of 40 Jews, including four women (later this was increased to 80 people) was selected and ordered to report for a secret assignment. They were first told to build a bunker in an already prepared hole. They worked at it for three weeks until it was completed. Each day they were marched back to the Lukiszki jail, and in the morning

Joseph Bielic

Shlomo Gol

Dr. Moshe Okuniew

Isaac Schwarc

Ponary before the war. An excursion of a group of Vilna Jewish teachers
in 1927.

they were taken out to work. Then they became permanent inhabitants of the Ponary bunker.

One day an officer told them: "You will be employed at a special government job. You must therefore be chained. Don't ever try to run away from here, because no one has ever escaped from Ponary. The chains will be checked, and if there are signs that the chains are not in order, you will be shot. Do good work. If we see any sabotage, laziness—you will be shot. You must fill every command at once. The chains must clank wherever you go. Remember what I have said."

At Ponary, a special vocabulary was used:

FIGURES—the murdered victims had to be called "figures," nothing else.

UNCOVERERS—these were the workers who dug up the graves. (Working at this were Ozur, Owsaitchik, Sheinuk, the elderly Dogim brothers, Singer, and others).

FIGURE-PULLERS—these used to throw iron hooks into the bodies of the figures and pull them out of the graves to the flat surface. (Workers: Shumelin, Motel Seidel, Motel Goldberg, the younger Itzik Dogim, etc.).

DENTIST—checked the teeth of the figures and pulled out the gold fillings which were given to the Germans. (Abraham Wishaiski, Dogim's brother-in-law, by trade a tailor.)

BONE-GATHERERS—these were four 13-14 year old children who had to gather up loose bones.

CARRIERS—these had to carry away the corpses on heavy wooden stretchers to the burning grounds (Sheindels, Kliatring, Blasser, Yuri Farber, Senin).

BURNING-MASTERS—they would lay the corpses in order, under directives of the German officers, in a pile (Cooperstock, a Warsaw printer, and Motzkin from Swenciany).

FIRE-MASTERS—when the pile of corpses was completed (exactly 3,000 bodies) they would pour oil and gasoline on it and place fire-bombs to light the pyre, watching that every little bit should be burned completely. Shlomo Gol and Eli the Black One.)

PYRE-BUILDERS—they would arrange the pyre so that it would be easier to climb it and place wood and gasoline on the corpses. (Potanin, Moshe Rudenski, Joseph Bielic, Gol and others.)

GOLD-DIGGERS—as the pyre burned down, the gold-diggers would gather up whatever did not burn. They would screen the ashes of the corpses, mixing it with sand so that it would be unrecognizable. The gold reclaimed by the sifting would be given to the Stormtroop leader. (Shepsel Portnoy, Magun, Novogrudski, etc.)

KITCHEN-WORKERS—the only four women, who would cook lunch and wash clothes. (Basya Smukler, Sabina Becker, Gita Blumberg and Sara of Podbrodz.)

That is how work was divided. This was the new kind of occupation that the Hitlerites created in their New Europe. This was the "very important government work" that the Storm troop leader spoke about to each newcomer.

That this work was top secret can be proven by the fact that the entire German guard consisted of officers of the most loyal Nazi stripe, and no ordinary soldiers were permitted to be there.

The officers, too, were like captives, for they were not allowed to leave the precinct of Ponary. However, they enjoyed all luxuries including liquor and women. But when they got tipsy, they would sometimes speak frankly in the presence of the slave laborers, that they did not believe that they themselves would get out alive, and would share the fate of the Jewish slaves.

Occasionally, high ranking visitors would come from the outside: Hingst, Kittel, Murer, Neigebauer, Weiss. They would always leave new instructions. They would always complain that too few "figures" had been burned (that is what they called the martyrs). They would hurry, as they complained that time was

Massacred Jewish People in Ponary.

Killed Soviet War Prisoners in Ponary.

not standing still and the Bolsheviks might make an unexpected attack. After such talk, the officers would increase the terror and the work proceeded at a faster pace. One day, Hingst appeared with his cohorts and addressed all the assembled workers:

"Today is a great holiday for us. Our speed of work is the fastest in the entire Baltic region. With you I acclaim our great achievement. One day you exceeded the norm with over 800 figures. That is truly a victory. Work, mein herrn, like this in the future, and you will be transferred to other places for work." As a token of appreciation, Hingst gave to each slave a gift of two cigarettes.

The officers were also pleased with the accomplishments and they too were rewarded for their efforts with special gifts. But after all this talk, one of the officers could be heard muttering, "All the same—we shall none of us leave this place alive."

Some Jews began to have different thoughts. What they faced, after the "work" was completed, was quite clear. They decided on a risky plan, to dig a tunnel that would lead out of the murder zone. A top secret group of ten, which included Shlomo Gol,* Itzhak Dogim, Joseph Bielic, David Kantorowicz, Kostia Potanin (a non-Jew), Cohen and others worked for three months, night after night, until they finished the tunnel. On Easter night, 1944, they figured that the guard would be in a holiday mood and get drunk. That was when they would try to escape.

The chosen moment was favorable and one after the other, nearly all crawled through the tunnel which ended several yards past the fence around the death camp. But when the last group was about ready to leave the tunnel, a drunken guard awoke and opened fire. Several inmates were killed and others wounded and recaptured. However, about 15 men succeeded in vanishing in the dark of the night.

* * *

*Shlomo Gol was a witness for the U.S.S.R. at the Nuremberg trial. Now he lives in the U.S.A.

Once I was on duty at our base, in charge of the guards inside and outside the base. One of the guards came to tell me that some strange people had come to the far outside guard and said that they were from Ponary. They wanted to speak to the head of partisans. I went to the guard post and met the people there. I interviewed them on the spot, and heard the above. unbelievable tale. I accepted their story, but I could not stand too close to them as their clothing gave off the stench of death. I took them into the base, informing the proper authority, who had them tell the story all over again in detail. They were immediately admitted into the partisan ranks where they had an opportunity, with weapons in hand, to repay their erstwhile murderers.

*　　*　　*

I proposed to the forest editors to publish in our paper the eye-witness reports about the horrors of Ponary, and it was agreed to do so. In front of this story the reader will find a facsimile of the article on Ponary.

The special ladder on which the workers used to carry the "Figures" to the fire.

Ponary "Figures" are carried to the flames.

The official newspaper of the Soviet-Lithuania Republic, *Sovietzkaja Litwa* one day in March 1966, carried a photostat of an official German report from the Vilna Gestapo commandant addressed to the central office in Berlin and to its chief, Heinrich Himmler.

The report is quoted verbatim:

"All the Jews were herded, and those who were still able to work were selected and sent off. The remaining 4,000 were sent to Ponary, where they arrived on April 5, 1943, for 'special' treatment.

"By the action were present Muler, Bormak, Schtuetz, and also Willi and Hock from the Vilna administration. One of the Jews all of a sudden attacked Willi with a knife, and gave him two wounds—one in the head and one in the chest. His life was in danger. He was immediately sent to a hospital in Vilna.

"Fifty other Jews made an attempt to escape and Lithuanian police started to shoot, but several of the policemen were injured."

The report has the signature of Horst Volf, the Gestapo-commissar of the Vilna region.

305

Jews are not aware that they are digging pits for themselves.

Ponary. The bunker and ladder where the corpse-diggers were living. On
this ladder they used to climb up to work. Under the bottom of the wall
they dug a canal and escaped to the nearby woods. Some of them
made it to the partisan lines.

SPIES AT THE BASE

A T the base where the staff headquarters were, a tall, thin man in his early forties, appeared one day. I would notice him walking around day after day and I did not know who he was. Eventually, I found out that he was not a partisan, but a spy who had been dropped in our vicinity and who had to make his way into Kovno where he was to engage in important espionage work against the Germans.

I never managed to speak to him because he kept to himself and had nothing to do with any of the others—with one exception. That was my good friend Gabik Sedlis. Gabik, who was in the Jewish "Revenge" fighter unit, was, like me, transferred at the staff headquarters. He was the son of the well-known Dr. Eliahu Sedlis, who, before the war, was the director of the Jewish Hospital. Gabik was an expert in copying stamps for the U.P.O. and his copies were as good as the originals. Here, however, conditions were different and, while they needed him, they could not avail themselves of his experience. Gabik was, therefore, like all the other partisans and, with his youthful enthusiasm, he participated in all partisan operations.

Gabik would spend hours with the espionage agent, Boris, arguing with him over the theater and other art subjects. Through Gabik I learned who this Boris really was. The spy stayed around the base a number of weeks with apparently nothing to do and I could not understand why he did not proceed on his mission in Kovno. It turned out that his picture on his identity papers was not on the right kind of paper and he was waiting for the arrival of a photographer-parachutist who would prepare a picture on the proper paper. This took time.

Finally, the photographer arrived. A few days later, Boris was escorted to the outskirts of the forest and from there he proceeded to Kovno.

The partisans who accompanied Boris later told me that they carried a radio transmitter for him and, at his direction, they buried it at the edge of the forest where he could later dig it up to transmit information to Moscow. But, a few days later, I saw that Boris was back at the base, hanging around by himself.

I later found out what had happened.

Before the German-Russian war, Boris had been an important personality in the theatrical world in Kovno and was friendly with many Lithuanian Germans who were repatriated to Germany during the period of amity between Hitler and Stalin. When the German armies occupied Lithuania, these same Germans were appointed to key occupation posts in Kovno.

Boris' mission was to come to them in Kovno and tell them that he was won over to Hitler and that, for some time, he was hidden in a village. He was now returning to his friends, the Lithuanian Germans, and wanted to work for them and with them in his field—the theater.

The Germans received him warmly because they were on good terms with him before the Nazi invasion. They would walk arm in arm with him in the corridors of the Kovno Gestapo headquarters where they had considerable authority.

Later, however, he was called to Gestapo headquarters and told that they had investigated his stay in the village where he said he was hidden and that he was now suspected of being a spy.

He was told to undress and to wait for interrogation. While he was waiting, the Gestapo officer left the room and went to the next room. Boris immediately put on his trousers and ran out. None of the sentries stopped him since only a few minutes earlier he had been seen walking arm in arm with the Gestapo officials. They even stood at attention when he passed.

He made it outside of the Gestapo headquarters building and headed straight for the forest in his shirtsleeves in spite of the fact that it was the middle of the fall. He covered the entire distance back to the base without any mishap and once again continued to hang around the area.

*   *   *

Another stranger also made his appearance on the base. About six feet tall, he appeared to be in his late forties, apparently a new partisan. I noticed, however, that he was never sent out on any missions. I could not understand what might have brought such a man to the partisans. He went about wearing a good pair of officers' boots, a leather coat and a Persian lamb fur hat without the usual crease in the middle. To me he looked like a member of the firing squad that would execute victims at the city's Ponary. It was my impression that they would dress like that.

I did not recognize this type and I was naive enough to accept at face value his explanation that he came to fight the Germans.

Among the staff, however, there were experts in the security field and they were better able to evaluate such characters. They immediately suspected him.

One day, as we were sitting by the fire outside, keeping ourselves warm, he asked me where in Vilna I came from. When I told him I was from Stefanska Street, he said he also lived there and, when I told him the exact address, he said that we were neighbors. When I told him I was Kowalski of 17 Stefanska Street, he said that he used to patronize the haberdashery store which we had and he described exactly my mother and the saleslady. We soon were talking to each other like close friends.

Even after my first meeting with him—he told me his name was Waclaw—I could not understand what brought him to the partisans. He did not say that he was a fanatical communist. His age ruled out the possibility of his being drafted by the Germans. One could readily see that he was not suffering from malnutrition and he certainly did not lack clothing. So the mystery remained. What had brought him to the partisans?

The partisans were recruited mainly from Jews; Soviet peoples who were in captivity had tasted Nazi brutalities and had succeeded in fleeing from their German oppressors; young peasants who were to be sent to slave labor camps in Germany or pressed into military service where they would have a slow but sure death; or from former communists who came to us out of deep conviction.

Waclaw, however, did not impress me as being among any of these categories. But since my task was operating the printing press and I was not supposed to poke my nose into other matters, I accepted what he told me at face value. So, like Boris, Waclaw used to hang around the base.

One day, an order was posted naming Waclaw as "Starshina," the person charged with responsibility for the economic functioning of the base. I immediately congratulated him and noticed that he seemed quite satisfied with the appointment.

A few days later, however, Waclaw rushed over to me and told me that he was called into the staff bunker and ordered to surrender his revolver which he had brought with him. They also searched him and found a smaller gun hidden up his sleeve. He seemed quite nervous and he did not know why he had hidden the second weapon. Only then did it become clear to me who my former neighbor really was.

The following day I learned that Waclaw had been sentenced to death by a court martial and that the sentence was immediately carried out.

* * *

In those days I used to leave the base whenever I had the chance, to visit with friends from the ghetto days who were now serving in the Jewish "Revenge" partisan unit. On one such walk through the woods I recognized from a distance a fellow by the name of Goldin whom I remembered as a schoolmate from my younger days. When I tried to approach him, he backed off and shouted to me: "I don't like it here. I'm leaving the woods."

By the time I made out what he said, he was gone. I did not attach too much importance to the incident and thought to myself: "Whether he likes it or not, the Germans have made partisans of us all."

A few days later, when I again visited the Jewish unit, I heard that Goldin had been spotted around the area where he was not supposed to be and that he disappeared when they wanted to question him. He was, in fact, spying for the Gestapo.

This I could never understand—a Jew like myself and the others, in the forest among Jewish partisans, who would prefer to trust the Gestapo rather than fight to the end, weapon in hand. But, apparently, there were also such people.

One day my friend Gabik Sedlis came over to tell me that he was going on a mission to Vilna. This surprised me. I knew that generally the only partisans sent into the city were either girls who would go on reconnaissance missions or large, well-armed groups, not all of whom would return. Some time later Sedlis returned and I was glad to see him alive.

He later told me that one of his tasks was to finger Goldin and to render him harmless.

In the city at Zawalna precinct, we had planted a partisan in the Lithuanian police who would, incidentally, cover us when we emerged from the sewer enroute from the ghetto to the city. Gabik pointed out Goldin to the policeman who immediately shot him dead in the street.

The policeman then reported to his headquarters that he had just shot a Jew who was without his yellow star. Naturally he could not possibly have known what documents Goldin had in his pocket where they later probably found a Gestapo card.

His colleagues at the headquarters congratulated him for his work and he soon acquired a reputation among his fellow officers. If all police were like him, the Vilna Jews would have been considerably better off.

*   *   *

In another incident, the partisans who went to a village some miles from our base, found a man there who said that he had for some time been seeking to make contact with the partisans. They took him along and, on the way he told them that he was a colonel from Siberia who was dropped by parachute some time before but was blown off his target by the wind. He said that he had been hiding in the nearby villages.

When he was brought to the base he repeated his story. This was immediately checked by radio with the partisan staff headquarters in Moscow. A few days later a reply came by radio that no such partisan was dropped by parachute. The command was instructed to bring him alive to the Russian side of the front.

The "officer" was kept among us for a number of weeks and he was allowed to participate in a few of the less important missions. Those accompanying him, however, were under orders to keep a close watch over him and that, if a situation should develop in which there was danger that not all the parti- sans would return, they should not hesitate to shoot him. He was allowed to take part in these unimportant missions in order to allay any fears he might have that he was under suspicion.

He suspected nothing, therefore, when they later took him to the Narocz forests where, in the beginning of 1944, Soviet planes would land almost daily in the fields. He was then brought over to the other side of the front.

I later learned that he really was a Soviet colonel who, after being captured by the Germans, went over to the Nazi side. He was trained in a special espionage school in Germany and sent to spy at the headquarters of the Lithuanian brigade. Un- doubtedly, he was able to furnish the Soviet authorities with considerable valuable information after he was recaptured.

Evidently, the "efficient" Gestapo and its espionage unit were not clever enough to train their agents how to deal with the partisans. They were naive enough to believe that the agent's story would be accepted without checking or they just did not know that the Lithuanian brigade had radio contact with Moscow.

I had occasion to speak with him a number of times. While

I may not have suspected that he was a Gestapo agent at first, I detected in his manner that something was wrong. If I finally suspected him, it was no wonder that our security people caught on to him in due time.

These were only four examples of espionage activity on behalf of both sides. Some were on the side of the devil. Others fought the devil.

Ejfe

A group of Jewish Partisans.

A PARTISAN'S WISH . . .

In the forest a story was making the rounds which is worth relating: Goebbels had severe headaches. No German specialist could give him the right diagnosis. Without any choice he called a Jewish specialist from one of the concentration camps.

After examining the patient, the Jewish doctor said to Goebbels: "In order to get completely well, you have to take three baths." "Why three?" Goebbels was puzzled.

"Quite simple," the Jewish doctor replied. "You have to put your head under water three times and bring it up only twice."

(As told by Dr. Peisachowicz)

*　*　*

Dr. Peisachowicz was a well-known surgeon-specialist in the Vilna ghetto and when the time came for the ghetto partisans to join those in the forest, he went along. In the forest the Rokosowski Brigade later took him in as their surgeon and he performed valuable services in his field.

Partisans destroy a railroad track.

LENA

THERE were very few women in the partisan units. These served as nurses, cooks, etc. However, there were some who performed the same tasks as the male partisans. They carried weapons and accompanied the men on many dangerous missions. But, as I said before, these women were far and few between.

On the other hand, in the Jewish units named "Revenge" and "Fight Against Fascism" which were found in the Rudnicki wilderness, there were a considerable number of Jewish young women. That was because these units consisted of members of U.P.O. recruited from the ghetto. In these units the women were sent on all missions usually assigned to men. They went against the enemy with gun in hand.

Whenever the commanding officer of the brigade needed a girl to perform a task in Vilna or some other cities, he used to "borrow" a girl from the Jewish divisions of the partisans, and entrust her with important and responsible missions.

One evening I saw the guard escort a Jewish girl-partisan with whom I was well acquainted in my ghetto days. I greeted her as she disappeared into the bunker of the brigade headquarters. Her name was Lena.

Even though I slept in the bunker and had my underground printing outfit there, and therefore had the right of entry whenever I wished, I did not go in. After a while she came out under guard. Lena came over to me and we had a short conversation. She wanted to take advantage of the opportunity to talk with one of her own people, because it was quite possible that we would never see each other again . . .

Lena told me that she was going into the city on a dangerous mission. I smiled and observed that I would have deduced that even if she hadn't told me, because of the clothes she was wearing. We were dressed differently in the forest.

The thought crossed my mind to tell her that if she would be successful in her mission to the city, and if she wanted to do me a favor, she should visit a former family servant of ours who was 100 per cent trustworthy. From this servant she was to find out what happened to my family who remained in a ghetto hiding place. I, myself, had closed the camouflaged door of their hideout a few minutes before I had abandoned the ghetto.

I knew that under the most favorable conditions they could only exist a few weeks in that hideout, and that if any one of them would chance to rescue himself, the first place he would run to would be the home of the Christian servant. If it were at all possible for the girl partisan to bring back any one of my family, she would do so. Later on I would know what to do.

Lena readily agreed to do my bidding. We both knew that it was strictly against regulations to carry out unauthorized side missions. But as long as I saw that she was willing to do it with all her heart, I gave her the address of the Christian servant. Lena took it down in code and we took leave of each other. An armed guard escorted Lena to the periphery of the city.

Lea Guberski
destroyed 15 locomotives
and railroad trains.

316

After a few days I saw a guard bringing Lena back again to brigade headquarters and I greeted her from afar. She shook her head in the negative—which meant no good news. (At the time I did not grasp her meaning.) After she had taken quite a long time to report on her mission to the city, she was free to return to her unit. Now she had more time to talk to me. The guard was not standing at her heels waiting for her to get through talking to me, as was the case before she left on her mission. One of the guards told me that when she was ready to go she should call for the escort. In the meantime they would take it easy.

Lena told me that her official mission was a complete success and that the staff had expressed their deep gratitude . . . However, Lena continued, she could scarcely talk with our Christian friend, because the latter kept on weeping uncontrollably. She had seen nobody. In fact, she had stood for days from morning till dusk near the wall to catch sight of anybody coming out of the doomed ghetto. She kept on watching ceaselessly for any one of my family. But she saw no one; nobody came to visit her. Now she cried for joy at the news that I was alive.

The Christian servant, Masha, no longer lived in her own apartment, but was compelled to sublease a place with a family who had moved into the location where my family had lived for years, where I, my brothers and sister were born.

Lena also told me of the dangers she had faced in doing my bidding. Danger number one was for Lena to inquire of a second person as to where Masha Iwaszkiewiczowa lived. for everybody in the surrounding area knew that she had no other friends outside of the Kowalski family . . . Lena was directed to the right address, and a landlady admitted her when she asked for Masha. She had introduced herself to Masha as a Christian, who knew the peasant who took care of her "baby," etc.

Danger number two came when she was leaving the apartment. She looked down the staircase from the third floor and she saw a Lithuanian policeman coming up the stairs.

It was dark and Lena took her revolver out of her bosom to be prepared; but to her great surprise, the policeman just smiled at her and went ahead to his own apartment in the building.

After she told me everything, I realized to what dangers I had exposed her in order that she do me a private favor.

Let me express my gratitude to Lena right here for her willingness to risk her life as a favor to me.

Doba Deweltow

Chaya Shapiro-Lazar

LADY-COURIERS ON THE MOVE...

A SHORT time after Lena visited my base, I noticed a peasant-type woman on the premises. After I looked closer, I recognized that she was **Dinah Grinwald**. She was one of us and came from the Vilna ghetto. She was together with me in an intelligence unit at the ghetto gate.

Lena was dressed in city clothes with a beret on her head. But Dinah carried a small basket of eggs and wore a peasant shawl which covered her blonde hair. She was supposed to be some sort of speculator who went to Vilna to sell eggs.

I engaged her in conversation and she asked me to greet my companions for her, for I was the last to see her before she left the forest on her way to Vilna.

On the road she met up with her girl friend and fellow-partisan, Doba Deweltow, and they went to Vilna together.

After traversing a few kilometers, they were stopped by a Lithuanian Police guard in the neighboring city of Rudniki. They established their identity as Christians who were on the way to Vilna to sell their wares.

They were cross-examined and questioned as to why they were wandering around in a zone which was "infested" by partisans; and how could they be engaged in speculation in a time of war when blood was being spilled at the fronts?

These lady-couriers were very experienced as regular partisans. In case of emergency, they could use effective weapons. But as lady-couriers they had to face another trial. They had to play the role of private citizens who carried documents of identification. (Of course these documents were counterfeited by our printing press in the forest.)

They were taken to the Rudniki police precinct and told to sit down on a bench to wait for the local sergeant to whom they would have to recount all the details they had told previously to the guard.

The two girls had quietly decided to "dispatch" the two Lithuanian policemen stationed at the post. Just at the moment of decision the two policemen went into another room to consult each other and the two couriers were left alone for a second. They made use of the second and ran away.

The two policemen fired shots after the fleeing girls. The latter shot right back with real bullets and not with eggs . . . They disappeared behind the small houses along the way and succeeded in reaching the nearby forest.

After this terrifying experience, the two couriers rested and took counsel together as to their next move: should they return to their base or continue their journey to Vilna? They decided to go ahead, and they arrived in Vilna without further mishap.

The couriers came to the fur factory-camp Kailis in which there still remained some two thousand Jews, and where we had stationed a unit of the U.P.O. The two girls led out the entire U.P.O. unit from Kailis and brought them to the forest in safety.

The unit brought along the local commander, Aaron Aronowicz, the activist Nionka Telerant, the blonde "Aryan" scout Dr. Tolia Krakowski, and a contingent of 80 fighters who carried a substantial amount of guns, revolvers and a large sup-

Jewish Police of the fur factory Kailis.

ply of medicaments and other necessities for the partisans in the forest.

At almost the same time the lady-partisans Chaya Shapiro and Vitke Kempner set out on another mission. Chaya used a mine to blow up an electric transport motor on Subocz Street and Witka blew up a transport motor on Orzeszkowa Street.

In another locality the partisans Mattathias Levine and Yisroel Rosow blew up water installations. The combined team left a great sector of the city of Vilna without light and without water. Thus the city population were "apprised" that partisans were active in the very heart of Vilna.

After carrying out these successful sabotage missions, the partisans came as representatives of the forest into the Kailis camp and they led out the remaining U.P.O. members and guided them to the forest in safety. There they were integrated into regular partisan units.

It would take too much space to recount the activities of the lady-partisans: Zelda Treger, who walked 18 times from the forest into the city and vice versa; Niusia Lubocki, Cesia Rosenberg, who were among our leading scouts and many, many others.

From left: Zelda Treger-Nisnelowicz, Dina Grinwald-Kagan

Abrasha Tchuzoj

Abrasha Sabrin (Resel)

Alexei Kapler

THE FIRST MINE IN THE RUDNICKI FOREST

AFTER several weeks in the forest, a group of Jewish partisans were given some explosives to be used for blowing up a German transport. The transports used to flash by on the railway line linking Koenigsberg and Kovno to the Russian-German front. These, of course, were military transports that included soldiers, tanks, artillery and bombs. On the locomotive wheels and on the wheels of every car there were inscriptions proclaiming: "On to Victory!"

The group assigned to this task consisted of the following partisans: Aba Kowner, Abrasha Sabrin, Abrasha Tchuzoj, Ruszka Korczak and Raszke Markowicz.

They could trace the railway line on the map, and they knew the directions and roads leading to the line. But the main thing was to find a good spot for the mine, a high place where the explosives would rip up the rails and force the train to roll downward at high speed. Then, there was the problem created by the Germans, who had chopped down the trees along the railway tracks and had mined the area so that the partisans who ventured on acts of sabotage would be blown up before they could accomplish their goals. In addition, the Germans, together with Ukrainian and Lithuanian collaborators were patrolling the length of the line where the transports passed. In order to avoid all these dangers and to find the right place they had to have someone on our side who lived nearby.

Armed with guns and hand grenades, and carrying the mine on their shoulders (they would take turns carrying it, as it weighed tens of kilograms) they went on their mission. They had to cover about twenty kilometers in one direction, and they had to return home that night after blowing up the transport.

At that time the transports used to go by quite frequently. Two months later they slowed down, and five months after that they stopped running at night altogether because of the partisan activity.

They arrived in the dark of night at the nearest village

which was about three kilometers from the railway. They called on the peasant who lived in the first house at the edge of the village and told him what they were going to do. He would have to be their guide. He was not anxious to do it but he had no choice.

The peasant led them to a point on the track that was excellent. Soon, in the stillness of the night, they heard a train approaching. Three of them remained with the peasant at the edge of the woods two hundred meters from the tracks. Aba Kowner and Abrasha Sabrin took the mine, crawled carefully but quickly to the tracks and attached the fuse, then slid down the embankment with the other end of the long fuse in hand. The train was coming closer, speeding toward them with its bright lamps in front of the locomotive. The wheels went over the mine. Sabrin pulled the fuse. There was a coal-blue flame, a second passed, then a thunder clap heard miles around. The railway was paralyzed and they ran back to the forest, in the direction whence they had come. They heard the ringing of the metal parts as the train hurled over the side and the air was filled with rockets going up to the skies. There was shooting. The German troops were in turmoil.

They bade farewell to the peasant at the village edge. He will certainly keep his mouth shut for his own sake . . .

They returned safely to their base. A few days later our scouts reported no transports went by for twenty-four hours. There were many tens of dead and large numbers of wounded German soldiers. The transport suffered great casualties before it ever got to the front.

*　　*　　*

As long as I took it upon myself to tell the story of the part the Jews played in the anti-Nazi resistance movement in Vilna and environs, I have to include the episode told by Svetlana Stalin in her sensational book, *Twenty Letters to a Friend*. She reveals that her Jewish boy-friend, Alexei Kapler, functioned as a partisan around Baranowicze about 200 kilometers

324

away from Vilna, and some 150 kilometers from the Rud-nicki forest.

After looking at his photograph, I remembered that Kapler, together with a group of partisans assigned to diversive actions, was billeted in our bunkers once overnight; but I did not know then, or later, that this diversive operator was carrying on a love affair with the daughter of the then mighty Stalin.

To his credit it must be said, that the Russian Jew, Kapler, dared to go to the most dangerous places. As we gather from Svetlana's account, we see him in Stalingrad, then in our part of the world in the hinterland of the bloody enemy.

We must not forget that Kapler came from a warm and comfortable home in Moscow.

And this is the type of Jew who fought against the Nazis.

A group of Jewish Partisans in the Naliboki forests (between Vilna and Baranowicze).

I AM WOUNDED

ONE day a 28-year-old Lithuanian named Jozas descended upon the forest.

In 1940-41, Jozas had been a militiaman in a nearby town. After two or three years of undisturbed life among the Germans, he decided to go out to fight against the occupiers. He knew that there were partisans not far away, so he left his parents, two brothers and a sister to join them. He was a welcome guest. He brought along his own weapons, but most important, he was a genuine Lithuanian of the type that the Lithuanian command looked for desperately. He made a good impression on me and I got to talking with him often.

His two brothers did not wait long. A wild party took place in the village where the family lived, and as frequently happened, a fight broke out. The local Lithuanian-German policeman mixed in, and Jozas's two brothers hit him so hard that he dropped dead . . .

The two brothers, Vincas and Antonas, ran away to their older brother Jozas, as they could no longer remain in the village. They became partisans, two more genuine Lithuanians. They did not have to be taught how to shoot as they were already skilled marksmen. How many Jews they had on their conscience before they came to the forest I do not know, but that their hands were not free of Jewish blood, of that I am sure. But no questions were asked and no one was interested in their past.

The brothers quickly adapted to the forest life and participated in various regular partisan ventures. I had not exchanged any words with either of them although they had been at our base for several weeks. Simply: they avoided contact with me. While the eldest of the brothers had made a favorable impression on me, and I spoke to him quite often, I instinctively could not tolerate the other two characters, especially Vincas.

After their flight to the woods, the Gestapo had come to the village to arrest the two brothers. Since the pair were not to be found, the Gestapo returned to the village at night to search for them again. A neighbor informed the Gestapo that the two had joined the partisans. Thereupon the Gestapo set fire to the house with the entire family trapped in it. When the brothers heard of this, they found out which peasant had been the informer. They received permission of the partisan commanders to seek revenge, and more partisans were assigned to accompany them to the village, to burn the entire family of the informer and all his livestock. The account was settled . . .

Once, while I was in the bunker where our printing press was located, a partisan dashed in, all excited. He was one of the parachutists who had dropped down from the skies, one of the tallest, a healthy, fine fellow, a Lithuanian who had lived all his life in Latvia. He announced that Vincas was lying on his bunk and singing an anti-Semitic song, and his younger brother helping him enthusiastically. Some of the others were laughing out loud or smiling to themselves. Almost all the commanders and commissars were there, including Yurgis, but nobody reacted. Later they only smiled at each other and ignored the entire incident.

In general my relations with the men were quite good. I used to meander around the headquarters and had the right to go wherever I wished, because that was where my workplace was. The commanders and commissars had a good opinion of me. Small wonder . . . They had sent more than one report to Moscow, even earlier, when we were in the ghetto, about the achievements of the secret press. In the ghetto the U.P.O. was already an official part of the Lithuanian partisan organization.

Only the singer of the Nazi song did not acknowledge me. He maintained that I was a Jew and that I should go where all Jews were going in those days . . . and he wanted to earn this good deed as soon as possible. One day I sat outside near a fire with a group of partisans, to warm up. I was the only Jew among them. Suddenly there was a shot. A tumult. They lifted me up. Blood dripped from me. The bullet had entered my backside. I was conscious, and saw what had happened. My condition was not serious. The whole company came running. It was the first time I had ever seen Yurgis so pale . . . Our doctor, Vassia, prowled around me. I asked that they call Dr. Salek Gorfinkel, who was in the Jewish detachment, a few kilometers from our base. He came immediately and took whatever measures were necessary. He told me confidentially that if I did not get another bullet, I would remain alive . . .

As they carried me, I saw that Vincas was standing by our table with a gun in hand, but his facial expression was that of an innocent bystander. The security officer called him in and interrogated him about the incident. He said that he was cleaning his weapon and that it went off accidentally . . . It was clear to all. However, he was a genuine Lithuanian, with two brothers at his side—so nothing was done to him, since I was lightly wounded and the matter was closed.

When I was well again, Yurgis explained to me that since I already had one bullet in me and it did not kill me off, I had a chance now to live forever. I also agreed with that . . .

Shortly after this affair, our intelligence reported that the Germans had brought reinforcements and had made dispositions at various points around the forest. The situation was deemed serious and it was decided to abandon the bases. We retreated some tens of kilometers further, to the area under the control of the partisan commander Genis.

Forty-eight hours passed and there was no sign of bombardment of the forest. It was decided to send a five-man scouting squad to our old post to see what the Germans were doing. Jozas was named leader of the squad, which included his two brothers, myself and another Lithuanian. A fine social mixture for such a task . . . But I thought: not so bad, if things repeat themselves I shall know what to do . . .

We returned with a report that everything was in order, and we immediately went back to our previous base. It had only been a German maneuver to scare us. Later, just when not expected, we had a picnic. We were bombarded, but soldiers did not enter the forest to comb it as they used to do during such operations.

Until we left the forest Vincas did not speak one word to me. He never apologized for his "accidental" shooting at me. It was not his fault that the bullet did not hit the target that he aimed at.

Shmuel Shapiro

Sanke Nislenowicz

Peneusof family repairnig arms. *Left*: Boria, Abraham, Shmuel (Father)

329

A HORSE'S LUCK

A COLUMN of peasant wagons driven by partisans arrived. The wagons were filled with all kinds of produce, brought from a peasant village, not far from our base in the woods. Some of those who accompanied the wagons ran over to the fire to warm up, while other partisans busied themselves with transferring the provisions into makeshift storage bins.

I noticed that the partisan Kolia lagged behind the rest and looked down and out. I asked the other partisans how they fared with their foraging mission, and they told me that their task was accomplished without any incidents and there was no shooting.

When we sat down to supper, I saw that Kolia did not touch a morsel of food. He sat sunk in thought without eating anything. I slid over to him and asked why he did not partake of the meal. He answered that he did not feel hungry and I went back to my place. But when I saw that he left the table without touching a thing, I engaged him in conversation and asked him what was the matter with him. This time he replied that he was all tied up in knots and that's why he could not eat.

When I asked him what happened, he told me this story. As he was returning from his foraging mission, he went off the road, landed in swampy ground and could not extricate the horse and wagon from the mud. No matter how much he pulled and tugged, he could not get the horse to crawl out of the bog.

Some of the other wagoners came over, sized up the situation, threw the food from his wagon into their own and went on. He remained behind and with the help of other partisans tried to help the horse lift himself and the empty wagon out of the mud, but to no avail. Since he did not wish to be left behind by the caravan, he gave up and abandoned the horse and wagon. But on the way, his conscience plagued him. Sooner or later the horse would be engulfed in the mud, and it was a living creature.

I tried to console him with the thought that he had done everything in his power to pull the horse out of his predicament.

330

But it was of no use. "Be glad," I said, "that you came out of it unharmed."

Kolia admitted that he nearly tore a gut trying to get the wagon out of the mud, and both he and the horse used their last ounce of strength, and nothing helped. But as he walked along the road to our base, the thought crossed his mind that he could have taken another measure: that is, to cut the harness that bound the horse to the wagon. Maybe that would have helped the horse to get out by himself. That was the reason he was under tension, could not eat, and was conscience-stricken... I then told him that if it was not too late, I was ready to go with him to cut the harness loose, and then everything would be all right.

Kolia's face became animated. It gave him a new lease on life. I approached our commander-in-chief, told him what bothered Kolia and we obtained permission to go and make an attempt to free the horse.

It was almost a two-hour walk to the sinking animal and we saw that three-fourths of the rope and the wagon were already under the mud. During the terrible period which was supposed to be "A thousand years of the Nazi Reich," I saw many instances of human extermination, but I never came across such a pitiful situation involving a living creature.

The horse's eyes seemed to plead for mercy. They bulged out of their sockets. From the movement of his head you could tell that he knew he was going to die in the mud.

On the way we agreed that one would keep an eye upon the other, so that we should not sink in the mud ourselves. Kolia and I lost no time and we cut all the leather bindings of the harness. We also spurred the horse on to make him crawl out of the ooze. But the horse was so weak and so far gone, that he could not do it.

Then the idea flashed through my mind to remove the ladders attached to the side of the wagon and push one down between the wagon and the horse's feet. After a tremendous effort we pushed one ladder deep into the mud, and the second ladder under the horse's head. Both of us began to whip the horse to urge him to push himself out of his tight spot. How relieved we both were when finally he gained a footing by touching the hard substance with his hindlegs and then with his forelegs. He then gave a tremendous shove and appeared upon the surface. Kolia began to tug at his mane and pulled the horse a few steps toward a dry spot. The horse stood still and began to shake convulsively. After 10 or 15 minutes he appeared in full view. We brought him back to the base, fed him and watered him and kept him as an official partisan horse.

Kolia remained a true and loyal friend to me because I encouraged him to go and rescue the horse. I also felt much easier, that after the exertion and danger we went through, we had succeeded in rescuing an innocent living creature.

From left: Dwora Reckin; Abrasha
Labit, Meier Ickowicz

THE VILLAGE—KONIUCHI

KONIUCHI was the name of a big village that was some 30 kilometers from Vilna and 10 kilometers from the periphery of our partisan base.

The Germans convinced the wheeler-dealers of that village that if they would be obedient they would receive security, riches and peace, and they would be able to live thus through the entire war.

All they had to do was to inform the Germans of the activities of the partisans in the region.

The villagers did the best they could to please the new occupants.

Whenever our partisans crossed in groups of five or ten men to important and dangerous missions, they were met by sniper fire and always suffered casualties.

The individual commands then decided that their men should pass the village in groups of about 40 or 50, and when shot at by snipers should chase after and destroy them. The rest of the group would guard the village.

For a while the situation was so. But then the Germans supplied the villagers with rifles and machine-guns. A permanent guard was established, whose purpose was to shield the village day and night.

It became so bad that bigger groups could not be safe crossing the village on the way to an important mission, or passing the village on the way to the railroad, highway, etc. We always ended up with casualties.

The brigade-staff decided to remove the cancer that was growing on the partisan body.

Our base commander gave the order that all able-bodied men should be prepared in an hour to leave for an operation.

The order was that all men, without exceptions, including the doctor, the radio-telegraphers, the workers of the brigade staff, and people like myself who were working in the propaganda and printing department, be ready on time.

At the correct time all of us were ready in full battle-gear, and left for our destination.

When we were closing in on our destination, I saw that the partisans were coming from all directions, from various detachments.

We stopped and our commander, a Lithuanian parachutist, told us about the behavior of the Koniuchi villagers.

Our detachment got the order to destroy everything that was moving and burn the village down to its roots.

At the exact hour and minute all partisans from all four corners of the village started pouring rifle and machine-gun fire, with incendiary bullets, into the village. This caused the straw roofs of the houses to catch fire.

The villagers and the small German garrison answered back with heavy fire, but after two hours the village with the fortified shelter was completely destroyed.

Our only casualties were two men who were lightly wounded.

When, later, we had to go through Koniuchi we did not encounter any sniper shots, because it was like crossing through a cemetery.

After the villagers of this region found out what had happened to Koniuchi which had attempted to live at the expense of the partisans, they were very careful not to accept arms from the Germans and a cardinal change occurred in their minds. This was of great benefit to the partisan movement.

One day one of our contact men gave us the message that a German post near the burned down village of Koniuchi authorized him to ask the partisans if the latter wanted to live in peace with the German post. The answer was—Yes. The result was a gentlemen's agreement: that the Germans would not obstruct our passage through the village and we would not burn down their bunkers in the night.

The agreement was honored by both sides and the German group was one of the lucky ones that lived through the entire war.

THE LOVE AFFAIR

B-s was one of the very few Lithuanians who retreated with the Soviet armies before the Germans invaded Lithuania. A long-time progressive labor leader, he was trained at the partisan training school in Moscow and parachuted back to his country in 1942. A man in his early forties, he became a deadly menace to the Germans.

One day he offered the headquarters staff in the forest to take a journey to his village deep in Lithuania to establish a contact that would be useful to the partisans; at the same time he would be able to visit his wife.

The leadership was always extremely careful in dealing with such offers. As a rule, no partisan was ever sent on any mission alone; there were never less than three men on any assignment, especially deep in the country, where the people were hostile to Soviet partisans and where the danger was therefore particularly great.

However, since B-s was a tried and trusted fighter, the staff permitted him to set out on his double mission of visiting his wife, whom he had not seen for three years, and of establishing contact with other peasants who could provide the partisans with important information.

A group of partisans combined their mission in the interior of Lithuania with his journey and accompanied him to the vicinity of his village, leaving him there to continue on his way by himself.

From a nearby hill he spied out his wife with binoculars as she walked to a well for water. He quickly hid his automatic, his grenades and other equipment under his sheepskin coat and went toward her. When his wife recognized him from the distance she almost fainted. He asked whether anyone was at their house, and when she said there was no one there, he carried her in and she soon recovered.

Their reunion was like all reunions under such circumstances. They kissed and embraced and kissed again. His wife looked at him as if he had returned from the dead, for she had never known where he had disappeared to after war broke out. She thought that he had retreated with the Soviet armies, but she was never sure of it. He might have been dead, and she had no way of finding out.

B-s told her his story. He also said that he intended to remain with her two or three days and rejoin the group of partisans on their way back to the Rudnicki wilderness in the Vilna region after their mission had been completed.

His wife became hysterical. She cried and laughed and cried again, and he could not calm her down. She finally told him that she had grieved and waited for him for weeks and months after his disappearance. In the end another man of their village began to court her, and, unable to endure her loneliness any longer, she had become his mistress.

B-s listened to her story in silence. She said that if he decided to stay with her, she would send her lover away and continue as his wife.

He reproached her violently for betraying him while he had been risking his life daily to fight the Germans. She tried to justify herself, but he became more and more agitated, threatening to shoot her lover when he came to her at night. She burst into tears and begged him not to do it. If he killed the man his family would surely kill her, and he himself would not get away alive either.

Obviously this complicated and painful love affair interfered with the second part of his mission. If he did anything to harm the lover, he would be unable to establish contacts in the village to help the partisan cause. Besides, his own escape would be jeopardized.

All day they talked and planned and weighed the situation. In the end B-s told his wife that he understood the circumstances and the only thing that remained was for her to continue her love affair with the other man. B-s would spend the night in hiding and then leave the house and village quietly, so that no one would know what had happened.

He instructed his wife to behave exactly as usual, promising that no matter how he felt, he would remain silent and neither she nor anyone else would be harmed. He told her to be careful in playing her part, to make sure that her lover did not sense the change or suspect anything out of the ordinary.

In the evening, after a day's work in the village, the peasant, her lover, came to her and she received him as usual with smiles and kisses.

Her husband lay hidden on the oven, warming his bones and listening first to their conversation and then to their passionate lovemaking, which seemed to go on and on endlessly. Finally B-s could endure it no longer, seized his automatic and wanted to finish off both of them. At the last moment, however, he restrained his anger and kept his promise not to interfere even when they engaged in the most intimate activities.

Besides, it became apparent that the lover was a Lithuanian "Shaulist" and Nazi sympathizer who was pleased with the whole war which made it possible for him to carry on this love affair undisturbed.

The front lines were then still far from Lithuania and their village life went on as usual, quietly and peacefully. Those who were not of military age continued their customary work, cultivated grain and raised pigs. The German military, it is true, sometimes confiscated their products—with a word of thanks, or, on occasion, with a bullet in the head as payment. On the whole, though, the peasants had enough to eat and tried to sit out the war.

After the wild sex orgy, the wife and her lover fell fast asleep for the rest of the night. But B-s, in his hiding place on the oven, did not close an eye for fear that he might snore and so betray his presence.

In the morning the peasant left the house and went home to work.

The wife could not look her husband in the eyes. But now he consoled and reassured her, saying that he understood her situation, whether he liked it or not. She kissed him fervently and begged forgiveness. She also thanked him for his patience in witnessing all he had witnessed without shooting both of them like dogs.

B-s told her that he forgave her everything. From now on, he said, she would be a partisan, under his command.

He appointed her as liaison between the village and the partisans. She would have to fulfill various assignments. He would not come again, to spare himself the painful sight of her love-making with the peasant, but other partisans would come to visit her with instructions, and she was to supply them with information as to the strength of the German forces in surrounding areas; she was also to tell them who collaborated with the Germans, and do other intelligence work.

The wife declared herself willing to do anything in order to expiate her betrayal. He left his house and village to meet the partisan group on its way back from its mission and join it on the long journey to the Rudnicki base, some two hundred kilometers away.

General Jacob Szmuszkiewicz, a Jew from Lithuania was the Commander-in-Chief of the Soviet Air Force. He insisted on leading his airmen personally into battle at the outbreak of World War II and was shot down and killed several months later while in action against the enemy.

B-s, who had several days off after his mission before returning to active partisan duty, dropped in at the bunker which housed the field printing shop to talk to me and tell me the story.

I comforted him, saying that under wartime conditions such things were only natural. After the war, I said, he would still have many happy years with his wife. He only shook his head, as if to say, "It is easy to talk when somebody else is suffering."

When the war was over B-s was appointed director of the first men's clothing factory. I was still wearing my partisan forest outfit, and he ordered a suit to be made for me at once, without any formalities or waiting time.

B-s also told me later that his wife, with whom he was then already living in Vilna as though nothing had happened, had indeed done most useful partisan service. And so the mission he had undertaken, in its own strange way was fully successful.

Typical partisans in the winter

COMBAT INVALIDS

Chaim Lazar

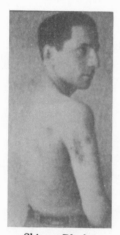

Shimon Bloch

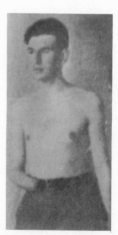

A. Kot

СПРАВКА О РАНЕНИИ

В боях за Советскую родину _____

_____ _____ _____

тов. _____ _____ _____

был ранен _____ _____

_____ _____ _____

_____ _____ ранен

(Равицкий)

Военком госпиталя
полковой комиссар
(Терик)

Certificate in Russian that Israel Liman
was wounded in combat **serving**
in the Lithuanian brigade.

THE WAR INVALID

AFTER our units had withdrawn, expecting a great attack, we came upon Commander Genis' units which were twenty kilometers away. There we remained three days, ready to withdraw eventually with Genis, if our intelligence brought word that a major open battle faced us.

In the forests of Rudnicki our forces were not prepared to engage in such combat. We adhered to the tactics of choosing the time, place and conditions of fighting and not allowing ourselves to be drawn into an open battle with an army equipped with tanks and planes.

Meanwhile a small group of partisans returned to Genis. Among them was a Russian by the name of Viktor, who had been severely wounded in the knee. Since our unit at the base had a doctor, Vassya, he examined the leg and decided that under the circumstances it would be necessary to amputate it. After the matter was explained, Viktor agreed to the operation which would cost him his right leg.

Suddenly I was transformed into a "surgeon." Vassya, who slept in my bunker, had to have a helper and he asked me to be it. Without further ado, I agreed to serve.

The three of us came to a bunker that had been left empty, and placed a pot on a chair to catch the blood. The amputation was done in the most primitive manner. It is unnecessary to mention that there were no anesthetics available. The wounded man had to watch the operation and even help a bit. It was tragic, indeed, for me to carry away Viktor's leg as he watched. I took it and buried it nearby.

The three of us stood there for a while, in order to change bandages and do what we could to alleviate the pain. Again I was forced to witness the brutality of war, to see a casualty who would remain a permanent invalid.

Some of the other units had well organized hospitals with doctors and nurses, who rendered outstanding medical service and performed surgical miracles. But we somehow lacked all this, and had to resort to the primitive operation by a non-qualified team. While Vassya was called doctor, he was actually only a medical student in the third semester at Kiev University when the war broke out and he was taken as a prisoner to do sanitation work in an army unit. Later, he escaped from the Germans. Although he was not a lover of the Soviet regime, he came to the partisans because he was convinced while in German hands that "they" were not humans at all.

* * *

Viktor told me what had happened. He had gone with a few more men on an assignment and they had entered several peasant homes to get something to eat. There was nobody around. Suddenly he heard some shots which his three companions were exchanging with a large police force. He did not know whether this was the result of a betrayal or not, but he saw about twenty police armed with automatic weapons coming closer, some of them carrying burning torches to set fire to the straw roof.

He had two alternatives: to die by surrendering or to take a chance and also save the innocent peasant family. Viktor kicked the door open with his foot and sprayed bullets left and right while dashing forward. The police fell like flies and he heard groans as he ran the several hundred yards to the edge of the forest and fell to the ground. When his colleagues found him they brought him to our base. The other three partisans were lucky and succeeded in shooting their way out of the entrapment to reach the forest safely.

Although Viktor now had only one leg he told with pride that the Lithuanian Nazis had paid for the other one with many lives.

Soon after the liberation I met Viktor in Vilna, and he told me that only then was he being sent to the Crimea where he would be fitted with an artificial limb. He was in a good mood and thanked me for taking care of him when he was in a bad plight.

Kovno Partisans. *From left*: Yerachmiel Berman, Kalmen Goldstein, Berl Kis, Shimon Bloch, David Safer, Aaron Nisnowitz, Isaac Jochnikov. *Kneeling*: Jacob Ratner.

Partisans in search and destroy action.

THE KOVNO FIGHTING GROUP

ARLY in 1944 I noticed a new face at our base. It was not so
much a face as a man with a long, black moustache point-
ing upward. His left hand did not move, as it was shot through,
following a shooting match with German ghetto guards that took
place when he once left the ghetto through the fence to get to a
meeting of the underground fighters in the city.

I found out that this was Chaim Jelin (Wladas), commander of the fighting organization of the Kovno ghetto, who
had come to the brigade staff to report on the resistance effort in
Kovno.

Later I had almost daily contact with Jelin, who spent several weeks at our base and had a lot of free time. He had not
been sent on any partisan missions. He told me of various incidents in the Kovno ghetto and of the preparations of the
armed youth there.

With Jelin came several dozen well-armed young men and
women from the Kovno ghetto. They had been organized into a
unit that went to various places in the Rudnicki wilderness,
where they excelled in their sharp battles with the Nazis.

One day Jelin approached me and said goodbye. He was
returning to the Kovno ghetto where he would continue to lead

Chaim Jelin and Moshe Muslis,
members of the underground,
confer in a conspirative room.

344

Statue of Chaim Jelin (located in Vilna museum)

the resistance and prepare the youth who were leaving the place with weapons, in order to join us in the woods.

A wagon was loaded with dynamite and other "good stuff," which Jelin and two companions, one of them a woman, took along to Kovno, a trek of about 150 kilometers. They made the trip safely and Jelin threw himself into his work immediately. The ghetto was seething. It was actually no longer a ghetto but a concentration camp, for the ghetto as such had been officially liquidated.

Some of the Lithuanian underground in the city had been arrested, just as it had happened in Vilna. On the way to a meeting with his colleagues in the city, Jelin was detained by two Nazis. He broke away and shot one of the agents. However, Jelin was already surrounded on all sides by the Gestapo. He returned their fire, cutting some of them down before making his escape. But the Gestapo knew of his hiding place and brought bloodhounds for the hunt. In four hours, they discovered Jelin in the bushes. Knowing what awaited him, he cut his wrists and throat and thus ended his life.

THE LAND ARMY (A. K.)

THE Land Army (Armia Krajowa) started to function in our area before the advent of the first Soviet partisans.

It is not my intention at the present writing to analyze the internal or external structure of this army as it was known in Poland in general, and in Vilna, in particular. One thing must be made clear: that to the everlasting disgrace of the underground Land Army, it was rabidly anti-Semitic. As if it were not enough to contend against the common Nazi enemy, it turned against the Jews as well.

In the Rudnicki wilderness, where the survivors of the Vilna ghetto were operating, many untoward scenes of contention occurred. But that is not the problem here. When the armed groups met, both sides paid with bloody casualties. The partisan Shlomo Brand wore the uniform of a Polish infantry officer all the time he was in the forest. He had obtained it from an A. K.-officer when he was attacked by the latter. The problem became more acute when the Land Army found scattered, unarmed Jews in the forest who had run away from the bestial Nazi hordes. Here the Jews were pursued and destroyed by so-called "patriots" as well as by the Nazis, who had smashed Poland and enslaved her inhabitants.

One day I received instructions to make myself ready to set out as an escort to Brigadier Gabris, who was going to meet the commander of the Land Army of our area. We were seven men in all. Our instructions were as follows: five of us were to hide behind the meeting house and two of us would act as a bodyguard in front of the house. This was done in the event the party of the second part would start any tricks.

This was the first time I saw Gabris wearing his military insignia. It was then that I learned that he had the rank of a colonel. (Gabris, as well as the rest of us, never wore any insignia of a military rank.) We set out on our journey and walked a few miles into a village.

At the appointed time, a Polish colonel arrived with his

guard. (They also had a secret watch who stood near another side of the peasant's house.)

The negotiations went on for hours. On our way back Gabris told us that he had accomplished nothing.

It is common knowledge that in the months of March and April, 1944, the Germans had suffered heavy defeats. It was more than certain that our area would be liberated from the yoke of the Germans in the course of the oncoming summer. Realizing that the Land Army would then remain up in the air, they turned to the Soviet-Lithuanian partisan leadership at this late date to discuss terms of possible union. They had the unmitigated gall to demand that they be paid for having fought against the Soviet partisans in the heat of the war against the common enemy. This was not taking into account their murder of refugee Jews.

The two colonels met again at a later time. The second meeting produced no results either.

I could not comprehend the fact at that time, that after the liberation of Vilna when the Soviet partisans were already demobilized, Polish partisans within the city still went around with guns on their shoulders. Nothing was done about them. Like the others, they were shortly after ordered to demobilize and the majority obeyed. Some began to rebel against the Soviet power. Many were arrested, and whoever remained in the woods to fight against the Soviet army, was destroyed.

From left: Szlomo Brand
Elchonon Magid

347

Generals Speak

(As published in our Underground Press)

ODEZWA GEN. ŻELIGOWSKIEGO DO NARODU POLSKIEGO

Znany na terenie Wileńszczyzny, przebywający obecnie w Londynie gen. Żeligowski wystąpił z odezwą do narodu polskiego, w której wzywa Polaków do współpracy ze Związkiem Radzieckim i przystąpienia do bloku zjednoczonych narodów słowiańskich, gen. Żeligowski wskazuje bezsensowność izolacji narodu polskiego od Państw Zjednoczonych co jest korzystnym tylko dla naszego wspólnego wroga, hitlerowskich Niemiec.

Wspólnota Zjednoczonych Narodów gwarancją zwycięstwa nad hitleryzmem.

PROCLAMATION BY GEN. ZELIGOWSKI TO THE POLISH NATION

Well known in Vilna territories and now in London, Gen. Zeligowski came out with an appeal to the Polish Nation in which he called the Poles to collaborate with the Soviets and form a bloc of the Slavic nations. Gen. Zeligowski explained Poland's non-realistic policy of isolation from the United Nations that brings only profit to the enemy, Nazi Germany. *Togetherness of the United Nations is a guarantee for victory over Hitlerism.*

ODEZWA GEN. EISENHOWERA

Dowódca sprzymierzonych wojsk inwazyjnych, gen. Eisenhower w dniu ich lądowania, wydał odezwę do swych żołnierzy.

W odezwie gen. Eisenhower zaznaczył, iż rozwścieczony wróg jest przygotowany do przyjęcia wojsk inwazyjnych. Walka będzie ciężką i trudną, lecz trud nasz przyniesie zwycięstwo narodów sprzymierzonych i zagładę hitleryzmu.

PROCLAMATION BY GEN. EISENHOWER

Commander of the United States Army, Gen. Eisenhower, on the day of their landing, issued a Proclamation to his soldiers.

In this proclamation Gen. Eisenhower pointed out that the mad enemy is prepared to meet the invasion armies. The battle will be a hard and a difficult one, but the Allies will be victorious and Hitlerism will be destroyed.

KRONIKA

WILNO. Niemcy ostatnio stosują nowy sposób łapanek na młodzież. Na fabrykach lub warsztatach niemieckich były wypadki, że po skończeniu pracy "przychodziło gestapo i zabierało pracującą młodzież wileńską zatrudnioną u Niemców. Ostrzegamy przed podobnymi łapankami.

RUDOMINO. Żandarmeria niemiecka ograbiła całkowicie z żywego inwentarza dwie wioski, położone na szosie Wilno—Lida, Mariampol i Tatarka. Po przyjeździe, żandarmeria okrążyła wioski, pozabierała cały inwentarz żywy, nie zostawiając w wiosce ani jednej krowy. Mężczyzn, którzy nie zdołali uciec, żandarmeria zabrała na wywóz do Niemiec.

RUDNIKI. Oddział partyzantów napadł na więzienie w Rudnikach. Spalono 2 baraki, z których zwolniono 27 osób aresztowanych przez Niemców. Zabito 2 policjantów, wzięto do niewoli naczelnika więzienia, Mikołę Jonasza, oraz 2 policjantów.

STASIŁY. 300 m. od stacji Stasiły grupa partyzantów wykoleiła pociąg z wojskiem, zdążający na front w składzie 4 wagonów i lokomotywy.

OLKIENIKI. Partyzanci trzema silnymi minami wysadzili piece olkienickiej smolarni, wskutek czego smolarnia, produkująca smołę i inne materiały dla wojska niemieckiego, zatrzymała 'produkcję. STASIŁY. Grupa partyzantów wykoleiła pociąg z wojskiem niemieckim w składzie 7 wagonów i lokomotywy.

JASZUNY. Między Jaszunami i Stasiłami partyzanci 33 wybuchami zniszczyli 66 szyn na drodze kolejowej Wilno—Lida. Zniszczono 412,5 m. drogi kolejowej.

ORANY. Pod Oranami grupa partyzantów wykoleiła pociąg w składzie 7 wagonów i lokomotywy, wiozący wojsko z frontu na odpoczynek. Ponad 100 Niemców zostało ciężko rannych.

OLKIENIKI. Silna grupa partyzantów urządziła zasadzkę na szosie Wilno—Grodno, około wsi Piercupie, na przejeżdżające auta niemieckie. Silnym ogniem karabinów maszynowych i broni automatycznej zatrzymano maszynę, wioząca 20 oficerów niemieckiej żandarmerii polowej. 10 niemieckich oficerów znaleziono śmierć w zaciekłych kul, 5 wzięto do niewoli. 4 Niemcom zdołało uciec, i próbując uciekać, skacząc z maszyny, zawisł i udusił się na swoim własnym płaszczu polowym.

OLKIENIKI. Niemcy w tchórzowski sposób odemścili się za swoje ofiary pod Piercupami na mieszkańcach tejże wsi. W dwie godziny po wypadku przyby[ł] tapowski oddział egzekucyjny, który okrążył wieś, spędził lud[ność] wsi do stodół i podpalił wie[ś]. W płomieniach zginęła cała [...]. Śmierć znalazło 105 mieszkańców, w tem kobiety, starcy i dzieci.

WILNO. Samolot radziecki, zrzucił bombę na Depo Wil. Dyr. Kolejowej wskutek czego nadjakiś czas zatrzymano przez v wartach.

(dokończenie kroniki)

— Na drodze kolejowej Wilno—Grodno grupa partyzantów wykoleiła pociąg, wiozący amunicję na front wschodni w składzie 12 wagonów i 1 lokomotywy.

— Na drodze kolejowej pod Olkienikami grupa partyzantów wykoleiła pociąg, naładowany mąką, wiozący wojsko z frontu na odpoczynek w składzie 4 wagonów i lokomotywy.

— Na szosie Wilno — Ejszyszki grupa partyzantów zasiadła z zasadzki na niemieckie auta, kursujące na tej drodze. Około godz. 8 rano przejeżdżało auto ciężarowe, przeprowadzane przez samochód pancerny. Partyzanci silnym ogniem broni przeciwpancernej i broni automatycznej obstrzelali i zatrzymali maszyny. Od partyzanckiej broni zginęło 13 hitlerowskich żołnierzy i 1 podoficer. Zdobyto 2 karabiny maszynowe, 6 karabinów, 4 granatomioty, 1 pistolet, granaty ręczne i naboje karabinowe.

— Na drodze kolejowej Wilno—Grodno, pod Rudziszkami, grupa partyzantów wykoleiła pociąg wiozący wojska na front. Ilości wagonów nie ustalono.

— Grupa partyzantów wysadziła w Żygarynie tamę na rzece Mereczance. Tama zatrzymywała wodę, którą kanałem skierowano do Grzegożewa dla poruszania maszyn, znajdujących się tam fabryk. Po jej wzerwaniu, woda rozlała się po pobliskich polach, i zatrzymanej doprowadzenie do Grzegożewa. Wskutek tej operacji, zatrzymały pracę fabryki papieru i bandaży, oraz tartaka.

— Między Waką i wsią Melechowicze, grupa partyzantów urządziła zasadzkę na Niemców, zwołujących z lasu drzewo. Śmiałym atakiem na przejeżdżającą grupę, ruszyli partyzanci z wezwaniem 'poddania się: Za wyjątkiem podoficera i jednego żołnierza, który przy stawianiu oporu został zabici, reszta w ilości 7 żołnierzy, przeszła na stronę partyzantów. Zdobyto 1 karabin maszynowy i 7 karabinów.

— Na drodze kolejowej Wilno—Kowno oddział partyzantów silną miną zatrzymał pociąg, zdążający na front, wiozący niemieckich oficerów i podoficerów. Silnym ogniem broni automatycznej obstrzeliwali partyzanci wrogie wojska. Niemcy w panicznym strachu częśc uciekać pcd gradem kul. Na polu boju zostało około 150 trupów niemieckich oficerów i podoficerów, około 90° zostało ciężko rannych.

— W rejonie Kaiszedary, na drodze kolejowej Wilno—Kowno, grupa partyzantów wykoleiła pociąg z lokomotywą, wiozący na front sprzęt wojenny.

— — —

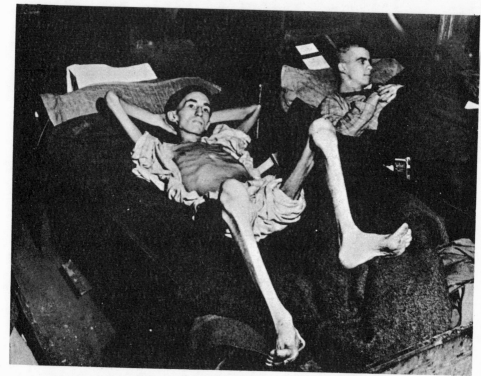

This is not a picture of a Jewish concentration camp victim. This is an American GI resting after he and other Yanks were liberated from a Limburg prison camp by the U.S. First Army. His daily ration as a prisoner of war was one slice of bread and a bowl of soup made of dried peas and unpeeled potatoes.

KRONIKA

— Wilno. W Wilnie odbywają się stałe obławy na młodzież i starszych, zdolnych do prac fizycznych, których Niemcy wykorzystują dla kopania rowów obronnych.

— Wilno. Coraz częstsze napady na niemieckich oficerów i żołnierzy, zmusiły Hingsta do skrócenia godzin policyjnych do godz. 20. Jednocześnie Hingst wydał odezwę do ludności, prosząc o pomoc w wykrywaniu sprawców zabijania lub rozbrajania niemców. Płacząca odezwa Hingsta, spotkała się ze śmieszną ironią ludności Wilna.

— Grupa partyzantów przeprowadziła niszczenie szyn na drodze kolejowej Wilno—Lida. 25 wzrywami zniszczono 50 szyn, co stanowi 700 m. drogi kolejowej,

— Grupa partyzantów wzrywem zatrzymała lokomotywę z wagonami, naładowanymi materiałem drzewnym. Ochronę pociągu zlikwidowano. Zabito 5 niemców, 3 wzięto do niewoli. Zdobyto karabin maszynowy i karabiny. Pociąg przewoził opał i budulec dla zaopatrzenia szeregu fabryk w Jaszunach i Wilnie.

— Grupa partyzantów na drodze kolejowej Wilno—Kowno wykoleiła pociąg z niemieckim wojskiem w składzie 4 wagonów i łożemem

(dalszy ciąg kroniki na str. 8)

—o—o—o—

The Story of the Jewish United Partisan Organization in Vilna

Free translation of Chronicles on the activities of our partisans as they were registered in our partisan publication, *Za Wolnosc*, in the Rudnicki wilderness.

This is a small fraction of the activities related in only two of many issues of our Underground Press.

VILNA. Lately the Germans used a new method to catch youths. Sometimes after work hours, when people left the factories, Gestapo came and took away young working people who were laboring for the Germans. We warn you to be careful of those catchers.

* * *

RUDOMINO. German police robbed, completely, two villages which lay between Vilna-Lida, Marianpol and Tatarka. They surrounded the village, and took away all the belongings. Men who didn't have a chance to hide or run away, were caught by the Germans and deported to Germany.

* * *

RUDNIKI. A group of partisans attacked the Rudniki jail. They burned two barracks, and twenty-seven people who had been arrested by the Germans went free. Two policemen were killed. The prison commander, Mikolaj Jonasz and two policemen were taken prisoner.

* * *

STASILY. Three hundred meters from the station, partisans derailed a train of four cars, and a locomotive, with soldiers on their way to the front.

* * *

OLKIENIKI. With powerful mines the partisans destroyed the ovens which produced pitch and other stuff for the German army. Production was halted.

* * *

JASZUNY. Between Jaszuny and Stasily, with thirty-three explosions, partisans ruined 66 rail tracks on the Vilna-Lida road. 412½ meters of railroad were destroyed.

* * *

ORANY. Partisans derailed a train with soldiers who were on the way from the battlefield for a rest. Over 100 Germans were badly wounded.

* * *

OLKIENIKI. A strong group of partisans ambushed German autos on the road Vilna-Grodno, near the village Piercupi. With heavy machine gun fire they stopped an auto carrying 20 officers. Ten died from the partisan bullets, four of them managed to escape. One, trying to escape, accidentally strangled himself in his military garb.

* * *

OLKIENIKI. A special German execution squad came two hours after an incident and chased all the people out of Piercupi, into the barracks and burned them alive. Among them were 105 women, children and old folks.

* * *

VILNA. A Soviet plane dropped a bomb on the railroad depot. Because of this, all work stopped for a time.

* * *

On the Vilna-Grodno railroad partisans derailed a twelve car ammunition train and a locomotive which was on its way to the Eastern front.

* * *

Near Olkieniki partisans derailed a four car train loaded with flowers.

* * *

On the Vilna-Ejszyski road partisans ambushed a German truck, at around 8:00 A.M. When a troop carrier passed by, the partisans stopped it with a heavy barrage. 13 Hitlerites and one corporal were killed. The partisans gained 2 automatic rifles, 6 rifles, 4 mine-throwers, 1 pistol and bullets.

* * *

On the Vilna-Grodno road near Rudnicki, partisans derailed a troop train going to the front.

* * *

Partisans destroyed a dam on the Mereczana river. The dam regulated the amount of water that flowed into the canal, and this in turn, operated the machines in the factories of Grzegozew. The water splashed on the nearby fields and did not reach Grzegozew. Because of this paper factories and some mills stopped work.

* * *

Between Waka and the village Melechowicz partisans ambushed Germans who were shuffling out of the forest with cut wood. Partisans attacked them and called to them to surrender. One corporal and one soldier who refused to surrernder were killed. The rest, seven soldiers, went over to the partisan side. The partisans gained one machine gun, 7 rifles.

* * *

On the railroad between Vilna and Kovno, a partisan mine stopped a train that carried German officers and sergeants to the front. The partisans ripped into the enemy soldiers with strong fire. In panic they started to run, but 150 German troops were killed and about 90 were badly wounded.

* * *

In the area of Koszedary, on the Vilna-Kovno railroad partisans blew up a train of six cars and a locomotive that carried war supplies to the front.

* * *

VILNA. In Vilna, youths and the elderly, who are able to do physical labor were sent by the Germans to dig trenches.

* * *

VILNA. There were frequent attacks on German officers and soldiers. Hingst proclaimed that the people should help him by not hiding those who kill the Germans. The tearfull proclamation from Hingst met with ironic laughter.

* * *

Partisans wrecked the Vilna-Lida railroad with 25 explosions, they destroyed rails for a distance of 700m.

* * *

Partisans stopped a locomotive and cars loaded with food. They liquidated the guard, killed 5 Germans and took 3 into captivity. They gained automatic rifles and rifles. This train delivered heating material to the Jaszuna and Vilna factories.

* * *

STASILY. Partisans derailed a train of 7 cars and 1 locomotive with German soldiers.

* * *

June, 1944.—The following appeared in the Russian-Nazi newspaper "Viestnik" which was published in Kovno. There was a written order, signed by Heinrich Loshe, General Commissar of Ostland, that anybody who knew of a partisan in hiding, must report the fact at once on pain of death. The announcement referred to partisans in Lithuanian territory. If the ordinance had also included White Russia, then a large sector of the population would have been executed. This would not have been a deterrent to the Germans, but the partisans would have resented and prevented any such action. Therefore, the order was directed at Lithuania, where the partisans did not, as yet, obtain a strong foothold.

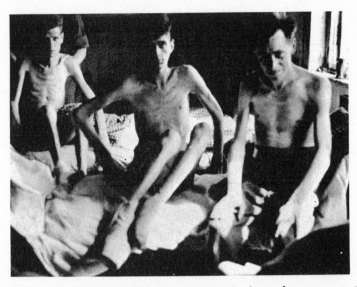

Prisoners-of-war fared little better at Nazi hands than other concentration camp inmates. English PWs from Stalag II-B show their malnutrition plainly.

Russians used as forced labor turned on a Nazi guard after their liberation. They beat him up badly.

INTERVIEW WITH KUBE'S ASSASSIN

WILHELM KUBE was the Commissar General of White Russia with headquarters in the city of Minsk.

Before the war Vilna was the nearest city to Minsk on the other side of the border between Poland and the U.S.S.R. There was a distance of 200-kilometers between the two cities.

Our first partisans were sent to the Narocz forest which was near Minsk.

Wilhelm Kube, like others of his ilk, wielded tremendous power in his district. The question of life and death for all the inhabitants of his sphere of influence was in his hands.

Rumors were spread around that Kube was a little partial to German Jews and tried to get better conditions for them than were meted out to other Jews.

The truth of the matter is that he wanted the German Jews exterminated later than the East European Jews, but he was just as gruesome as the other "Gauleiters" of his rank.

As far as the partisans in White Russia were concerned, he was Enemy Number One, and the partisan field-court issued a death sentence against him.

Our base served also as a billet for partisans from time to time. These brave souls had to pass by our section on their way to some dangerous diversive mission, far away from their own base and they found it necessary to sleep over for a few hours or to take a short rest in order to be able to continue on their way.

As I was stretched out in my own sleeping quarters, I saw the guard lead a group of 6 partisans. With his flashlight he indicated 6 vacant spots for them to occupy for the night.

There was a vacant spot near me and one of them lay down at my side.

We began to talk to each other in the darkness. He told me that they were on their way to a far-away point with the mission to explode an important ammunition depot near the old Polish-German border.

In the course of our conversation, he introduced the members of his group to me with the comment that they were hardened veterans. Among them was the one who organized and carried out the attack on Wilhelm Kube.

When I heard this, I insisted that he introduce me to the perpetrator of the deed, David Kemach.

In a second I was laying at his side and I told him that I was the head of the illegal forest press, and since I was well acquainted with the subject of Kube, I would appreciate his telling me how his execution came about.

Kemach, a Soviet Jew, was dropped by parachute into the forests of Kazan, which surround Minsk; he had conceived and executed the details of the assassination by himself.

A girl partisan had been assigned as Kube's housekeeper a long time ago. Her name was Halina Hazanik. It seems that Kemach himself sent another White Russian girl partisan with an explosive mine to Minsk. She handed it over to Halina who put it under Kube's bed.

A terrific explosion resulted and Kube was blown to bits. The courier took Halina and her entire family into the woods where Kemach was stationed as the commanding officer.

After the explosion the Germans were terrified and afraid to stick their heads out in the dark.

Abt. IIa Nr. _2407/428_

Geheim! Minsk, am __31. Juli 1942__

Der Generalkommissar
für Weissruthenien

Herrn

..eichskommissar für das Ostland
Gauleiter Hinrich L o h s e ,

Abtlg. Gauleiter/G. - _507/42g._

(Bei Beantwortung unbedingt anzugeben!)

R i g a

Der Reichskommissar für das Ostland
Tgb. Nr._____ 1122/42 g.

Geheime Reichssache!
.-.-.-.-.-.-.-.-.-.-.

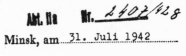

Reichskommissar
Ostland
7. VIII. 1942
Hauptabt

Betreff: Partisanenbekämpfung und Judenaktion
im Generalbezirk Weißruthenien.

Bei allen Zusammenstößen mit Partisanen in Weißruthenien
hat es sich herausgestellt, daß das Judentum sowohl im ehemals
polnischen wie auch im ehemals sowjetischen Teil des Generalbezirks
zusammen mit der polnischen Widerstandsbewegung im Osten und den
..otkommisten Moskaus im Osten Hauptträger der Partisanenbewegung
ist.

(Translation on the next page)

A small part of an official secret letter from General Commissar Wilhelm Kube.

AS SHEEP TO THE SLAUGHTER?...

(*Not according to the Germans*)

Translation: "In all clashes with partisans in White Russia it turned out that both in the former Polish and in the former Soviet parts of the General District, Jews, together with the Polish resistance movement in the West and the Red Army men in the East are the main carriers of the partisan movement."

(*Signed*): The Commissar General
for White Russia *Kube*

As one can see from the above paragraph from a secret letter that Kube wrote before he could not write any more, to his superior the Reichskomissar for Ostland, Heinrich Loshe, a year after the Germans conquered Vilna, Minsk and hundreds of other towns in our vicinity, the Germans were very much engaged in combatting the partisans. He said, *"The Jews are the MAIN carriers of the partisan movement."* (my italics).

* * *

From the "Oberkommando der Wehrmacht," a letter came to all units in the Ostland (Ostland was comprised of Latvia, Lithuania, White Russia), on February 12, 1943, with the signature of General Field Marshal Wilhelm Keitel, and read, in part:

" . . . The soldier must therefore fully understand the necessity of hard but just expiation on the part of Jewish sub-humanity. He further aims to nip in the bud revolts behind the front of the Wehrmacht which, *according to experience, are always instigated by Jews . . ."* (my italics)

THE LATE COMERS

WHENEVER I had some free time, I would usually visit the Jewish units which were recruited from the former U.P.O. members of the ghetto and other Jews. When I asked permission for such visits, I would always receive it from my superiors who were parachutists from the other side of the front.

I remember one such visit I made to the Jewish unit known as "For Victory" when the front had already come close to Vilna and we were able to hear the artillery bombardment about 100 kilometers away.

As I came close to the unit's base, I came upon a couple with their daughter—a girl about 14 to 15 years old—who were going away from the base. They were walking softly. I saw that they were not partisans since they carried no arms. They appeared quite dejected.

I stopped them and asked who they were, what they were doing there and where they were going.

The man introduced himself as Dr. Moshe Feigenberg and said that he was with his wife and daughter. I knew the name well and he recognized my name. He told me that he had been at the base of the Jewish unit and had met with the commander, Krauklis, and asked him to let him join the ranks of the partisans. Krauklis refused to accept him on the grounds that he had come too late—he had not joined the partisans earlier when they needed him most.

Krauklis then told him to leave the base and to keep away from the entire area. Their wandering in the strange forest exposed the family to considerable danger. Dangerous "White Poles" were known to be active in the area. They would shoot anyone they came across, particularly unarmed Jews.

When I heard Dr. Feigenberg's story I told them to remain where they were or to proceed back to the base at a very slow pace while I tried to persuade Krauklis to change his mind. If I succeeded, the Feigenbergs could remain in the area.

I found the commander as soon as I arrived at the base.

357

We knew each other quite well because he would frequently visit our base for meetings with the staff officers. He was a parachutist—a real Lithuanian—who now led the Jewish unit which, under his command, had become a Lithuanian unit. I greeted him and told him whom I had met not far from the base.

Krauklis was quite a personality. He even had a Jewish girl friend whom I knew. He told me the same story that Dr. Feigenberg had related and bitterly deplored the fact that they were asking to join the partisans when the latter were just about ready to leave the forest. The Feigenbergs had remained in the ghetto or in some other secure place earlier in the war.

I told him that he was wrong and that the matter was more complicated than he thought. Not everyone could always leave the ghetto to join the partisans. I told him about a group of eight men and two women who had just come to our base and nobody asked them why they came so late. On the contrary, the next day they were attached to one of the units and they went through their first battle with the Germans.

When he heard how the brigade unit had handled such a case in a similar situation, he admitted that his conscience bothered him and that he regretted having sent the Feigenbergs away.

I then suggested that he assign one of the partisans to help me find the family and bring them back. He agreed, and an hour later they were all back at the base.

When the partisans joined the regular army a few days later, Dr. Feigenberg was one of them and he was able to render medical aid to many of the wounded partisans who took Vilna.

Boris Jochej preparing
to blow up a railroad track.

Editorial Staff of the Lithuanian division "Rodina Zavyot" (Fatherland Calls). *From left, standing in rear*: Zeif, Salfeta, Esradom. Shaulis, 1944.

In the order of May 1st, 1944, the following figures showed what the "Vilna" unit achieved in the vicinity of Narocz during the ten months of its existence:

51 rail cars destroyed.

991 vehicles full of soldiers and weapons destroyed.

2 rail bridges blown up.

1 electric power station in Swienciany blown up.

1 peat works destroyed.

3 trucks destroyed and a colonel seriously wounded.

In battle, more than 30 Nazis were killed and 50 wounded. Among the killed was a lieutenant colonel with three decorations on his chest. How many officers and men were killed in the destroyed rail cars was not reported, but it is assumed to be in the many hundreds.

"SAM NACZALNIK" (ON MY OWN)

WHEN the fighting front approached Lithuanian territory, almost the entire brigade staff, headed by Yurgis, went on an assignment deep inside the country. En route they were attacked by armed forces which were hurrying to the front and suffered heavy casualties in dead and wounded. But the greater part reached their goal. I remained with the staff headquarters with a few minor commanders who did not understand the importance of fighting through the use of the printed word.

In 1958, in Argentina, one of the best books about the partisan movement in the Ukraine was written by Melech Bakalczuk-Fellin. Referring to another press where he was one of the editor's, he says: "The type was guarded by *all* partisans more carefully than precious stones."

We see from this quotation that they understood very well the importance of the printed word provided to the oppressed population.

In the absence of Yurgis I was left on my own. Then I issued the already mentioned appeal in the German language, in which I gave all the details of the opening of the Second Front in France under the command of General Eisenhower. Political officers insisted that we end with the statement that all this was due to the clever policies of Stalin.

After the Liberation, when I met Yurgis for the first time after he had resumed his right name, he praised me for my activities after he had left the base, but he was unhappy with my last proclamation in German, because I had made such a big fuss about the Second Front.

The last proclamation that I issued was to the residents of my native city, Vilna, urging them to help the attacking Soviet army and point out where the German troops were hiding; that they should not stop working; that they should prevent conflagrations; etc.

Part V

Liberation

ON THE EVE OF LIBERATION

IN the long drawn out hours when I was alone, I tried to figure
out what things would look like if we survived until liberation. The "if" was a big item in my thinking.

The first thing I did was to try to become a strategist. *How*
and *where* would the German army be forced to retreat?

I received reports that on many other fronts on the entire length of White Russia, the retreating armies frequently
avoided the main roads, where they were being bombarded, and
used side roads through the forests. If our region was in the
line of retreat, then the "*if*" about my living to see the liberation would become a real question.

Every partisan who could hold a gun in his hands had
already left to meet the attacking armies near Vilna. The badly
wounded were left behind, with a handful of men to care for
them.

My forest printing press was then in full operation and I
was among the select few who were ordered to remain at the
base, to work the press and care for the wounded.

361

A partisan returning from Vilna told me of the bloody fighting that had been going on for five days and nights around Vilna, and that the Nazis had dropped parachutists and surrounded the city in an effort to help their encircled troops. It was a surprise to me although I was only 40 kilometers away. I knew nothing of these developments. We no longer had a radio as the command staff and the radio operators had left us. We were like an abandoned group which had to maintain itself.

I thought to myself that the Soviet army had gone all the way from Moscow to Vilna and that it would soon go a bit forward so that Vilna and "my forest" would be free one day. But here came the "if"—if the remnants of the Nazi troops retreated through the woods . . .

While engrossed in such thoughts. a partisan came by and related that he had met some cavalrymen of the regular Russian army. I could not believe it. He told me that here and there were some scouting parties.

I did not waste much time to think it over and went two miles through the woods and saw about ten horses being fed by a soldier. However I did not approch them, as I knew that if I came close with weapons on my shoulder and in civilian clothes he might get scared and not knowing the password the incident might have fatal consequences.

I went right back and told the several wounded men what I had seen with my own eyes. Not something I had heard second hand. but what I had seen with my own eyes . . .

The spirits were high. But I thought to myself: these worn out, small horses have turned back the mighty tides of German panzers. It was not easy to understand.

A few hours later, three jeeps full of officers arrived with lightning speed. I came out of the bunker where I was working on the press and greeted them. I told them that there was no one left at the base except for the wounded men. a nurse and myself, who was printing the last appeals to the city dwellers.

I was astonished when one by one they began to salute me, introducing themselves as Major General so and so, Lieutenant General so and so, Colonel so and so, etc. Before I could say a word the oldest among them began by saying that he knew about the vital role of the partisans in general and of the partisans in this particular sector. When he meets a partisan he gives him the highest honors because he knows of the tremendous handicaps the underground had to face as they fought the enemy. I tried to answer that the true burden of the war was carried by the military forces and not the partisans. They did not agree with my viewpoint and insisted that it was the partisans who had a more dangerous task in fighting the Nazis than the regular army.

I did not quarrel with them too long. If they meant it, so be it. But why did they have to hail me, a small man, and salute me as though I were a general and they were the plain soldiers? ... This was what was on their mind. It was not just a singular case, but *all* of them, the entire group of officers was of the opinion that the least of the partisans was more important than the highest ranking officer of the regular army.

They did not have much time for conversation. This was a war zone. They visited the wounded men and bade us a hearty farewell. They left us some delicatessen and cigarettes and took off.

After that visit of the top brass, other jeep loads of lower ranking officers came calling. The senior officer asked various questions, such as whether I knew if there were any Germans in the forest and where the nearest brigade post was located. I told them that there was several partisan bases in the vicinity but all the men were now in Vilna, and that a brigade post led by Genis was about twenty kilometers away. However, that unit was also engaged in cleaning up the small towns where German soldiers might be hiding and I did not know exactly where they were.

While I was speaking to the officers, a large scouting patrol arrived. They went through our base and did not even stop. With weapons at the ready, dust on their grim faces, they just looked ahead. They were the real front liners, first to meet the enemy fire and they had no time to be sentimental. Behind them came a formation of trucks with nurses and doctors, wearing the Red Cross. Further behind were a lot of soldiers.

A group of five tardy partisans from another brigade, who came from an assignment to blow up a railroad, arrived at our base and told me that they were hurrying back to their unit which was now on the edge of Vilna. They also told me that en route a peasant had informed the.n that he had seen several hundred Germans with field guns and tanks leave the highway the previous night and enter the thick forest about 15 kilometers from the base.

Although all was quiet and it appeared that there were no German troops in the area, I decided to take no chances and gave this information to the attack army. I was afraid that if the German army unit was well camouflaged, it could lure the Soviet forces into a trap and there would be many casualties. I therefore mounted an emaciated horse which had been hanging around like a lost sheep, and rode in the direction taken by the fighting unit.

I told the senior officer what I had just learned. The whole unit came to a halt. I told them approximately where, according to the account of the peasant, the large camouflaged German unit might be located. By radio, the commander contacted the tank units which were rolling along parallel to the highway in the direction of Grodno and Bialystok. In a half hour a column of heavy tanks appeared.

They took up positions and I was in the middle . . .

After a Russian barrage of anti-tank shells the Germans replied with heavy fire. This proved that they were actually there and that my guess was correct.

When it seemed that I would go through the war without being involved in a frontal attack by a regular armored division, I was given the privilege of participating in this kind of a battle. There were Russian casualties, but the end result was that in the two-hour battle an entire S.S. unit, with its twelve medium tanks, several cannon and 635 soldiers and officers were destroyed.

It was later learned from the surviving officers that the Germans had not intended to attack the marching troops but wanted to hide in the woods and valleys until the first units of the Red Army had gone by, when they could attack from the rear . . .

Fate, however, decreed that the five partisans, not meeting up with any Soviet forces in the woods because they had followed the narrow dogpaths usually taken by the partisans when they were moving in small groups, should stop for a rest, find out what was doing in that neck of the woods, and off-handedly giving me the information which I hastened to forward to the right parties in the nick of time.

After the battle a certain colonel and I were thanked in front of a large military formation, and on my request, I was taken by jeep back to my bunker where the printing press was kept. I had to finish my interrupted work; between twilight and sunset, I had taken time to participate in a regular frontal attack.

* * *

While still in the ghetto I knew that the Germans were most afraid of the Russian frost and of the "Katuscha." I did not know exactly what a "Katuscha" was so when I saw one for the first time, it was a pleasant surprise. Just as the skinny horses did not make much of an impression, so did the "Katuscha" fail to impress a viewer although it was considered one of the greatest artillery inventions of the Soviets during World War II. The shrapnel blew up in phases, that is, after one part of the shell exploded and caused widespread damage, a few seconds later another section exploded and compounded the effect in another spot.

An officer explained to me how it works, which he did in

"Katuschas" in action.

Yiddish. He gave me a shell to hold in my hand, telling me to place it on the carriage from which it was launched. The shrapnel hit an area in a fire break. It was then that I got first hand knowledge of this weapon that struck so much fear into Nazi hearts. In the ghetto, I, Yitzhak Kowalski, never dared to think that some day I would hold one in my hand, and scrawl on it with chalk my name in Hebrew before sending it to our "best friends," the beleaguered S.S. unit which now paid the full price for its good deeds prior to July of 1944.

Marshal Ivan Konev (left) confers with General Omar Bradley (center), 1945.

Three Crosses on the hill of the peaceful Wilenka river, before the war.

Army and Partisans in Battle of Vilna Streets

From left: Noima Markeles, Szmerke Kaczerginski, Aba Kowner, Isaac Kowalski.

Ilya Ehrenburg in Vilna with Jewish partisans after the liberation. *From left to right*: Chaim Zeidelson (part face), David Ehrlich, Abraham Sabrin, Schloma Kowarski, Yichiel Warszawczyk (part head), Ilya Ehrenburg (with beret). Isaac Kinkulkin (part face), Dr. Sola Gorfinkel, Ema Gorfinkel, Hirsch Gurwicz, Isaac Alter, Rivka Karpinkes, Israel Weis (part face), Dr. Leon Bernstein, Rachel Mendelshon-Kowarski.

THE BATTLE FOR VILNA

An order arrived, via radio, directing the brigade in the Rudnicki wilderness to leave the forest on July 8, 1944, and approach the outskirts of Vilna.

During the last phases of our partisan activities, there had been formed at my base a unit called "Adam Mickiewicz," under the command of Margis. Nominally, I also belonger to this unit. For political reasons, it had been named after the Polish author and patriot, who had written "Dziady" 113 years ago to celebrate the Vilna revolt against Russia. In the unit were many Jews, Poles and Lithuanians.

Under the command of Brigadier Gabris and Captain Wasilenko (the latter being a very assimilated Jew from Kiev who was a submarine commander captured by the Germans; he managed to escape and join the partisans), my unit left the base. En route, it met up with the other units in the area, and they closed ranks for the march on Vilna.

The battle for Vilna was a bitter one. The enemy was entrenched on the strategic "Three Crosses" hills and other points, and the attacking forces paid a heavy price in hundreds of lives. Partisans also died, including Borowicz and Jelecki of the "Adam Mickiewicz" unit. The Germans lost 8,000 men in their effort to hold the city. They destroyed forty percent of Vilna, and went so far as to drop reinforcements by parachute, to help out their beleaguered army. But the last desperate effort was of no avail. That July, Vilna was redeemed by the Soviet troops and the partisans.

Later, I heard on the German radio that the Germans had retreated from Vilna for strategic reasons, in order to straighten their front lines . . .

*   *   *

Isaac Kowalski/A Secret Press In Nazi Europe

The great War Correspondent ILYA EHRENBURG writes about the recapture of Vilnius: *

". . . On 12th July, towards evening, I glimpsed the first houses of Vilnius; there was shooting on all sides and a Major whom I did not know shouted: "Down." On that day our tank-men were already far ahead, halfway to Kaunas; ** but in the woods to the east of Minsk groups of Germans still roamed, unaware that the distance between them and the German army was far now than that between the Soviet tank-men and the German frontier.

"Somewhere near Molodechno I spent the night at Marshal Pavel Alexandrovich Rotmistrov's quarters. He told me: 'Last summer the tanks played a different role, at that time they flushed the enemy out, but now we encircle and destroy him. In these days one can't do without technical equipment. Nor without using one's head either, naturally. Our people are intelligent but slow to get going: there's not much room for initiative. Let's hope that after the war we'll live more sensibly.' I liked the marshal: young and keen, he knew how to appraise not only military operations but many other things as well: the politics of our Allies, literature and even various kinds of Rhine wine. I met him two or three times after the war and came to the conclusion that he was as bold in everyday civilian life as he had been on the battlefield, and that is perhaps the harder of the two.

"I had never been to Vilnius before. The Germans had not had time to set fire to the town and it was extraordinary to see the houses, baroque Catholic churches, narrow old streets. Here and there a little old woman creeping out of a cellar and immediately darting back. The wounded being carried in. Prisoners being led to the Ros cemetery. There were few soldiers about, they were busy clearing the Germans out of a coppice on the outskirts. Only the day before the Germans were still holding the centre of the town, the old prison of Lukiszki. Even now many of them were hiding and there was sporadic machine-gun fire.

"General Krylov was sitting over a map, his eyes red from sleepless nights. On seeing me he shook his head: 'You oughtn't to be wandering about, they're shooting from windows. Of course I realize that you find it interesting, but still . . .'

"At the command post I met the writer Pavlenko. I had first met him in 1926 when I was passing through Stambul and he took me to see Santa Sophia. We seldom ran into one another: he was an excellent raconteur and I enjoyed listening to his incredible stories but, as so often happens, we did not meet for years on end, and I never gave him a thought. Now we talked about the town together. In the main square the Germans had abandoned hundreds of motor vehicles loaded with an incredible assortment of objects: Cine-cameras, French liqueurs, detective novels, lavatory paper. At the Ostrobramsky Gate women were on their knees praying to the Virgin. We went to St. Anne's Church. Pavlenko said that Napoleon had expressed regret that he could not remove this church to Paris. We made our way to the house where Mickiewicz had lived. Every few steps we came across the bodies of local inhabitants who had been killed; I remember an old man with a small pointed silver beard who

*Lithuanian spelling of Vilna.
**Kaunas—Kovno.

looked like a scholar of the past century; by his side lay a stick with a white knob. Pavlenko examined the white knob, the statues in the church and a German radio-set with great attention; suddenly he said: 'It's raining. Let's go. I've got a bottle of French brandy.'

"Later I wandered about alone. A sergeant came up to me and asked to see my papers; after reading them he broke out laughing: 'So that's who you are. I've read your articles, I don't think I've missed a single one. What I want to ask you is to tell them to make the papers print every day how many miles still to go to Germany. I keep asking and nobody really knows—some say a hundred, others say a hunderd and fifty. If it can't be done in the Moscow papers, let them print it in the army sheets. I think we'll get the job done for the November celebrations. My mother's in Biysk, she writes that she's waiting from day to day, she's ill and she's afraid she won't live to see the end.'

"*I came across a group of Jewish partisans; they were helping to clear the Fascists out of the cellars and attics. I got into conversation with two young girls—Rachel Mendelsohn and Emma Gorfinkel. They told me that they had been in the ghetto. Almost daily the Germans had sent groups of people to Ponary where they put them to death. Those who remained alive had to work; they were sent out under escort. In the ghetto itself there was a secret resistance organization; its members burnt stores, laid mines, killed Nazis. A mass escape was being organized. The leader of the organization was a Vilnius worker, the Communist Wittenberg. The Nazis found out about him and demanded that he should give himself up or they would destroy the whole ghetto. Wittenberg told his comrades: 'You'll be able to work without me. I don't want everybody killed because of me.' He was tortured to death. Five hundred of the prisoners in the ghetto managed to escape; they fought in groups called: 'For Victory,' 'The Avengers,' 'Death to Fascism.' Rachel and Emma had been students before the war and were greatly interested in literature. Now they held in their hands not books but grenades. They laughed gaily; I have still got a photograph of myself amongst a group of partisans.* (I. K. italics).

"On the morrow there was an Order of the Day announcing the liberation of Vilnius: the Germans in the copse began to surrender. I roamed about the streets again and stopped to talk to people; they looked horrifying after five days spent in cellars, often without food or even water; but everyone smiled—the worst was now behind them. There were no longer any corpses in the streets. The soldiers were removing the loot from the German cars. People said that bread would be issued."

*　　*　　*

After the war, Margis invited me to his home to meet his parents. I took with me the poet-partisan Abraham Suckewer. To our astonishment we found that Margis and his parents had lived during the Nazi period in a building whose backyard was adjacent to Gestapo headquarters at Mickewicz Street and many sentries were all around their building during the war. They protected the Margis home from where he was directing sabotage activities against the occupants. A bigger irony could not be imagined . . .

General (later Marshal) Chernickowski with Ilya Ehrenburg
at the front in 1942.

An American MP and a Russian policewoman guard a bridge on the
river Elbe.

k Times.

LATE CITY EDITION
Partly cloudy and continued warm today with moderate winds.
Temperatures Yesterday—Max. 80; Min., 7
Sunrise, 5:39 A. M.; Sunset, 8:26 P. M

apany.

Y 16, 1944.   Including Magazine and Book Sections.

TEN C
New York City and Subur

S FLANK GRODNO, KAUN
REPORTS DRIVE ON LV
CANS IN LESSAY OUTSK

RUSSIAN TROOPS ENTER VILNA

2 FOR

Red Ar
River
Eas

LONG

Soviet
Bialy
Pu

LOND
a deep
nine pa
Red A
flacked
Nazi h
proache
of Germ
the Ru
ful nev
ress at
Poland
While
the e

elf-propelled gun of the Red Army passes a disabled German howitzer in the city captured
e Nazis after five days of fierce street fighting.

The New York Times (Sovfoto Radiophoto)

WITH MARSHAL CHERNICKOWSKI

THE General Staff of the Third White Russian Front had set up its provisional base in the forest near the townlet of Woronowa, which was about 60 kilometers from Vilna. After the liberation of Vilna, I was named technical director of the Polygraphic Trust, and thus supervised all the printing plants in Lithuania. One day I was visited by a Soviet official who told me that recently their field press that was carried on trucks, had been badly damaged. They were in urgent need of printing equipment. He told me that he was the chief editor of the frontline newspapers and had been ordered to get such equipment in liberated Lithuania.

After hearing the problem, I asked him if he was ready to take the machinery with him right away. He answered that below, at the entrance, an officer and some soldiers were waiting. I immediately boarded one of their autos and we drove to the largest printing plant, *Spindulis*, where I showed the soldiers which equipment they could dismantle.

After finishing the job I wanted to say goodby to the editor but he told me that he wanted me to be present when the machinery was being assembled, and especially, he wanted to introduce me to Marshal Chernickowski, who had heard of my record during the war. I was taken aback but agreed to go along.

My talk with Marshal Chernickowski, one of the greatest Soviet Jewish heroes, lasted fifteen minutes. The marshal spoke very slowly and friendly. He asked about everything that had happened during the Nazi occupation. I felt that he had a very sensitive heart. He was serious and concerned, and mentioned that if we needed anything we should freely ask him for it. This we did, and he helped a great deal, for example, in getting furnishing for a Jewish children's home. He sent it through the Jewish psychiatrist, Professor Rebelski, who had his hospital in Vilna.

The next day a circular arrived in all factories stating

374

that nothing should be given to the military as they had their own sources of supply. I thought to myself: if the Russians came to me with a similar request again, I would lead them to the former well-known printing plant of the Widow Romm and Brothers, in which the machines of my father's plant had been placed when the Soviet regime was established in Vilna, and I would gladly give them equipment for the front, rather than worry about the future of the Lithuanian economy.

* * *

I go along the streets of liberated Vilna and see here and there the large proclamations of the Third White Russian Front, signed by Marshal Chernickowski, and my proclamation which was issued during the hours when Vilna was stormed. Hundreds of Jewish partisans participated in the liberation of the Lithuanian capital. We liberated Vilna, but it is no longer our Vilna, the Jerusalem of Lithuania.

* * *

Chernickowski was killed on the front in Prussia. The army command brought his body back to Vilna, and buried him with great honor in a newly created military cemetery, in Orzeszkowa Place, near Mickiewicz St. in the heart of the city, where many thousands of Soviet soldiers and some partisans, who fell in combat while liberating Vilna, were buried.

It was a mystery to me, why Chernickowski's body was brought back from Prussia to Vilna, when there were many military cemeteries along the way.

One possibility was that it was his last wish. If it was so, it remains a mystery to me to this day, as to why he chose Vilna as his final resting place.

Jewish partisans are reading news of the front
in a street of liberated Vilna.

To the end of the war these fourteen year old children were Hitler's soldiers, because the mature soldiers were already dead, wounded, or in captivity.

Soldiers of the Lithuanian Brigade consisted mainly of Jewish fighters.

A memorial to the martyrs of Ponary. After the liberation, the remnants of Vilna Jewry were gathered together at the place in the Ponary Forest where the massacre took place and the people of the city who were murdered by the Nazis were commemorated.

A crowd of Jewish people came to the pits of Ponary for prayers. Professor, Colonel Rebelski, a Jew from Moscow, weeps.

These tots lived as Aryan children and survived

Actor Berman

Jacob Prener,
principal of the childrens home

Teachers and Governesses of the Jewish school and children's home after the war. Prof. Colonel Rebelski (*in uniform*) was a patron of the school.

WOJSKO POLSKIE

Tymczasowe zaświadczenie Nr 23340

Okaziciel niniejszego *podpułkownik Muszkat Marian s. Marka*

<small>(Stopień, nazwisko, imię, imię ojca)</small>

odznaczony *Rozkazem Personalnym Naczelnego Dowódcy W. P.*

<small>dekretem lub rozkazem</small>

Nr *548* z „*13*" *lipca* 194*5* r.

ZA BOHATERSKIE CZYNY i DZIELNE ZACHOWANIE SIĘ
W WALCE Z NIEMIECKIM NAJEŹDŹCĄ

Orderem medalem *Krzyż III kl. Grunwaldzki*

Szef Oddziału Pers. W. P.

Podpis wręczającego:
ZAWADZKI Stanisław
Zajmowane stanowisko i stopień
pułkownik

M p. „*18*" *lipca* 194*5* r.

Temporary certificate that Prof. Marian Muszkat is promoted to Lieutenant-Colonel in the Polish army for his heroic combat against Germany.

ПРОЛЕТАРИИ ВСЕХ СТРАН, СОЕДИНЯЙТЕСЬ!

Год издания 2

№ 166 (846)

ПЯТНИЦА
14
ИЮЛЯ
1944 г.

Цена 20 ко

ИЗВЕСТИЯ
СОВЕТОВ ДЕПУТАТОВ ТРУДЯЩИХСЯ СССР

ПРИКАЗ
Верховного Главнокомандующего
Генералу армии ЧЕРНЯХОВСКОМУ

Войска 3-го БЕЛОРУССКОГО фронта сегодня, 13 июля, в результате пятидневных боев уничтожили гарнизон немцев, окруженный в городе ВИЛЬНЮС, и освободили столицу Литовской Советской Республики от фашистских захватчиков.

В боях за овладение городом ВИЛЬНЮС отличились войска генерал-лейтенанта КРЫЛОВА, генерал-майора КАЗАРЦЕВА, генерал-майора ПЕРЕКРЕСТОВА, генерал-майора ПОПЛАВСКОГО, генерал-майора ГЛАДЫШЕВА, генерал-майора ЛАСКИНА, генерал-майора КАЗАРЬЯНА, полковника ДОНЕЦ, генерал-майора КАЛИНИНА, генерал-майора АЛЕКСЕЕНКО, полковника ЖЕКОВА-БОГАТЫРЕВА, полковника БАБАЯНА, генерал-майора ГОРОДОВИКОВА; артиллеристы генерал-лейтенанта артиллерии БАРСУКОВА, генерал-майора артиллерии ФЕДОРОВА, генерал-майора артиллерии ВЛАДИМИРОВА, полковника БАРЫШЕВА, полковника РАХМАНОВА, полковника ЧЕРНЕТА, генерал-майора артиллерии ЮДИЧЕВА, генерал-майора артиллерии РОЖАНОВИЧА, полковника ГАЦКО, полковника СЕДОВА, подполковника ТИХОМИРОВА, майора ГУЖВА, подполковника ЛИТВИНОВА, подполковника КОЗЛОВА, майора РЫЖИКОВА, майора УСОВА, подполковника НИКИТИНА, подполковника НАУМЕНКО, майора КОЛУПАЕВА, майора ШАРКОВА, полковника МЕЖИНСКОГО; танкисты генерал-лейтенанта танковых войск ОБУХОВА, генерал-лейтенанта танковых войск РОДИНА, полковника РОДИОНОВА, полковника КРЕМЕРА, полковника СОКОЛОВА, генерал-майора танковых войск АСЛАНОВА, генерал-майора инженерно-танковой службы СОЛОВОГО, генерал-майора танковых войск ВОВЧЕНКО, генерал-майора танковых войск ФОМИНЫХ, полковника ГРИЦЕНКО, подполковника ЕСИПЕНКО, полковника ДОЛГАНОВА, подполковника МОЛЧАНОВА, подполковника КУРНОСО-ВА, подполковника МИЩЕНКО, подполковника ДЬЯЧУКА, полковника КРУТИН, подполковника СОЛТЕРА, майора БОРЩЕНКОВА, подполковника НЕМКОВИЧА; летчики генерал-полковника авиации ХРЮКИНА, генерал-лейтенанта авиации БЕЛЕЦКОГО, генерал-лейтенанта авиации САВИЦКОГО, генерал-майора авиации АНДРЕЕВА, полковника САВИНА, подполковника ГОРБАТЮКА, подполковника ОРЛОВА, подполковника ДОРОШЕНКО, подполковника ЗАЙЦЕВА, полковника ЧУЧЕВА, майора КАТКОВА, полковника ВАСИЛЬЕВА, полковника ЧУМАЧЕНКО, полковника РОДИНА; саперы генерал-лейтенанта инженерных войск БАРАНОВА, полковника МОЛЧАНОВА, майора РАБИНОВИЧА, полковника ЮСУПОВА, полковника ЛУКАШЕНКО и связисты генерал-майора войск связи БУРОВА, полковника ПРИХОДАЙ, подполковника БЕЛОВА, полковника МИНИНА, полковника ТКАЧЕНКО, майора ТАРАСЕНКО, майора СЕМЕНОВА, майора СУХИНИНА.

В ознаменование одержанной победы соединения и части, наиболее отличившиеся в боях за овладение городом ВИЛЬНЮС, представить к присвоению наименования «ВИЛЕНСКИХ» и к награждению орденами.

Сегодня, 13 июля, в 23 часа 30 минут столица нашей Родины МОСКВА от имени Родины салютует доблестным войскам 3-го Белорусского фронта, овладевшим столицей Советской Литвы — городом ВИЛЬНЮС, — двадцатью четырьмя артиллерийскими залпами из трехсот двадцати четырёх орудий.

За отличные боевые действия ОБЪЯВЛЯЮ БЛАГОДАРНОСТЬ руководимым Вами войскам, участвовавшим в боях за освобождение города ВИЛЬНЮС.

Вечная слава героям, павшим в боях за свободу и независимость нашей Родины!

Смерть немецким захватчикам!

Верховный Главнокомандующий
Маршал Советского Союза
И. СТАЛИН

13 июля 1944 года.

Izvestia about the liberation of Vilna—a commendation of General Czerniakowski, and many other soldiers and officers. *Signed*: J. Stalin.

A HELPING HAND

DURING the period of over three years that Vilna was under the Nazi occupation, the city escaped heavy destruction because the Russian army retreated with almost no resistance. Things were quite different when the time came to drive Nazism out of my native city.

It was a great surprise for me to find out that the Germans had decided to stage a terrific, stubborn resistance to the attacking Russian army and the partisans.

The Jewish partisans as well as the others were assigned to regular Russian army units on the periphery of the city. They knew the city in and out—her streets, alleys and passageways. They acted as guides from the periphery into the heart of the city. When bloody battles took place, when they had to fight for every street and courtyard, the Jewish partisans proved of inestimable value in guiding the regular army soldiers through various back-streets to break through to the enemy.

There were heavy losses in the ranks of Soviet soldiers and partisans and after many days of bloody battle, the city was recaptured by the combined efforts of the Jewish partisans and the Soviet army.

The park on Orzeszkowa Place was turned into a tremendous cemetery for the fallen soldiers and partisans.

The high partisan command had temporary headquarters in a large building, where the daily Polish newspaper *Curier Wilenski* was located before the war. The *Klucz* High School was also located in this building, in the vicinity of the historic Vilna Cathedral.

In those days I was assigned the job of collecting the weapons which the partisans had to return, because their services to the city were terminated. Every one of us was assigned a responsible civil service position.

It was my first opportunity to see such a varied collection of weapons from all over the world; from the short Japanese rifles to the small revolvers with ivory handles for ladies; from World War I long French rifles, to American colts. I had one thought in mind then—if we only had these weapons one year earlier while we were still in the Vilna ghetto, how useful they would have been . . .

One by one the partisans came to return their weapons. They were no more partisans. Now they were civilians. More than one found it difficult to part with his weapon. Many never let their weapons out of their hands during all those years of bloody warfare. This was their way of life! Therefore I was not surprised to see tears well up in their eyes—not because they had to part with their weapon, but because it represented memories of the heroic occasions when the weapon had to be used.

A few feet away from my station an anti-aircraft battery was installed. During the course of my service I used to visit the anti-aircraft outfit and chat with the soldiers and officers on duty. I used to tell them things about the city of Vilna which were entirely strange to them. They came from all over Russia and they told of their experiences behind the cannon. I told them they would be unemployed here because the front was far from the city. One officer burst out laughing. "Don't be so sure," he told me. "An airplane has no fronts. We may have many guest-appearances."

I was right for a few days. But one afternoon a squadron of German airplanes came and began to bombard Vilna. That one occasion made up for lost time.

The entire city quivered, but some of the planes never returned to their base. I ran over and lent a helping hand to the anti-aircraft unit, which shot down nine airplanes.

When the struggle was over I tried to figure out, together with the commanding officer, where the planes fell down. One fell in Tielatnik, I told them; a second, in Antokol; a third, in Pospieszki; a fourth, in Wolokumpia; a fifth, on the way to the small town of Niemenczyny; a sixth fell into the Wilja river, etc.

A short while later they received an official report about the results of their efforts and where the airplanes fell down. It tallied more or less with my prognosis . . .

A group of former U.P.O.-members. Photographed on the day of the liberation of Vilna. *From left*: Elchonon Magid, Jacob Prener, Bluma Markowicz, (x) killed in a bombardment a few days after the picture was taken), Aba Kowner, Ruszka Korczak, Leib Sapirsztein, Vitka Kempner. *Kneeling from l.*: Gerszan Griner, Pesach Mizerec, Motl Szames.

Zarecza cemetery (x), the place where we buried Bluma Markowicz. At the gates was standing Agronom Jacob Szabad.

383

THE LAST BOMBARDMENT

AFTER living for several days as a civilian in the liberated city of Vilna, I was employed as director of the Polygraphic Trust. One day Bluma Markowicz, a former art student at the University of Vilna and a partisan, came and told me that she was assigned to a room in a nice apartment, in which before the war lived the Deiches family. Their daughter Miriam was considered the Shirley Temple of our town. Even as a child she made guest appearances in the U.S.A. This family had lived on top of our former apartment. Bluma told me that she had been living there several days already in the apartment, which was occupied by a Catholic family.

I was waiting till Masha, who had served our family faithfully for 40 years, would come back from the hospital, where she was confined due to general weakness. Then I planned to move into Masha's apartment which was on top of Bluma's present room. I was born in the building and lived there prior to the war.

Bluma complained that because of the curfew that started in the early evening, she was compelled to stay alone in her lonely room. She had come to ask whether I would move to Masha's apartment immediately so we could be neighbors and could talk together so as to break the monotony of her drab life.

I told Bluma that I had the keys to the apartment for quite a long time and I would move in the next morning. I would bring along my bundle of bones, for at that time I didn't have much else, and await the arrival of Masha at her apartment.

Happy Bluma left with the thought that a fellow member of the U.P.O. would be in the same building to keep her company.

Unfortunately I had business to take care of in Kovno which compelled me to break my promise to Bluma.

That night, when I had this mission to take care of, the building in which I, my brothers and sister were born, was destroyed by a German bombardment. Among the ruins was Bluma's body.

The following day a group of U.P.O. members, along with their former commander, Aba Kowner, had to perform the burial rites at the pre-war Zarecza cemetery.

There were no Jewish undertakers to take care of the burial, so we dug the grave ourselves. At the bottom of the pit the young girl was handed to me so that I should lay her down. As she was being handed to me, an arm fell out of the blood-soaked blanket and I put it back in position, so that it and the rest of her might rest in peace.

*   *   *

After the destruction of the building of 17 Stefanska Street I lived in an apartment at 16 Stefanska Street with the old Masha, after she had returned from the hospital. I fed her at my expense and helped her to convalesce from her serious illness. I no sooner settled down when a second bombardment took place which shattered the entire Vilna railroad station.

The teacher Miriam Ganiszczyker was visiting me at this time and was caught in the middle of the bombardment. Due to the heavy vibrations the wooden frames of my windows were loosened. One of those frames fell on my guest's face and the glass fragments bloodied it. This was the last flow of blood which I saw upon the face of a Vilna Jewish girl. No more German planes appeared over Vilna. They had to defend their own railroad stations in Germany.

A street in Vilna after the war.

JEWISH NAMES

IN Jew-free Vilna there appeared immediately after the liberation from the "Thousand-Year Third Reich" a small poster, only twelve by seventeen inches in size, with the announcement that a whole list of heads of various factories and businesses had been appointed by the city committee, as though it had been a City Hall. By itself this would not have been worth mentioning. However, since the entire group of ten consisted of partisans, former U.P.O. members, they were all Jewish names.

I happened to overhear a conversation on the street between two Vilna Christians. One said to the other: "See, we thought the Germans had killed all the Jews of Vilna and here you have such names as Chava Glezer, Feige Milstein, Jakob Prener, Ruszka Korczak, Niusia Lubocki, Paul Bagrianski." The second man answered: "Yes, I'm beginning to believe that the Jews are really an eternal people!"

The head of the city committee was Petrajtis. He was one of the few Lithuanians who voluntarily came to the forest to fight the Nazis and he was shortly thereafter named commander of the almost exclusively Jewish unit, "Nekamah." So, when he became a very high official in the town's civilian affairs, he appointed "his Jews" to various important economic posts.

Incidentally I know that in the circles of the Lithuanian city fathers it was considered "politically inconsistent" to publish a list with such genuine "Lithuanian" names as those mentioned above.

Whoever wishes to see in this evidence that the Jews are an eternal people, may do so.

MY MEETING WITH PRESIDENT PALECKIS

ONCE I came on an official mission in August 1944 as the representative of the Polygraphic Trust to my former brigade commander Zimanas (Yurgis). He had attained a very high position in the Lithuanian government. I had to see him about important matters relative to my polygraphic office. In the middle of our conversation he lifted up a telephone receiver to call somebody. When I rose to take my leave, he told me that he had just spoken with President Paleckis, who asked that I come to see him.

The president had his office in a temorary quarter, one-floor above Zimanas, in the same building. The guard was apprised of my coming and I was ushered in.

As I entered he greeted me with the Hebrew words of welcome, "Sholom Aleichem," (Peace be with you) and then he went right over into Russian (Paleckis knew how to speak and write Yiddish very well. He had learned the language when he was confined for many years in the pre-war jails of Lithuania for his political revolutionary activities.)

Paleckis told me he had heard quite a bit about me when he was the President of the Lithuanian Government-in-Exile in Moscow, during the war years. He had received many reports about the underground partisan activities. On his agenda there was a list of partisans he had intended to invite to a gathering and my name was among the others. But since I was in the building, according to information given him by Zimanas, he had expressed the wish to see me personally.

Paleckis praised and thanked me for my activities in the period of the Nazi occupation, and after we finished our conversation, he escorted me down the length of the corridor to the staircase.

Isaac Kowalski/A Secret Press In Nazi Europe

On July 9, 1945, in the official paper of Lithuania, "Tiesa" (Truth), there appeared a speech delivered by the Soviet-Lithuanian President Yustas I. Paleckis. This excerpt is a reference to Jewish participation in the resistance movement:

"The Jews of Vilna wrote a heroic chapter in the history of Judaica of Vilna with the story of the struggle of the Vilna Jews against the German occupation forces. Jews did not go to their death passively; they fought bravely against the German aggressor. A partisan battalion was organized in the Vilna ghetto with Wittenberg as its head. After they escaped from the ghetto, the Jewish partisans derailed a train carrying a military echelon by blowing it up with improvised mines, put together in the city of Vilna. The partisans organized a series of diversive actions in ammunition plants and in other places where they worked. At the risk of life and limb they gave help to war prisoners and to the wives and children of Soviet soldiers and officers. On the day of the final liquidation of the ghetto, a group of Jewish partisans escaped to the forest, integrated with their Lithuanian brothers and continued their struggle. This day, together with the Lithuanian partisans, they joyously welcome the Red Army on liberated Lithuanian soil."

Russian newspaper in Estonia about "Lager of death in Klooga"

EPILOGUE ESTONIA

THE Vilna Jewry account did not terminate with the ghetto. Deported to Estonia and Riga, the survivors landed in the notorious Baltic labor camps, in which life was worse than death. The unhappy slaves were distributed among various places of work and torture. Near Riga there were at least half a dozen such camps, including Kaiserwald, which absorbed the last transport of 1,500 Vilna women. Near Vilna there were also Dundagien and Strasenhof, which absorbed the overflow of Vilna transports. The Estonian concentration camps were drenched with the sweat and blood of Lithuanian Jewry. The camps—Veivara, Goldpilz, Portkunde, Klooga, Kivioli, Narva —evoke horrible memories.

With the approach of the Soviet armies, the Nazis accelerated the tempo of exterminating the Jews. In August, the Jews from Latvia and Estonia were rushed to Stuthof and Magdeburg, in a race against time. Whole columns were slaughtered with hand grenades or drowned in the Elbe.

In Klooga, near Revel, where the Jews had worked under the most brutal conditions, the Nazis selected from among the inmates the most robust individuals and assigned them to labor gangs, to cut lumber. While other prisoners stood at attention, these men cut and brought in logs, which were arranged in rows and spaced to cover an entire field. The Jews were then ordered to lie down on the log grills, face down. About 1,800 people were machine gunned, and their bodies cremated on the logs. This happened on September 29, barely a few hours before the first Soviet units arrived.

Zelig Kalmanowicz, the "Prophet of the Ghetto," a famous sixty-year-old writer, scientist and linguist, was among those deported to Estonia. He worked in Kivioli and died in Camp Narva.

A no less horrible crime was the massacre and drowning of some 4,000 Jewish survivors gathered from the northern camps. After a forced march from Fischausen on January 29,

Zelig Kalmanowicz

1945, these people were shot or drowned in the Baltic Sea. Some of the victims, shot but still alive, pleaded for another bullet before being thrown into the sea. They cried: "Ya Zhivu!" (I am alive), But the Ukrainian escort lacked ammunition and the sea was impatiently waiting for its victims.

In the northern reaches, tucked away in far off places, the rest of the best of Vilna Jewry died.

Protocol

A commission composed of the following persons: First Lieutenant Ochrepow, Chairman; Major Leibowicz; First Lieutenant Pawlenkow; the former concentration-camp doctor Buzanski; Mendl Balberiszki, pharmacist; Ratner, an engineer; and Dondes, an electrician.

In the area east of Padiszki, in the town of Klooga, during the retreat of the German army, the following atrocities were committed: September 19, 1944, at five o'clock in the morning they "selected" inmates of the camp; among them were some 700 women, 750 men, and 60 children up to 14 years of age. Aside from those, they added 1,500 people brought over from other concentration-camps. During the entire day, all of them were driven out in groups to the nearby woods and shot. In the evening at 7 o'clock, they set fire to the place where the shooting occurred and burned the victims' bodies.

Despite the burning and the will to erase proof of their animalistic crimes, marks were left over, that testified to the massacres. Of the lot, only about a hundred people managed to survive.

Town of Klooga-Camp, 11:40 o'clock. September 25, 1944.

Russian troops surging towards Berlin march prisoners past a dead Nazi.

German officers are paraded in Moscow as War Prisoners in the beginning
of 1945.

Corpse of the Fuehrer and Reich Chancellor Adolf Hitler in box
as released for the first time in 1968 from the official
Russian archives.

Autopsy Commission with corpse of Reich Propaganda Minister
Dr. Joseph Goebels, as released for the first time in 1968
from the official Moscow archives.

IMPORTANT DATES

1939–1941

Before SEPTEMBER 1939—60,000 Jews lived in Vilna. With the addition of war victims, the Jewish population rose to about 80,000. After being occupied for a short time by the Soviet Army, the city was turned over by the Soviet Government to the independent Lithuania of President Smetona on OCTOBER 10, and remained under its sway until AUGUST 3, 1940, when it came under Soviet Lithuania and belonged to it until the invasion of the German Army on JUNE 24, 1941.

The first Jewish Council (Judenrat) was formed JULY 4. On JULY 11, occurred the first mass shooting of Jews on the Ponary. The order to wear yellow patches was issued on JULY 15. On AUGUST 3rd, Jews were forbidden to walk on the sidewalks. On AUGUST 6th a 5 million ruble assessment was imposed on the Jews.

AUGUST 25.—Dr. Jacob Wigodski, 86 years of age, the elder of Vilna Jewry, was arrested and sent to Lukiszki prison, where he was a few days and later with others sent to death.

On AUGUST 31 occurred the "great provocation," during which 8,000 Jews were slain. On SEPTEMBER 6th, about 30,000 Jews were driven into Ghetto No. 1 and 10,000 more into Ghetto No. 2. A day later the Jews of various streets (Pohulanka, Jasinska, Kalwariska, Antokol, Mickewicza, etc.) were led directly to the Lukiszki jail instead of the ghetto.

SEPTEMBER 15, 3,000 Jews were put to death on the pretext that they were being led from Ghetto No. 1 to Ghetto No. 2. On OCTOBER 1st, on Yom Kippur night, 2,250 Jews were taken to their death from Ghetto No. 1, and 1,750 from Ghetto No. 2.

On OCTOBER 3rd—2,000 Jews from Ghetto No. 2 were led to their death. On OCTOBER 16th—3,000 more Jews. On OCTOBER 24th, there occurred the first action of the "Yellow Certificates" in Ghetto No. 1, and 5,000 Jews were wiped out. On OCTOBER 28, 29, 30—Ghetto No. 2 was liquidated, 2,500 Jews were killed. The second action of the "Yellow Certificates" took place on NOVEMBER 3rd and 4th, nearly 1,200 Jews died. An action took place DECEMBER 4th with 600 Jews dead. The DECEMBER 5th action against the so-called "Jewish underworld," 90 dead Jews. DECEMBER 20-21 the action of the "Pink Certificates"—400 dead Jews.

1942

The United Partisan Organization was definitely established on JANUARY 23, 1942. Then came a relatively quiet period in the Vilna ghetto, and a number of institutions were established in it. At this time, mass slaughter of Jews in the province of Vilna took place.

APRIL 15—Organization of a group called Esther (a fighting group) which later became known as the Ilya Scheinbaum group.

1943

FEBRUARY 17, 1943. Lisa Magun was executed.

The "Kovno" action took place on APRIL 5. Fearing that the remnants of the youth in the Vilna province would run off to join the partisans, the Gestapo transferred them to the Vilna ghetto. After being there a few days they were removed and sent to the Kovno ghetto, where there was more room. On the way to Kovno they were taken to Ponary. The misled youth saw where they were and broke out of the freight cars and tried to escape. They were massacred in the cars and on the railway tracks. Of the 5,000 healthy and educated youths, only a handful were saved.

The Glazman days were during the first half of JULY (see story).

On JULY 9, 200 Vilna Jews were shot in the work camp Kena, and 350 in the Besdan camp. These camps were near Vilna.

Wittenberg day—JULY 15 (see story).

JULY 27 was the beginning of the end of the existence of the first ghetto. All the bridges of the labor units were then wiped out. On AUG. 1, all Jews were released from slave labor and were put into the hermetically sealed ghetto. The situation was catastrophic. Mass hunger ruled. On AUGUST 6 the first transport was shipped to Estonia, about a thousand Jews. From the 19th to the 24th AUGUST, a second transport was shipped to Estonia.

On SEPTEMBER 1, there was the first and last battle with the Germans at the ghetto gates. The last Jews were deported. At 12 Straszuna Street, there was one of many points in the ghetto held by the U.P.O. fighters. (see story).

On SEPTEMBER 10-13, groups of U.P.O. left the ghetto for the forest.

Jacob Gens, the Gestapo aide, was shot on SEPTEMBER 14th. On SEPTEMBER 16th, a thousand Jews were transferred to the H.K.P. camp (Army Vehicle Park) and a thousand more to the Kailis camp

(Fur factory). Both of these camps were inside the city itself, and were separated from the ghetto.

SEPTEMBER 23rd, the Vilna ghetto was liquidated. Seven thousand Jews were led out. The old and sick were sent to be slaughtered at Ponary. Groups of women and children were sent to Majdanek. The last group of partisans left the beleaguered ghetto through the underground canals, and thence into the forest. (see story).

1944

On APRIL 15, 1944, a group of Jews who had worked at digging up the Jewish and non-Jewish corpses at Ponary and burning them, make their escape. (see story).

APRIL 28—Tens of Vilna Jews revolted in the concentration camp Dautmargen, when they were preparing for an evacuation to Dachau (Germany). Some of them survived.

JUNE 19—Vilna Jews were shot and burned in concentration camp Kloga, Esthonia. A group of approximateiy 800 Jews gathered together in Vilna's Great Synagogue.

JULY 2-3, liquidation of H. K. P. and "Kailis." 2,000 Jews were killed. Tens escaped and reached the partisan lines, where they were incorporated in fighting units.

On JULY 13, the partisans helped the attacking armies to storm the city and they were among the first to enter the liberated Vilna, showing the army the way.

SEPTEMBER 19—1,800 Jews killed in concentration camp Revel, Esthonia.

1945

JANUARY 29, 1945—A few thousand were shot and thrown into the Baltic Sea near Koenigsberg.

In other concentration camps in Germany, the survivors, including the Vilna Jews, were liberated in the following days, by the victorious Allied Armies.

In a little red schoolhouse at Rheims, where Eisenhower made his headquarters, Germany surrendered unconditionally at 2:41 on the morning of MAY 7, 1945. The capitulation was signed for the Allies by General Walter Bedell Smith, with General Ivan Susloparov affixing his signature as witness for Russia and General Francois Sevez for France. Admiral Friedeburg and General Jodl signed for defeated Germany.

Germany surrendered to the Allies and Admiral Friedenburg (*left*) and General Jodl signed the surrender for the Third Reich.

Destroyed Berlin bunker
and corpse of a German officer.
The first to enter the bunker
was a Soviet Jewish officer

This was the end! General Weidling leaves the bunker after hearing of Hitler's death.

Martin Weiss (*right*) and August Hering, two Vilna Gestapo hangmen, are tried in Wurzburg, Germany, in 1950.

ELIJAH BEN SOLOMON ZALMAN (The Vilna Gaon; 1720-97):
Talmudic genius. His keen study of the sources, his critical insight,
enriched all branches of Jewish learning. Opposed Hasidism; approved
the study of mathematics and science (*As recorded in the Jewish Encyclopedia*).

WE ARE PRAISED!...

When the Jews of Vilna were forced to exchange their books for the sword and the great catastrophe befell them just as it befell the entire Jewish community of Europe, Vilna continued its glorious tradition and was the *first* to raise the flag of revolt against the Nazis.

The following commentaries of several prominent personalities on the role of Vilna in the Jewish underground movement add to our understanding of the historic pages inscribed by the "Jerusalem of Vilna" that was.

ANSWER TO A LETTER

... Girls, youths, old men escaped from the Vilna and Minsk ghettoes to join partisan detachments.

> (Article published in *Pravda*, September 21, 1948. Reprinted in *Jewish Life*, New York, June, 1949.)

VILNA—THE FOCAL POINT OF THE RESISTANCE MOVEMENT

"The city of Vilna played a vital role in the history of the Jewish resistance movement during World War II. *In this so-called Jerusalem of Lithuania, was born the idea of a resistance against the murderers of the German occupation forces.* (I. K.'s italics). There, too, came the first call to the Jewish masses to put up an armed resistance against the occupation forces and there the first Jewish United Partisan Organization (U.P.O.) was formed. Out of Vilna came the call of resistance which reached the Jews of Bialystok and Warsaw."

This excerpt is taken from the book, *Die Yiddishe Vidershtand Bavegung in Poiln*, 1941-1945, which appeared at the end of 1967 in New York. The book was edited by the scholar N. Kantorowicz.

Golda Meir Speaks at Madison Square Garden

President Nasser and other Arab rulers have had a slogan for years: "We shall drive the Jews into the sea." Menachem Begin, former commander of the Irgun Zvai Leumi, and now a member of the *Knesset*, reported that if the Arabs would try to push us into the sea, we would first drive them back into the desert. A close colleague of Begin, Joseph Klarman, who represented the *Yishuv* in Turkey during World War II and did important rescue work there, and incidentally was the godfather of my younger son, Martin, who was born in New York, warned the Arab warmongers that they would first be turned into dust . . .

Then came the Six Day War of June 1967. The Arab threat was repulsed. Shortly thereafter, Golda Meir, former Israeli Foreign Minister, and her country's first Ambassador to Moscow, addressed a mass meeting of over 15,000 persons in Madison Square Garden. She told about the Six Day War and declared that the Jews would never allow themselves to be led into the gas chambers again or be thrust into the sea. She hailed the stand of the Jewish underground in the Vilna ghetto against the Nazis. As one of the throng in Madison Square Garden that night, I felt proud of the compliment.

A group of Lithuanian high school students visiting our former partisan compounds. The secret press was located in this bunker, which was also my sleeping place. The Soviet Lithuanian government saved the compound as a historical site.

Former partisan leaders came to Poland in the 60's for a commemoration of the Warsaw Ghetto uprising. *From left to right*: Alexander Levi, Yugoslavian Jewish partisan, Colonel Senk-Malecki of the Peoples Guard (Warsaw division); Hersh Smolar, leader of the Minsk Ghetto underground; Aba Kowner, last U.P.O.-commander, Isak Parda, Bulgarian Jewish partisan.

Jewish Writers in Paris. Picture taken in 1950. *From left:* Leon Leneman, Mrs. Grinberg (from the U.S.A), Itzik Manger, Moshe Knapheis, Leib Rochman, Abraham Zak. *Second row:* Chaim-Leib Fux, Isaac Kowalski and Dr. Isaac Kantor

A group of former U.P.O.-members at the *Bar Mitzvah* of Samson, the son of this author. *Sitting fromm left:* Motl Szames, Mendl Tarle, Gabik Sedlis. *Second row:* Chaim Lewin (part face), Golda Lewin, Isaac Kowalski, Chaya Warszawczyk (a visitor from Israel), Rachel Mendelshon-Kowarski, Eta Lipenholc, Liuba Sabrin. *Last row:* Fania Warszawczyk, Abraham Sabrin, Henry Zagajski, Zalman Kaplinski, Mirocha Cheifetz. Missing at the picture, but who attended the *simcha* are MosheSzymeliski, Chaya Lipchic-Tarle, Mitcke Lipenholc, Schlomo Kowarski, Joseph Musnik, Jonas Wirszup, Sam Kowarski, Dina Abramowicz, Hirsch Warszawczyk (who took the picture).

Selected Bibliography

Ajzensztajn, Betti. *Ruch Podziemny w Ghettach i Obozach* (Polish), Warsaw-Lodz-Cracow, 1946

Arendt, Hanna. *Eichmann in Jerusalem*, New York, 1963

Bakalczuk, Melach. *Zichroines fun a Yiddischn Partizan*, (Yiddish), Buenos Aires, 1958

Balberyszki, M. *Stronger Than Iron*, (Yiddish-English), Tel-Aviv, 1967

Borwicz, Michal. *Arische Papirn*, (Yiddish). [three volumes], Buenos Aires, 1955

Brown, Zvie A. and Levin, Dov. *The Story of an Underground*, (Hebrew-English), Jerusalem, 1962

Cohen, Israel. *Vilna*, Philadelphia, 5704-1943

Charney, Daniel. *Vilne*, (Yiddish), Buenos Aires, 1951

Dworzecki, Mark. *Yeruschalayim d'Lita in Kampf un Umkum*, (Yiddish), Paris, 1948

Ehrenburg, Ilya. *The War: 1941-1945*. (English translation), Cleveland-New York, 1964

Friedman, Philip (editor). *Martyrs and Fighters*, New York, 1954

George St. George, *The Road to Babyi-Yar*, London, 1967

Goldfarb, Solomon, Rabbi (in collaboration with Scharfstein, Rose). *Ready-Reference Jewish Encyclopedia*, New York, 1963

Grade, Chaim. *Der Mames Shabosim*, (Yiddish), Chicago, 1955

Jelin M. Gelpern D. *Partizaner fun Kaunaser Ghetto*, (Yiddish), Moscow, 1948

Habe, Hans. *The Mission*, New York, 1966

Hilberg, Raul. *The Destruction of the European Jews*, Chicago, 1961

History of the *Second World War* (Weekly magazine), published by Purnell, London

Kaczerginski, Sz. *Khurbn Vilne* (Yiddish), New York, 1947

——————, *Ich bin Gewen a Partisan* (Yiddish), Buenos Aires, 1952

——————, *Partizaner Geen*. Munich, 1948

Kahn, Shoshana. *In Fajer un Flamen*, (Yiddish), Buenos Aires, 1954

Kantorowicz, N. *Di Yidishe Widerstand Bawegung in Poiln*, New York, 1967

Karski, Jan. *Story of a Secret State*, Boston, 1944

Katzenelson, Yitzhak. *Al Naharot Bovel*, (Yiddish), Tel-Aviv, 1967

Korchak, Reizl. (Ruz'ka). *Flames in Ash*, (Hebrew), Jerusalem, 1965

Krueger, Kurt Dr. *I Was Hitler's Doctor*, New York, 1953

Kruk, Herman. *Diary of the Vilna Ghetto*, (Yiddish), New York, 1961

Lazar, Chaim. *Churban Vemered*, (Hebrew), Israel, 1950

Leneman, Leon. *Der Cheschbn Bleibt Ofn*, (Yiddish), Buenos Aires, 1957

Mark, Berl. *Oifshtand in Bialystoker Ghetto*, (Yiddish), Warsaw, 1950

Markus, Peisach. *Der Vilner Gaon*, (Yiddish), New York, 1952

Mazur, Tadeusz and Tomaszewski, Jerzy. *We Have Not Forgotten*. (English-French-German), Warsaw, 1961

Morse, Arthur D. *While Six Million Died*, New York, 1968

Mul ha'oyev ha'Nazi (Face to face with the Nazi enemy), Editorial staff, (Yiddish and Hebrew), Tel-Aviv-Jaffa, 1961

Poliakov, Leon and Wulf, Josef. *Das Dritte Reich and die Juden*, (German), Berlin, 1955

Ran, Leizer. *Ashes of Jerusalem of Lithuania*, (Yiddish), New York, 1959

Reich, Joseph. *Wald in Flamen*, (Yiddish), Buenos Aires, 1954

Robinson, Jacob. *Eichmann and the Question of Jurisdiction*, Commentary Magazine, July, 1960.

Rolnik, Masza. *Ich Mus Derceijln*, (Yiddish), Warsaw-Moscow, 1965

Ryan, Cornelius. *The Last Battle*, New York, 1967

Schellenberg, Walter. *Hitler's Secret Service*, New York, 1956

Sefer Milchamoth Hagetaoth. Editors: Yitzchak Cukerman, Moshe Basok, (Hebrew), [two volumes], Tel-Aviv, 1954

Shabbetai, K. *As Sheep to the Slaughter*, Bet Dagan, 1962

Shirer, William L. *The Rise and Fall of the Third Reich*, New York, 1962

Shul, Yuri. *They Fought Back*, New York, 1967

Steinbeck, John. *Once There Was a War*, New York, 1958

Steiner, Jean-Francois. *Treblinka*, New York, 1967

Suckever, Abraham. *Vilner Ghetto*, (Yiddish), Buenos Aires, 1947

Tenenbaum, Joseph. *Underground*, New York, 1952

The Jewish Partisans, (Hebrew), [two volumes], Editorial staff, Merhavia, 1958

The Massacre of European Jewry (an anthology), editorial staff: Kibbutz Merhavia, 1963

Thorwald, Juergen. *Defeat in the East*, New York, 1967

Turkow, Jonas. *Azoi is es Geven*, Buenos Aires, 1948

————. *In Kamf Farn Lebn*, Buenos Aires, 1949

Uris, Leon. *Exodus*, New York, 1958

Vilner Almanach. Editor: Grodzenski, Vilna, 1939

Vorobeichic, M. *Ein Ghetto in Osten*, [Vilna], (German-Hebrew), Zurich, 1939

Wdowinski, David. *And We Are Not Saved*, New York, 1963

Weinreich, Max. *Hitler's Professors*, New York, 1946

Wiesenthal, Simon. *The Murderers Among Us*, New York-Toronto-London-Sydney, 1967

LIST OF
JEWISH PARTISANS IN THE RUDNICKI WILDERNESS*

Abramowicz, Dina
Abramowicz, Elijahu
Abramowicz, Mera
Alter, Isaac
Anglik, Moshe
Aranowicz, Aaron
Aranowicz, Eli
Aranowicz, Shlomo
Azgud, Chana
Bagranski, Pohl
Barancowski, Micha
Baron, Sioma
Bart, Eliezer
Bart-Lewinson Zenia
Bastomski, Mitia
Beker, Shlomo
Belkind, Jaob
Ben-Osher, Israel
Beniek
Berkowicz
Bernstein, Leon, Dr.
Bernstein-Scheinbaum, Pesia
Bielic, Isaac
Bielic, Joseph
Bielic, Zisla
Bigsun, Pesach
Bilbinder, Berta
Bilbinder, Motl
Binionski
Blazer
Bliacher, Jacob
Borowska, Chiena
Brand, Marsha
Brand, Shlomo
Breslin, Scholom
Bressman
Bursztejn, Mendl
Bursztejn, Sonia
Bursztejn, Zewke
Celnik, Abraham
Celnik, Natan
Celnik, Pola
Cement, Rachel
Charmac, Juliek
Chejfec, Mirocha
Deweltow, Dora
Didialis (Schmidt), Iser
Dogim, Isaac
Drewiacki, Melach
Drewiacki, Schmul
Druc, Nathan

Druzgenik, Berl
Epsztein, Moshe
Epsztein, Moshe
Epsztein, Rivka
Erlich, David
Erlich, Esther
Fajnberg, Sender
Farber
Faust, Janek
Faust, Rita
Fejgelson, Ruza
Fejkowski
Fejkowski, Reuben
Feldman
Feldman
Finkelstein-Schechter, Chwola
Finkelsztejn, Arie
Finkelsztejn, Cwi
Frida
Frida
Fridman, Boria
Fridman, Chasia
Galpern, Nachum
Galpern, Tewke
Geguzinski, Isaac
Geguzinski, Liza
Gejwusz, Jacob
Gelblum, Tajbl
Glezer, Chawa
Glezer, Gerchn
Glezer, Mania
Gol. Shlomo
Goldman, Leizer
Goldman, Pola
Gopsztejn, Motke
Gordon, Izia
Gorfinkel, Ema
Gorfinkel, Solia, Dr.
Gorniec, Zelda
Grinberg, Joseph
Griner, Gerchn
Grinwald, Dina
Grodzenski
Guberski, Joseph
Guberski, Lea
Gurwicz, Gricha
Gurwicz, Motke
Gurwicz, Rachel
Himeflarb, Alter
Ickowicz
Jacobson, Benjamin

*) Not included are the names of Jewish partisans in Narocz and other nearby forests.

Jafe
Jaszuner, Fejga
Jaszuner, Shlomo
Jaszunski, Jacob
Jaszunski, Mirjam
Jelin, Jacob
Jocheles, Fania
Josl, Schmuel
Jurkowski, Mendl
Jurkowski, Mira
Jutan, Genia
Kac, Lejzer
Kagan, Aaron
Kagan, Jaszka
Kaganowicz, Nachum
Kaganowicz-Zak, Sima
Kaliksztejn-Kowarska, Ula
Kalksztejn, Ignac
Kaplinski, Schmuel
Karpinkes, Abraham
Karpinkes, Rivka
Kas, Jejzer
Kejser
Kejser, Chaim
Kempner, Witka
Koniuchowski
Korczak, Ruszka
Kotler, Abraham
Kowalski, Isaac
Kowarski, Rachel
Kowarski, Shlomo, Engineer
Kowner, Aba
Kowner, Genia
Kowner, Niuta
Koziol, Siomka
Krakowski, Tolia, Dr.
Krasner, Codek
Kremer, Alek, Attorney
Kremerman, Chackl
Kresin, Musia
Krinski
Krinski
Kronik, Israel
Kulkin, Isaac
Kuperberg, Isaac
Kuszinski, Yehuda
Kwas, Szurka
Kwojowski
Lam, Ze'ev
Lazar, Chaim
Lewin, Baruch
Lewin, Beniek
Lewin-Swirski, Bluma
Lewin, Chaim
Lewin-Maze, Chaja

Lewin, Elijahu
Lewin, Golda
Lewin, Hirch
Lewin, Matitjahu
Lewin, Matla
Lewin, Schlumka
Lewin, Schmuel
Lewin, Shlomo
Lewin, Yechiel
Lichtenson, Meyer
Lichtenson, Schochana
Lipenholc, Mitia
Lubcianski, Israel
Lubocki, Danka
Lubocki, Imka
Lubocki, Iser
Luboki, Niusia
Lukuber, Chaim
Lukuber, Etl
Lukuber, Zacharja
Luski, Schimon
Magid, Batia
Magid, Elchonon
Markeles, Nojmi
Markowicz, Bluma
Mas, Abraham
Maze, Gita
Melamed, Bejla
Mersik, Cemeret
Mersik, Janek
Meszy, Moshe
Miaszczanski, Abraham
Miaszczanski, Eta
Miaszczanski, Israel
Mikliszanski
Milikowski
Milikowski,
Milikowski, Melech
Milikowski, Yerachmiel
Milsztejn, Fejge'le
Minikes, Micha
Mirkin, Wolodia
Mizerec, Pesach
Mizerec, Sara
Mostowicz, Isaac
Musnik, Joseph
Nemzer, Schike
Niedzwiedzka, Liuba
Niselowicz, Batia
Niselowicz, Berl
Niselowicz, Sanke
Nitlson, Gerchn
Okuniew, Moshe, Dr.
Peneusow, Abraham
Peneusow, Anna

Peneusow, Boria
Peneusow, Ema
Peneusow, Schmuel
Perlsztejn, Felka
Perlsztejn, Motka
Poczter, Joseph
Poczter, Lejb
Poczter, Rachel
Prener, Jacob
Pruchno, Liola
Prutka, Aaron
†Pszewalski, Wanda
Rabinowicz, Abraham
Rabinowicz, Reuben
Rachel, Tamara
Reznik, Jochewed
Rindzunski, Senia
Ring, Natek
Rodzewicz, Moniek
Rojtbord, Nisn
Rozow, Israel
Rubin, Tewke
Rubinsztejn, Note
Rudaszewski, Nachum
Rudnik, Batia
Rundbeken, Abraham
Ruwka
Sabrin (Resel) Abraham
Safar, Dorka
Sakir, Rachel
Sakir, Zalman
Sapirsztejn, Jejb
Sarchan, Pesach
Sedlis, Gabik, Architect
Senderowicz, Sender
Slawin, Ze'ev
Solc, Chaim
Solc, Chana
Solc, Micha
Solonojc, Jehudith
Stricianski, Moshe
Swicki, Schmuel
Swirski, David
Swirski, Mina
Szames, Motl
Szechter
Szelkman, Chaim
Szeroszeniewski, Berl
Szotan, Moshe
Szotan, Pesach
Szmerkowicz, Yekosiel
Szmerkowicz, Yisrolik
Szpiro, Batia
Szpiro-Burnsztejn, Schejndl

Szpiro-Lazar, Chaye'le
Szpiro, Schmuel
Sztul, Janek
Sztul, Matla
Szub, Baruch
Szwarc
Szwarc, Abraham
Szwarc, Isaac
Szwarc, Jacob
Szwarcbord
Tarbucin
Tarbucin, Lejb
Tarle, Mendl
Tatarski
Taubs, Chasia
Tchuzoj, Abracha
Tchuzoj, Isaac
Tejtelbaum, Genia
Telerant, Izia
Telerant, Nionka
Telerant, Sonia
Tkacz, Reuben
Toker, Zalman
Treger, Zelda
Twerdin, Raschel
Wajnsztejn, Lusia
Wajnsztejn, Michal
Warszawczyk, Fania
Warszawczyk, Hirsh
Warszawczyk, Liola
Warszawczyk, Yechiel
Weis, Israel
Weiskop-Sabrin, Liuba
Widucki, David
Wilenczyk
Wolozinski
Wolozni, Fania
Wolozni, Meyer
Wolozni, Zalman
Wulc, Samek, Engineer
Zac, Lena
Zagajski, Henrik
Zajdel, Motke
Zajdel, Shlomo
Zajdelson, Chaim
Zajdelson-Margolis, Liola
Zalcberg, Liutek
Zalcberg, Shulamit
Zalcsztejn, Webek
Zalmanowicz, Feifke
Zawelson, Cemach
Zeleznikow, Abraham
Ziner, Micha

Postscript

AFTER leaving my native city of Vilna, I lived in many countries of Western Europe. In 1945, looking for a way to kill an evening in Rome, I went with a friend to a movie. At the entrance there were no photos, only huge posters featuring a serious looking woman, and two white enevelopes with the inscription: *Due lettere anonime.*

I expected to see a love story. Two anonymous letters. Perhaps a rival sends a letter to her competitor. To our pleasant surprise, however, this was about a secret press in Italy.

Truthfully, they could have stated on the placards, "The Secret Press of Vilna" and it would have fit . . . Only here the Italians did their work in a friendly surrounding, in their own land, while we had to work in a hostile environment and not in our homeland . . .

The Gestapo was also here. They searched for the press and found it, in the end. Torture and death awaited those who did not get out in time, almost exactly as depicted in this volume. When the lights were turned on, I saw that almost all the audience had tears in their eyes.

All nations, wherever the Nazi cannibals ruled temporarily, produced great films about the partisans. Only we Jews, then without a country, had not done so. Our Jewish activities were diluted in the general underground struggle of those years.

     *   *   *

The foregoing paragraphs are from the epilogue of my little Yiddish book published in New York in 1953. All these years, my conscience has bothered me for not telling the world the entire story of the Jewish resistance to the Nazis—while millions of Jews perished, there were many who fought back valiantly. Now, a quarter of a century after the Holocaust, I am able to tell some details about the resistance in one small corner of the world, in Eastern Europe, and my small part in it.

"Barbarossa" was the code name for the war against the east. This proved to be the right name. The Nazis acted barbarously to the population and also their own German people paid with ten million dead and another ten millions crippled and wounded. It was "Barbarossa" also for the barbarians themselves.

Beside the 6,000,000 Jewish nationals also another 7,000,000 gentile people died in the concentration camps. Altogether the "New Order" massacred 13,000,000 people in the concentra-

408

tion camps alone, beside the millions that perished at the fronts and many other ways.

My city Vilna, belonged to many masters during the first and second World Wars. The Germans paid dearly—eight thousand dead and five thousand prisoners—in their last desperate effort to hold the city during the final days of the battle. Finally, the partisans in conjunction with the regular Soviet army liberated the city. When I emerged from the forest, toting my underground press equipment on military trucks, I found my Vilna in a sorry state of disrepair.

*   *   *

I left desolate Vilna convinced that out of the Holocaust must come the renaissance of the Jewish people in their own homeland. A Jewish State must rise again in Palestine. Otherwise, all this struggle to remain alive would be of no value. I did my share to attain this goal, but that is a chapter that must be treated independently of this acount of my underground work against the Nazis. I must mention, however, one example: one of my writings was included in a memorandum to the British mandatory government, in the form of an essay, for the 1947 U.N.-Commission.

*   *   *

The reader of this volume now has an account of what happened in one corner of Eastern Europe. It is proper to add a few words about what occurred during those dark days in the United States, the country which I was later to adopt. One can easily imagine how different the war could have ended were it not for the tremendous outpouring of help from America to the European allies. During the period that Vilna was under Nazi rule, the United States lent the Allies trucks, war planes, tanks, jeeps, motor vehicles, and miles and miles of railroad tracks, and other essential war materials. All in all, the Allies received fifty billion dollars worth of aid, of which only eight billion was repaid.

Who, more than I, knows what it means to acquire weapons with our bare hands. In the beginning we were happy to get a single bullet. We cherished every rusty old rifle, and we worked diligently to make it like new. I can therefore appreciate the value of America's expensive, modern weapons that saved the day for the Allies.

The American armed forces included 550,000 Jewish men and women. Eight thousand were killed in battle and 25,000 were decorated for valor. The Congressional Medal of Honor was won by many Jewish servicemen.

All this is told without any intention of glorifying militar-

From left: General Bernard Montgomery, General Dwight D. Eisenhower, General Ivan Susloparov, General Francois Sevez.

ism or making a cult of the partisan movement. I am against the methods of the partisans in peace time. Pope Julius III (1487-1555) once said. "Learn. my son, with how little wisdom the world is governed." Too often. it is ruled by the sword, by force, and not by reason. These ideas are found in the Bible whose ancient teachings against war should be hearkened to by the leaders of the nations. Let us listen to the voice of reason and get out of the business of war, of killing each other. Let us rather work for the betterment of mankind, and really beat those swords into plowshares. as our Hebrew prophets have urged.

*   *   *

I am now preparing an anthology about the Jewish resistance movement in Nazi Europe. It will cover all countries where Jews were in active combat against the evils of the twentieth century. In this anthology. I shall let the Jewish partisans speak directly to the reader, to describe the events they lived through. I shall try to make the anthology a forceful presentation of my own life's philosophy. which is to work for the co-existence of all nations, especially the super-powers, because I do not wish to see the world destroy itself.

In Memory
Of Fallen Partisans

Aronowicz, Aaron
Baron, Eliyahu, Engineer
Benski, Feivl
Bernstein, Miriam
Bialak, Tuvia
Big, Asia
Blum, Abraham
Bonk, Jacob
Boraks, Edek
Braunszweig, S., Attorney
Brauze, Moshe
Brauze (wife)
Burakiski, Chaya
Cepelewicz, Gricha
Chazan, Bela
Chwojnik, Abrasha, Attorney
†Dudziedz, Jadzia
Entin, Shlomo
Ezlagman, Chaim
Friedman, Boria
Frucht, Isidore, Major
Ganionska, Miriam
Glazman, Joseph
Gobstejn, Motl
Goldman, Mordechay
Gordon, Hirsh
Gordon, Lejbl
Jabrow, Isaac
†Jankauskas, Julian
Jelin, Chaim
Kaplan, Jacob
Kaziborowski, Liona
Kempner, Israel
Koniuchowski
Kowner, Michal
Kowner, Yasha
†Kozlowski
Kuniski
Kuricki, Mula
Lajzerowicz
Lewin
Lewin, Eliyahu
Lewin, Jona
Lewin, Mates

Lichtensztejn, Tosia
Lubocki, Daniel
Lubocki, Imka
Lukiszer, Rachel
Mackiewicz, Izia
Madejsker, Sonia
Magun, Iiza
Markowicz, Bluma
Markowicz, Rachl
Meller, Chaim
Mikliszanski
Milejkowski, Jacob
Napoleon, Chaim
Niedzwiedzki, Luba
Perlman, Cr., Dr.
Pinczewski, Yehuda
Plotnicka, Frumka
Pruchno, Lola
Pupinski, Frieda
†Pszewalski, Jan
Rachel,, Tomka
Raf, Jasha
Rodziewicz, Moniek
Sarachan
Scheinbaum, Ilia
†Schmidt, Anton
Striczanski, Moshe
Swirski, Sholem
Szapiro
Szapiro, Schmuel
Szerszniewski-Kas, Rosa
Szmere, Leib
Szneider, Boria (Dov)
Tajc, Leivik
Tenenbaum-Tamarow, M.
Tiktin, Zalman
Turgel, Jacob
Twerdin, Rachel
Wajner, Meyer
Warszawczyk, Lola
Widucki, David
Wilkomirski
Winiski, Toiba
Wittenberg, Itzik
Zilber, Reizl
Zilber, Sarah
Ziskowicz, Lova

†Gentiles (Only co-workers with U.P.O. in Ghetto)

411

Index